MW00638447

Newcastle and Gateshead

PEVSNER ARCHITECTURAL GUIDES

Founding Editor: Nikolaus Pevsner

PEVSNER ARCHITECTURAL GUIDES

The *Buildings of England* series was created and largely written by Sir Nikolaus
Pevsner (1902–83). First editions of the county volumes were published by
Penguin Books between 1951 and 1974. The continuing programme of revisions
and new volumes has been supported by research financed through the
Buildings Books Trust since 1994.

The Buildings Books Trust gratefully acknowledges
Grants towards the cost of research, writing and illustrations
for this volume from

ENGLISH HERITAGE

ENGLISH HERITAGE

Newcastle and Gateshead

GRACE McCOMBIE

with contributions by

ELAIN HARWOOD

STAFFORD LINSLEY

HUMPHREY WELFARE

PEVSNER ARCHITECTURAL GUIDES

YALE UNIVERSITY PRESS

NEW HAVEN & LONDON

For my husband and our family

The publishers gratefully acknowledge help in
bringing the books to a wider readership from
ENGLISH HERITAGE

YALE UNIVERSITY PRESS
NEW HAVEN AND LONDON
302 Temple Street, New Haven CT06511
47 Bedford Square, London WC1B 3DP

www.lookingatbuildings.org
www.pevsner.co.uk
www.yalebooks.co.uk
www.yalebooks.com

Published 2009
10 9 8 7 6 5 4 3 2 1

Set in Adobe Minion by SNP Best-set Typesetter Ltd., Hong Kong
Printed in China through World Print

Library of Congress Cataloging-in-Publication Data
McCombie, Grace.
  Newcastle and Gateshead / Grace McCombie.
    p. cm. -- (Pevsner architectural guides)
  Includes bibliographical references and index.
  ISBN 978-0-300-12664-8 (alk. paper)
1. Architecture--England--Newcastle upon Tyne--Guidebooks. 2. Historic
buildings--England--Newcastle upon Tyne--Guidebooks. 3. Newcastle upon
Tyne (England)--Buildings, structures, etc.--Guidebooks. 4. Newcastle upon
Tyne (England)--Guidebooks. 5. Architecture--England--Gateshead--
Guidebooks. 6. Historic buildings--England--Gateshead--Guidebooks.
7. Gateshead (England)--Buildings, structures, etc.--Guidebooks.
8. Gateshead (England)--Guidebooks. I. Title.
  NA971.N4M33 2009
  720.9428´76--DC22
                            2009024898

Contents

1. Newcastle and Gateshead, showing areas covered by walks and excursions

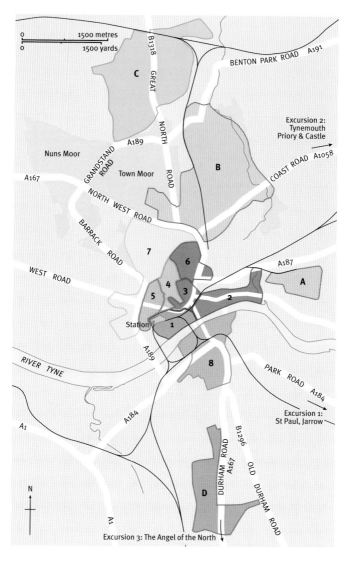

	Walk 1.	Sandhill and the Western River Banks		A. The Byker Estate
	Walk 2.	Quayside and East Quayside		B. Jesmond
	Walk 3.	The Historic Centre		C. Gosforth
	Walk 4.	Grainger Town		D. Shipcote and Gateshead Fell
	Walk 5.	The Town Wall and Western Centre		
	Walk 6.	The North-eastern Town Centre		
	Walk 7.	Newcastle University, and some Inner Suburbs		
	Walk 8.	Gateshead Town Centre		

2. Sandhill, with Tyne Bridge, Millennium Bridge, and the Baltic art centre

Acknowledgements

No book about Newcastle or Gateshead can be written as though the two places were isolated one from the other. After William Grey's *Chorographia* in 1639, many historical and topographical accounts were published up to the early 1800s and most covered both towns (*see* Further Reading). This book owes much to all those earlier writers, and especially to the scholarly histories written by Sydney Middlebrook (Newcastle, 1953) and Frank Manders (Gateshead, 1973).

Nikolaus Pevsner's *County Durham* (1953, revised by Elizabeth Williamson, 1983) and *Northumberland* (1957, revised by John Grundy, Grace McCombie and Peter Ryder, with Stafford Linsley and Humphrey Welfare, 1992), laid the foundations for this book. Pevsner acknowledged assistance from experts in both counties, and this City Guide has also benefited from such help. Planners, architects and owners are thanked for patiently answering many questions, including for both sides of the river Ian Ayris and Peter Derham of Newcastle's Historic Environment Section, with their colleagues David Heslop and Jennifer Morrison in Tyne and Wear Specialist Conservation Team. Barbara Harbottle, former County Archaeologist, long ago introduced me to urban research, and has kindly provided notes on faculty documents for the Newcastle Diocese. Gratitude is also owed to Martin Barlow, Debbie Harvey and Trevor Miller of the City of Newcastle. In Gateshead, Clare Lacey, Marie-Claire Robson and Geoff Underwood, as well as Dennis W. Robson, the Borough's Director of Architecture from 1973, gave much useful information. Professor Norman McCord kindly commented on the draft Introduction.

For help with specific aspects of the text, the author is indebted to the following: Bill Ainsworth (Ainsworth Spark Associates); Elizabeth Bennett, Eric Carter (Napper Architects); Kevin Poad; Neil Moat; Alan Moody (Douglass Wise & Partners); Adrian Osler; Lynn Redhead of the National Trust, and Peter Jubb, formerly Historic Buildings Officer for the County (Holy Jesus Hospital); R.W. Rennison; John Sanders and Tanja Romankiewicz (Simpson & Brown Architects); Capt. R. Shipley and Capt. S.C. Healy, Master and Deputy Master of Newcastle's Trinity House; and at St Nicholas' Cathedral, Geoff Scott and Canon Peter Strange, Hugh Richmond and Jane Kennedy of Purcell Miller Tritton, and the Very Rev. Dean Christopher Dallison, for permission to use their research. Fr Leighton at St Mary's Cathedral and Fr Dixon at St Joseph's church, Gateshead must also be thanked for their help.

For other information the author thanks David Baker, Joan Chilton, Colin Dallison, Kevin Doonan, John Gregory, Colin Haylock (Ryder Architects), Brian Jobling (Tyne and Wear Buildings Preservation Trust), Jocelyn Marriner, Steve Palmer, Glynis Pearson, the Rev. John Sadler, Mike Tilley and Cyril Winskell. Gratitude is also due to Craig Wilson at the University of Northumbria School of the Built Environment, and at the University of Newcastle to Dr S.D. Hogg and Prof. J.J. Murray (Dental Hospital; also to Alistair Telford of RMJM), Melanie Reed (Press Office), and Ian Ward (Medical School).

Local research starts in the Local Studies sections of the two libraries and continues in Tyne and Wear Archives. Staff at all three places were always most helpful, as were those who guided me through catalogues of diocesan records at Northumberland Collections at Woodhorn, and at Durham at the County Record Office and the University Special Collections. Invaluable help was also given by the staff of Gateshead Old Town Hall, Newcastle College, the North of England Institute of Mining and Mechanical Engineers, the Literary and Philosophical Society, Central High School, Messrs Johnson Tucker (Jesmond Towers), the Stephenson Trust and Silverlink Holdings (No. 20 South Street), the Society of Antiquaries of Newcastle upon Tyne, its Librarian Denis Peel, and Paul McDonald and the late Pat Blue (Black Gate and Castle Keep).

If any name or organisation has been omitted, thanks and sincere apologies are offered. Errors and omissions throughout the text remain the responsibility alone of the author, who begs readers to tell the publishers of any that they find.

The author is immensely grateful to Elain Harwood, Stafford Linsley and Humphrey Welfare for the sections and entries on the Byker Wall Estate, industrial and engineering sites and themes, and Roman Newcastle respectively. Fellow City Guide authors have given valued advice, and discussions with very many former students and colleagues have also played their part in the process of discovery. This City Guide draws on all of these, but could not have been written without the help of Yale University Press's splendid team, especially Sally Salvesen, the editor Simon Bradley, production editor Sophie Kullmann (who also designed the volume) and the picture researcher, Louise Glasson, who co-ordinated the maps. The Buildings Books Trust and its secretary Gavin Watson have been very supportive. Assistance was also received from Anthony Bucknall, Dr Julia Craig-McFeely and Peter Hodgkiss. The whole enterprise is indebted to English Heritage for support and encouragement and for the superb photographs taken by their staff, especially James O. Davies and Keith Buck.

How to use this book

This book is designed principally as a guide for exploring the buildings of central Newcastle and Gateshead, and selected suburbs or outer areas. The divisions between the sections are shown on the map on p. vii.

After a chronological introduction, the gazetteer begins on p. 45 with eight Major Buildings, six in central Newcastle and two in Gateshead, along with a section devoted to the seven Tyne bridges, described upstream from E to W. The next section covers central Newcastle in seven Walks, with an eighth Walk for Gateshead town centre. Each Walk has a street map, with the main buildings and landmarks marked and arrows indicating the suggested route. Descriptions of selected outer areas and suburbs begin on p. 231. Four of these districts lie N of the Tyne, two to the s. Some buildings off the main routes of these Walks are also included. A final section describes three Excursions further afield. Readers should note that the description of the interior of a building does not indicate that it is open to the public.

In addition certain buildings, topics and themes have been singled out for special attention and presented in separate boxes:

History and Trade: Trade and Coal, p. 6
Building Traditions and Types: Newcastle Plasterwork, p. 11; Building Materials, p. 12; Tyneside Flats, p. 33
Architects: Tyneside Architects in the Nineteenth Century, p. 30; Ralph Erskine, p. 232
Transport and Planning: The Metro, p. 38; The Post-war Plan for the City Centre, p. 190; Early Railways, p. 228
Major Buildings: Newcastle Cathedral Monuments, p. 56; Artworks at the Civic Centre, p. 79
City-centre Buildings and Institutions: Trinity House, p. 125; The Royal Arcade, p. 146; The Town Wall, p. 168–9; Newcastle University, p. 201

Introduction

Introduction

Newcastle and Gateshead form a wide arena around a grand array of Tyne bridges, the sides of the bowl filled with ever taller buildings above the old low centre. The settlements grew where the Tyne could most easily be crossed on the coastal plain, and stand on Carboniferous (Coal Measures) sandstones. They prospered because coal, layered between the sandstones, could easily be won from outcrops and then transported down river and beyond. Ships which took coal out brought other goods in; expansion and industrial and commercial success followed.

Pevsner, in 1953, thought 'no one would choose to investigate the sights of Gateshead for fun', and in Newcastle in 1957 saw 'thickets of factory, warehouse and slum'. That was the past: today's visitors see a clear river, splendid new and restored buildings, attractive public spaces and lively sculpture. But Pevsner did enjoy the drama of the topography, which still makes exploration a journey of pleasing variety. Changes of scale, texture and style reflect the pattern of building of many centuries, from narrow old streets near the river, uphill to palaces of c19 and c20 commerce, and out to broad sweeps of suburban terraces and villas, all woven through by roads and railways, and punctuated by ancient and modern churches and glimpses of distant green hills.

For most of their history Gateshead and Newcastle were towns in the counties of Durham and Northumberland respectively, united by the river and bridges that they shared; both were in the ancient Diocese of Durham until 1882. In 1400 Newcastle became a town and county in its own right; in 1882, a city and county. Gateshead became a municipal borough in 1835, a county borough in 1888. Both have been radically changed by post-war road systems and huge gaps left by the departure of heavy industries, and then by the regeneration of recent decades. In 1974, when local government boundaries were redrawn, they became two of the five districts of the new Metropolitan County of Tyne and Wear. The populations in 2001 of those districts, much larger than the historic towns, were Gateshead, 191,300, and Newcastle, 269,500.*

*Accounts of the buildings of the old counties and of other Gateshead and Newcastle suburbs may be found in the *Buildings of England* volumes for County Durham (revised 1983) and Northumberland (revised 1992).

3. The Tyne from the Castle keep; Newcastle Quayside roofs, and Gateshead Sage Music Centre, by Foster & Partners, 1996–2004; New Tyne Bridge, by Mott, Hay & Anderson with R. Burns Dick, 1925–8

Hadrian's Wall and Roman Newcastle*

Fragments of almost all of the elements of **Hadrian's Wall** – the great system of frontier defences erected from sea to sea to divide the Roman province from the barbarians to the N – are visible or are marked out within Newcastle, though not all are included in this gazetteer. (Only the ditch on the N side of the Wall would be needed to complete the set.) There is the curtain and a turret at Denton; more along the Shields Road; remnants of a milecastle in Westgate Road; a temple, and a causeway across the linear earthwork known as the Vallum, outside the site of the fort at Benwell; and parts of the fort under the Castle.

From Denton, on the western boundary of the city, and through Benwell and Fenham, the West Road follows the line of Hadrian's Wall. Its course continues down Westgate Road, where the rebuilt fragments of a milecastle (one of the series of fortified gates, a mile apart, attached to the rear of the Wall) are visible behind Nos. 69–73, and the line is marked outside the Neville Hall (the Mining Institute). To the SE, a section may have continued to the fort (under the Castle) but the main curtain probably swung E, across the foot of Dean Street to All Saints' church. Further E, it lies beside St Dominic's R.C. church (not included in this book), and along the S side of Shields Road and Fossway, towards the fort at Wallsend (Segedunum).

It appears that the Wall was originally to end at the bridge at Newcastle; the extension to Wallsend may have been an afterthought. The fort at Newcastle certainly seems to have been an addition for it was not built until about eighty years later, in the late C2 or early C3. Before that, a bridge – perhaps somewhere near the Swing Bridge – may have been guarded by a postulated fort in Gateshead. Occupation of the fort under the Castle Garth continued to the end of the C4.

The Middle Ages and Sixteenth Century

Both towns had pre-Norman **monastic settlements**. Bede, writing in the C7 further down the Tyne at Jarrow, mentioned Utta, an abbot, of Gateshead. Symeon, the C12 Durham monk-chronicler, referred to Monkchester, later called Newcastle: a Saxon cemetery has now been found above the Roman fort. At Jarrow the remains of Bede's own monastery can be seen at St Paul [178], where the C7 chancel is in origin one of two Anglo-Saxon churches which were linked by the later tower (the western church replaced in the C19).

In 1080 William Rufus ordered a **castle** to be built to guard the river crossing. Within its ramparts a stone keep was built in 1168–78, dominating today's riverside [44–47]. Of the enclosing castle wall, much was sacrificed to the C19 railway, but fragments survive to the W and S. Its C13 N gatehouse (the Black Gate) [4, 48] has C17 additions. A settlement grew around the Castle and St Nicholas's parish church

* By Humphrey Welfare.

4. The Black Gate, Castle Garth, c13; balcony and rear wing by R.J. Johnson, 1883

(since 1882 the Anglican cathedral), its spine a triangular market place, and spread out along the roads to the countryside. St Nicholas has c12/c13 origins, a c15 crown spire, and furnishings including a grand late Perp font cover [35–41]. Its three chapels, which became **parish churches**, incorporated c12–c13 fabric. Of these, St John's (now mostly c14–c15) and St Andrew's churches are reminders of the town's medieval phase [117]; All Saints' church was rebuilt in the 1780s. Some medieval church **monuments** survive, including the superb c15 brass to Roger Thornton, now at St Nicholas. Of Newcastle's nunnery and several **friaries**, the only substantial remains are the c13 Dominican buildings at Black Friars [120].

Trade and Coal

The medieval Port of Newcastle, from Tynemouth to the tidal limit (*c.* 20 miles), exported coal, grindstones, wool and hides. It was controlled by Newcastle's Corporation until the Tyne Improvement Commission took over in 1850. The Tyne was the largest East Coast port near Scotland, with Tynemouth Castle to guard it. Trade was national and international: Tyneside merchants routinely dealt with foreign countries, often sending sons to live in North Sea and Baltic ports.

In medieval times coal was dug from outcrops near the river. Later, from ever-deeper and more distant pits, it was taken to riverside quays and coal staithes or staiths (timber jetties; a spectacular late C19 example survives at Dunston outside of the area of this guide); first by horse-drawn wains, then on wooden-railed wagonways [153], and eventually by steam locomotives pulling trucks running on iron rails. From the C16 London became increasingly dependent on North East coal for domestic fires. The wealth generated by the sale of coal, and by payments for the right to construct wagonways between pit and river, brought prosperity to landowners, and also to many entrepreneurs who manufactured the machines and boats needed, and sold necessities and luxuries to the growing workforce.

5. A wagonway in Gateshead, and Tyne Bridge, 1775–81, by Robert Mylne; engraving from Brand's *History of Newcastle and Gateshead*, 1789

Gateshead's monastic site is not identified, but St Mary's church [6] (now a heritage centre) has some work of *c.* 1200; its C14 arcades are like those at St Nicholas and at St John, i.e. arches flowing directly from piers without capitals. St Edmund's Chapel at Holy Trinity church is C13, the front with lancet windows set in blind arcading. There is also a ruined medieval chapel in Jesmond [164], as well as the important medieval site at Tynemouth. The narrow headland overlooking the river here was a stronghold from early days. The present castle is chiefly

6. Gateshead, St Mary (now Heritage Centre), Church Bank; medieval and later

medieval, though the defences were being updated even in the c20. An early timber monastery within the defended site was superseded by a Norman stone one, and that by a grand c13 priory church, now ruinous [180–181].

Of secular urban buildings, one land arch of the medieval **bridge** survives in cellars on Newcastle's Sandhill, where the bridge chapel stood, dedicated to St Thomas Becket. The bridge was built by 1175; it had drawbridge and gate by 1219–20. Newcastle's late c13–c14 **town wall** [116], punctuated by gates and towers, ran from the river at the w, near Close Gate, round the town and along the Quayside to Sandhill. The Quayside stretch was demolished in 1763 to improve access to the Quay; the e walls were gradually dismantled, leaving three isolated towers: the Plummer and Sallyport towers, both remodelled for use by town guilds in the c18 [129], and part of the Corner Tower. At the w, towers and stretches of wall remain between roads and railways s of Gallowgate.

7. Newcastle, Castle Stairs. Photograph by Eric de Maré, 1960s

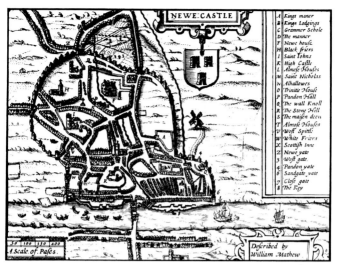

The key/legend in the image reads:

A Kings maner
B Kings Lodgings
C Grammer Schole
D The manner
F Newe house
H Black friers
I Saint Iohns
K High Castle
L Almese Houses
M Saint Nicholas
N Alhallowes
O Trinitie House
P Pandon Hall
Q The wall Knoll
R The Stone Hill
S The maisen deeu
T Almese Houses
V Wess Spittle
W White Friers
X Scottish Inne
Z Newe yate
3 Wess gate
4 Pandon yate
6 Sandgate yate
7 Close gate
8 The Key

A Scale of Paces. 50 100 150 200

Described by
William Mathew

8. Plan of Newcastle from John Speed's map of Northumberland, 1610

Medieval and C16 **houses** were timber-framed with jettied upper floors and, in Newcastle, with stone party walls, a medieval building regulation. Good examples survive on Sandhill and in The Close [73, 74, 76]. There is also the Cooperage in The Close, timber-framed and C16–C17 on the remains of an older, stone-built house. Some C16–C17 timber-framed houses are hidden by C18 brick façades (White Hart Yard in Cloth Market; No. 44 Sandhill) [73]. A single medieval house all of stone survives: it is in Newcastle's Trinity House complex. At the Quayside, piers formerly extended into the river. Dumping between them then raised the ground level, and the piers became chares (alleys) between buildings constructed on the landfill: excavations in 1998 found a C14 stone building some 16 ft (5 metres) below Fenwick's Entry. In Gateshead no comparable sites have yet been investigated, but a fine classical door surround of C16 type is incorporated into the forecourt wall at St Edmund's Chapel.

The towns' medieval **street plans** (*see* Speed's 1610 map [8]) remained unchanged until the later C18. The hilly topography of Newcastle, shaped by the Lort, Pandon and Ouse burns, is easily understood at the Castle, which rises steeply from NE (The Side) and SE (Sandhill). Five streets ran through the town: two on the waterfront, three to the countryside. The Close (a C13 enclosure between Castle and river) was upstream, and Quayside downstream, from the Sandhill bridgehead. The Side took vehicles up to the church of St Nicholas and the markets (Bigg etc.), then northwards past St Andrew, and through the New Gate to Sidgate (today's Percy Street). A second route crossed the Lort Burn on Sandhill, climbed to All Saints and Pilgrim Street, and passed through Pilgrim Street Gate to meet Sidgate/Percy Street at Barras Bridge. A third ran w from the Castle along Westgate, following the line of Hadrian's Wall past St John, and out through the West Gate. Narrow lanes (Pudding Chare, Denton Chare, High Friar Chare) and stairways linked the streets [7], and High Bridge and Low Bridge crossed the Lort Burn between the markets and Pilgrim Street. Gateshead, without defensive walls, was protected at least from northern raids by Newcastle's presence, the river, and the defended bridge. Its three medieval streets formed a T-plan.

Historically the two towns had an uneasy relationship. Gateshead was briefly annexed to Newcastle in 1553–4 when John Dudley wanted Edward VI to control towns and coal trade. A second attempt at annexation failed in 1576, only for Queen Elizabeth to lease the coal-rich manors of Gateshead and Whickham – 'the Grand Lease' – to a consortium of Newcastle merchants. That lease was in 1599 assigned to Newcastle's mayor and burgesses. The Bishop of Durham regained ownership by 1679 and from 1684 leased the manors out. While the Grand Lease was in operation, coal production was at its highest (*see* topic box, p. 6).

The Seventeenth and Eighteenth Centuries

Raids into Northumberland lessened after the union of the crowns in 1603, when James VI of Scotland became also James I of England. However, in the 1640s during the Civil War Scottish troops captured Gateshead, and eventually Newcastle, their cannon firing from Gateshead's Windmill Hills. Scottish occupation ended in 1647, coal trading resumed, and recovery began.*

Newcastle replaced the oft-repaired town hall on Sandhill with a larger stone building (1655–8) by *Robert Trollope* from York [13, 49–53]. He settled in Gateshead, where his mausoleum (rebuilt 1850) stands in St Mary's churchyard. Timber-framed **houses** were built or remodelled on the N side of Sandhill in the 1650s, the last such in the region [73]. New houses thereafter were usually brick, often with shaped gables, like the E gable of a house of *c.* 1700 in Rosemary Lane. Tyneside has no brick extravaganzas such as barley-sugar-twisted chimneys – those behind No. 41 Sandhill are of the 1930s – but Celia Fiennes described Newcastle in 1698 thus: 'it most resembles London of any place in England, its buildings Lofty and Large, of brick mostly or stone.' The economic recovery is shown by buildings such as the Holy Jesus Hospital almshouses (1681), with their moulded brick embellishments and long arcade [102], and the turreted brick Mansion House of 1691 (destroyed 1895), built in The Close for civic entertainments and the mayor's residence. In 1701 the Keelmen's Hospital was begun: four brick ranges round a courtyard, attic gables decorated with brick spirals [91]. It was a tremendous achievement for the keelmen, whose flat-bottomed boats ferried goods and coal between ship and shore.

*During the Jacobite risings of 1715 and 1745 Newcastle's Town Wall was repaired, but neither town was attacked.

The earliest surviving plasterwork in Newcastle is the most remarkable: the allegorical schemes used *c.* 1611 in Nos. 28–30 The Close, based on engravings published in the Low Countries. The 'branch' motif forming the oval compass in the Banqueting Hall of 1721 at Trinity House is used in 1658 in Trollope's Guildhall ('Mayor's Parlour') [52] and in the great c17 first-floor room of Alderman Fenwick's House, Pilgrim Street [9a]. There, strapwork surrounds cruciform branches, with small pendants. It is used as a corner motif in a mid-c17 room at No. 44 Sandhill, and outside Newcastle, at a c17 house in Hexham, the same moulds used over some seventy years. Mid-c18 work is more up-to-date [9b, 123].

9. a) Ceiling of Alderman Fenwick's House, first-floor room, c17 (left); b) medallion on staircase wall of 55–57 Westgate Road, mid-c18

James Corbridge's 1723 survey of Newcastle has margin pictures including some of old houses with irregular fronts, and some up-to-date with classical proportions. c17 and early c18 windows had mullions and transoms of timber or stone, with side-hinged casements as at the Holy Jesus Hospital. Later high-status buildings, such as the Banqueting Hall at Trinity House (1721), had vertical sliding sashes [85].

Good **interiors** of this period are few, but **woodcarving** is noteworthy. Trinity House Chapel has cherubs' heads carved in the 1630s, and fretwork decoration [86]. In Guildhall and Sandhill there are overmantels carved with biblical and mythical scenes of great sophistication; others of the 'Newcastle School' exist elsewhere [53]. Excellent c17 allegorical **plasterwork** appears in Nos. 28–30 The Close; there is strapwork plaster of the 1680s in Guildhall and more in a merchant's house in Pilgrim Street (Alderman Fenwick's House [98, 99]; *see also* topic box). Fine stucco decoration is seen in Nos. 55–57 Westgate Road [9b, 123], a stone-faced mid-c18 house. These two are the best surviving **houses** of the late c17 and c18.

10. All Saints, by David Stephenson, detail, *c.* 1786

For centuries, local sandstone ('freestone', because easily worked) was used for the most important buildings [10]. It was extensively quarried until the C20, especially at Kenton, Benwell and Elswick in Newcastle, and at Wrekenton on Gateshead Fell. Other local stones are harder to use: the creamy-grey magnesian limestone from the coast is beautifully pitted by fossils; the glossily dark whinstone from Northumberland's hills is difficult to dress to blocks. Houses before the mid C17 were commonly timber-framed; good timber became scarce, however, and after London's Great Fire of 1666 there was increased awareness of the danger of exposed wood. Brick was readily made on Tyneside, where both clay and coal were plentiful, and was already used as nogging within timber frames by the C16. So brick became the usual building material from the later C17 [91, 102], although ashlar was employed for major buildings. The great C19 urban building projects also used ashlar for main elevations, though brick returned to favour later in the C19.

Roofs of large buildings were lead-covered, probably using Durham's Weardale ores. Thin roofing slabs ('flags') included some of magnesian limestone from the coast, known from excavations, and others of local sandstone, seen on the SE porch of Newcastle's St Andrew's church, perhaps C16/C17. Thatched roofs were also known; a medieval charter allowed Gateshead people to take reeds for thatch. In the C17 bright red pantiles became popular, both imported from the Low Countries and made on Tyneside. Some good C18 buildings, such as Nos. 55–57 Westgate Road, had grey-green slates brought by pack-horse from Borrowdale, Cumbria. The most common roofing material of the C19 and C20 was Welsh slate, brought by ships on the 'tramping' circuit.

Wealthy patrons brought some **national architects** to the region in the C18. In 1730 *James Gibbs* designed a fashionable addition to Henry Ellison's Park House, Gateshead, the door with Gibbs's typical blocked surround (damaged by fires, dem. 2003). 1736 saw Newcastle's first Palladian building: the rebuilt s vestry and library of St Nicholas's church [11], also by *Gibbs* (his design slightly modified), for Sir Walter Blackett of Wallington. *Daniel Garrett* designed Newcastle's Infirmary (1751–2, dem. 1954), and worked at Newcastle's Fenham Hall for William Ord, at Gibside for George Bowes, and at Wallington for Sir Walter Blackett (all three outside the area covered by this guide). *James Paine's* works include Gosforth House for the Brandlings (*c.* 1755–64) [171], and alterations to Ravensworth Castle near Gateshead (dem.).

11. Cathedral Church of St Nicholas, Thomlinson Library, by James Gibbs, 1736

12. Charlotte Square, by William Newton, begun 1770

Of other C18 **church work**, the sw porch of St Andrew in Newcastle was in 1726 given a modest Baroque doorway [117], and in that year too a brick chapel was completed in Hanover Square for the Unitarian congregation (dem.). *William Newton* rebuilt St Ann's church on Newcastle Quayside in 1764–8, with a pedimented Doric portico. *Newton* and *David Stephenson* together rearranged the interior of St Nicholas in 1783–7. But the greatest achievement of *Stephenson* was the rebuilding of All Saints' church, 1786–96, in beautiful ashlar: a many-staged spire above a portico with perhaps the first fluted Doric columns seen in Newcastle, and with an oval nave [10, 88]. In Gateshead, St Mary's church tower was rebuilt in 1739–40 by *George Cansfield* in classical style [148]. Post-medieval **church monuments** of note are concentrated in St Nicholas, including mid-C17 costumed groups of merchant families. Later and more refined are *John Bacon Sen.*'s monument to Matthew Ridley, 1787, and *Flaxman*'s to Sir Matthew White Ridley, d.1813. *Rossi*'s bust of Admiral Lord Collingwood, d.1810, is on a majestic pedestal by *C.R. Cockerell*.

Assize balls and the Newcastle races were great C18 attractions, attended by gentry from both counties, and in 1793 the Literary and Philosophical Society was founded. Tyneside's first **town square**, Hanover Square, of the 1720s, was left incomplete (now only a fragment), but *Newton*'s Charlotte Square [12] of the 1770s, Newcastle's first successful square, retains classical doorcases and regular proportions. *Newton*'s Assembly Rooms, built by subscription in 1774–6, have a pedimented ashlar front and plasterwork of Adam type [122]. In the

13. Guildhall, north elevation, by Robert Trollope, 1655–8, centre by David Stephenson and William Newton, 1794–6, left addition by John Dobson 1823–5. c19 engraving

1780s *David Stephenson* built Newcastle's first **town improvement scheme**, Dean and Mosley streets: an E–W link between Pilgrim Street and Flesh (later Cloth) Market, and a N–S connection to Sandhill. These had three-storey brick houses with Tyneside's first purpose-built shops with display windows. In 1794–6 *Newton* and *Stephenson* altered Trollope's Guildhall [13], replacing the Gothic stair-tower with a pedimented entrance front (followed in 1823–5 by an extension by *John Dobson*) [50].

The new wide routes to *Robert Mylne*'s rebuilt Tyne bridge of 1775–81 [5], Church Street (Gateshead) and Dean Street [103], brought benefits for travellers and townsfolk alike. Yards and gardens of the medieval burgage plots were filled with new houses and additions. In Newcastle the centre became a solid mass of buildings of all periods: front properties were rebuilt in brick, often with added storeys. Open spaces outside the Town Wall filled with middle-class houses such as Saville Row, of the 1770s. In Gateshead, similar development was slightly later and less intense. Three houses of the late c18 or *c.* 1800 survive, altered, in the High Street (Nos. 270–274).

The industrial suburbs of Gateshead also grew. The Crowley iron-works on the rivers Derwent and Team were much admired by the Swedish traveller Angerstein in 1754. He, like Celia Fiennes and other travellers (even present-day writers), thought Newcastle was on both sides of the river. He also observed glass-making, a once-important local industry.*

* There are displays of local glassware in the Laing and Shipley art galleries. A late c18 glass-works cone remains at Lemington, w of Newcastle and outside the area of this guide.

The Early Nineteenth Century: Grainger and Dobson

Vast changes came in the first half of the c19, as industries grew and railways and the High Level Bridge approaches were constructed. Factories and workshops spread further along the river banks: chemical industries and foundries in Gateshead, shipbuilding and gun manufacture at Newcastle. Coal mining, glass-making and heavy engineering grew in both. William Howitt, *c.* 1842, saw 'Gateshead, on one side high and dense with houses and swarming with population, and cloudy with the smoke and soot of many a manufactory; on the other side, stands high Newcastle on *its* hills, and deep between them the Tyne, with all its ships and coal-boats . . . right and left, up and down the river, on this side of the country and on that, the kindred objects of coal-mines and railways and steam-engines, and a hundred thousand grimy buildings and creatures, smokes and fumes, noise and commotions, blend the two towns into one unique and indivisible existence. . . '

Industrial development brought more people, houses, banks, offices and shops. Francis Humble's *Directory of Newcastle and Gateshead* (1824) already listed fifty 'new streets, courts, places &c lately named and erected' in Newcastle, among them Stowell Street, Ridley Place and Ellison Place. The grander **houses** had stone doorcases, the lesser, timber door surrounds; windows had stone lintels. Newcastle continued to spread beyond old boundaries, too: Jesmond's fields filled with terraces at Brandling Village; off Westgate Road, nursery gardens became genteel Summerhill Square [145], with terraced streets around it.

The key figure in the transformation of Newcastle was the builder-developer **Richard Grainger**. In 1819–20 *Grainger* built some conventional Georgian houses in Higham Place, off New Bridge Street. But then he launched bold schemes in a new, refined style, perhaps

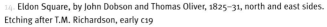

14. Eldon Square, by John Dobson and Thomas Oliver, 1825–31, north and east sides. Etching after T.M. Richardson, early c19

15. Central Exchange Buildings, Grainger Street, by John Wardle and George Walker, 1837–8; Grainger Market, by John Dobson, 1835 (left) and Grey's Monument, by Benjamin Green, 1838

influenced by Edinburgh's New Town, changing the entire scale and plan of Newcastle with his grand classical stone frontages. A forerunner worth mention here the Moot Hall designed by *William Stokoe*, Greek Revival of 1810–12 [82]. The first of Grainger's own major schemes was Eldon Square [14] (1825–31; only the E side surviving), to designs by *Thomas Oliver* and *John Dobson*. There followed Leazes Terrace [144] and Leazes Crescent [143] (1829–34), by *Oliver*. Grainger next built the Royal Arcade [100] in Pilgrim Street, 1831–2, a sophisticated design by *Dobson* (dem. 1963–9; *see* topic box, p. 146).

A wonderful opportunity then arose. The C17 town house of the Blacketts, with a large open space within the town walls – in origin the combined precincts of the Benedictine nunnery and the Franciscan friary – came on the market. In 1782 the property had been offered to Newcastle Corporation, but that body was committed to the expensive new bridge and its approach streets. It was bought instead by George Anderson, whose descendants put it up for sale (as Anderson Place) in 1831. Grainger raised the money, and in 1834 embarked on England's most ambitious **planned urban centre** of the period: a group of streets set within the Town Wall and the radiating network of medieval routes, demolishing street property only where new joined old. Grainger also persuaded the council to buy the New Market that he would build to replace the meat market of 1808, which stood in the way of his key street, Upper Dean Street (now Grey Street). This street was linked to Pilgrim Street to the E by Market, Hood and Shakespeare streets. From the N end of Grey Street, Grainger Street led diagonally SW to Bigg Market; further W and nearly parallel to that, Clayton Street ran from Blackett Street to the Forth, with much plainer elevations. Between Grainger and Clayton streets, Nun and Nelson streets framed the New Market – today's Grainger Market [15, 109]. Architects included *John Wardle* and *George Walker* in Grainger's own office, e.g. for the triangular Central Exchange Buildings at the hinge between Grey Street and Grainger Street [15, 107], *Dobson* for the severe but sophisticated New Market and much of Grey Street's E side, and *John & Benjamin Green* for the Theatre Royal block (*see also* topic box, p. 30).

Grainger brought Newcastle into the first rank of English cities, well-supplied with houses and hotels, shops, banks and offices. Particularly successful was the gentle rising curve of Grey Street, a magnificent composition in honey-coloured sandstone [113], leading the eye to the new Theatre Royal's projecting portico [114] and the eventual climax of the columnar Monument to Earl Grey [15, 105]. Harriet Martineau, an astute observer of society, wrote in *The Penny Magazine* in April 1840: 'That this row of shops, warehouses, and inns, sprung up within three years, should offer to the eye the same impression [as]. . . a line of palaces in Vicenza, is a wonder which may well excite and sustain admiration.'* The few exceptions to the classical rule at this time include the Lying-in Hospital [128] in New Bridge Street, Gothic of 1825–6, and the Neo-Tudor terrace of St Mary's Place, *c.* 1829–30, both by the versatile *Dobson*.

Meanwhile Neville Street opened in 1835, linking Collingwood Street (of 1811) to Scotswood Road, completing the E–W route across the town. On its S side, *Dobson*'s Central Station [58–61] was in use from 1849: one of the country's great engineering achievements, later supplemented by Dobson's simplified version of his grand frontage design. The station was built in conjunction with *Robert Stephenson*'s High Level Bridge (road and rail), recently restored and painted in its original stone colour [22, 70, 71]. (For the early history of **railways** in the area *see* topic box, p. 228). The bridge gave the towns their first easy road connection, and created a new focus for public buildings in the later C19 (*see* p. 20). The approach viaducts soar dramatically above the streets running down to the Quayside, and also skim the N side of the Castle keep [16, 103]. Many old houses were demolished for the railways on both sides of the Tyne, and other losses followed in 1854, when a huge blaze destroyed any remaining riverside houses in Gateshead. The burning débris also razed a large area of Newcastle's Quayside, including many timber-framed buildings, though the Custom House with its new front of 1833 by *Sydney Smirke* was spared [84].

In Gateshead early C19 **houses** spread down the High Street and W of it, most of the survivors now shops. In West Street is a single brick

* The shops included Emerson Muschamp Bainbridge's 1838 draper's and fashion shop in Market Street, where by 1849 takings were recorded by department: by this definition, probably England's first department store.

16. Railway Viaduct, by Robert Stephenson, 1849 and 1890s; The Side, and Milburn House by Oliver, Leeson & Wood, 1902–5

house of the 1830s with giant pilasters and big eaves [150]. To the s, brick terraces of grander proportions were built in Walker Terrace and Regent Terrace, and modest stone houses stand on Windmill Hill, high above the river. After the enclosure of the Town Fields and the Fell, 1807 and 1818, many terraced houses were built e.g. in Shipcote and Low Fell. On the High Fell, a fashionable suburb grew below the landmark spire of St John's church (*see* below). The Great North Road from Durham across High Fell, turnpiked in 1747, was in 1827 superseded by the 'New', lower, Durham Road. Along New Durham Road, stone villas appeared. Other **suburban developments** of this period in Newcastle and Gateshead are mostly brick, but Brandling Village had some terraces of stone, presumably quarried on site. An interesting shift is shown by Newcastle's St Thomas's Street and its neighbours, and the earliest terraces of Jesmond Road [138], where smart brick-fronted houses have rear walls of rubble sandstone.

New **chapels and churches** served the growing populations. The Brunswick Methodist Chapel of 1820–1 off Northumberland Street is brick, in simple Nonconformist classical style. *John Green*'s Presbyterian chapel of 1822 in Clavering Place is brick but Gothic, of C18 type. Newcastle's first true Gothic Revival church was *John Dobson*'s St Thomas, Barras Bridge, 1827–30 [135], a charming Early English design to replace Sandhill's medieval bridge chapel, demolished for street widening. Gosforth's medieval church of St Nicholas was rebuilt from 1799 [168]; Gateshead had St John, a new church on the High Fell, by *John Ions* with *Ignatius Bonomi*, simple Gothic of 1824–5 [177]. The advent of suburban garden **cemeteries** meant that a new type of chapel became necessary, represented by *Dobson*'s distinguished pair of 1834–6 at Jesmond Cemetery [162]. The C19 **monuments** in these cemeteries often repay exploration.

Victorian and Edwardian Developments

Sites near the new High Level Bridge and its approaches were preferred for **public buildings** in both towns in the years after 1850. Newcastle's Town Hall of 1858–63 (demolished), in St Nicholas Square, was an Italian Renaissance design by *John Johnstone*. Near its site, in St Nicholas Street, is *James Williams*'s former General Post Office, 1873–6, similarly with a giant order. *Johnstone* also designed Gateshead's Town Hall in West Street, 1868–70, which incorporated courts, police cells, refreshment rooms and a fire station [149]. Beside it in Swinburne Street, again by *Johnstone*, is the former Public Library, 1882–5, with an art school and art gallery above. Later public buildings in Newcastle included the Central Library in New Bridge Street, classical by *A.M. Fowler*, 1880–4 (dem.), and the adjacent Laing Art Gallery [127], splendidly Neo-Baroque by *Cackett & Burns Dick*, opened in 1904. Much more sedate is the former Northumberland County Hall [17] (now the Vermont Hotel) in Castle Garth, much enlarged between the wars by *Cackett, Burns Dick & Mackellar* from the first building by *J.A. Bain*, 1910.

Commercial architecture is seen at its best in Newcastle. **Banks** favoured the richer variants of the C16 palazzo style, as at the former Newcastle Joint Stock Bank of *c.* 1845, possibly by *Benjamin Green*, in St Nicholas Square, and *John Gibson*'s National Provincial Bank, 1870–2, in Mosley Street. This street and its continuation, Collingwood Street, were almost entirely rebuilt by the early C20 as the banking and

17. Vermont Hotel (former Northumberland County Hall), Castle Garth, by J.A. Bain, 1910, enlarged by Cackett, Burns Dick & Mackellar, 1929–34, converted 1988–93

insurance quarter of Newcastle. Here are offices by various combinations of the *Oliver, Leeson & Wood* partnership, such as the Sun Insurance building of 1902–4 [111]. The pedimented former Newcastle Savings Bank, 1862–3 by *J.E. Watson*, now belongs with the extension of Grainger Street sw from Bigg Market in 1869–70 ('Grainger Street West'). This new street, planned to link the Central Station to the northern part of the town centre, presents rich carving and varied roof-lines, styles abruptly changing from Gothic to the Northern Renaissance and Jacobethan of the 1870s–80s [110].

Newcastle's purpose-built **speculative offices** begin in the 1860s with *William Parnell*'s St Nicholas Buildings, St Nicholas Street, *c.* 1863 and his Exchange Buildings, Quayside, *c.* 1861–2 (part of the reconstruction following the fire of 1854 there); the former now rebuilt with a retained façade. The Quayside and approach streets were also favoured by banks and insurance offices, though these are less grand than later offices in Collingwood and Mosley streets. Of those of the speculative type elsewhere, *W.L. Newcombe* designed Worswick Chambers, a long 1890s brick-and-stone Neo-Gothic block on Pilgrim Street, and *Oliver, Leeson & Wood* designed Dean Street's Cathedral Buildings (1901) and Milburn House (1902–5) [16], while *Simpson, Lawson & Rayne*'s lively Emerson Chambers [106] in Blackett Street dates from 1903–4.

Other building types made an increasingly large contribution to the urban fabric. **Hotels** supplemented and eventually replaced the coaching inns. Grainger built the Turk's Head hotel in Grey Street *c.* 1836 (closed *c.* 1990), with Ionic order, opposite the Theatre Royal. The growing railway network brought Gateshead's Station Hotel by *G.T. Andrews*, 1844 (dismantled in 2003). *Thomas Prosser*'s Central Station Hotel, drawing on a *Dobson* design, was built in 1861–3, and greatly enlarged in 1888–90 and later by *William Bell*, with *Burmantofts* faience interiors. Across Neville Street, the imposing County Hotel by *John Johnstone* (1874, extended 1897) fills the w side of the extended Grainger Street between Westgate Road and Neville Street.

Pubs were always numerous in Newcastle: medieval taverns in the market streets and beside the Town Quay, then c17 and c18 coffee houses and coaching inns and c19 alehouses throughout. Many were rebuilt in the later c19 for big brewing companies; fashionable styles and furnishings increased the appeal of pubs in business areas. Notable examples include the Bridge Hotel beside the High Level Bridge, Free Style of 1901 by *Cackett & Burns Dick*, and *B.F. Simpson*'s exotic Half Moon Chambers in Bigg Market, 1904–5. *J. Oswald & Son* rebuilt the Beehive Hotel [96] in Cloth Market for Newcastle Breweries, 1902, with a faience pub front: such fronts were attractive and practical, pollution-resisting and always bright and shiny.

Some pubs continued the tradition of combining theatre or music hall with the sale of alcohol. In Newcastle, the Wheatsheaf in Cloth Market, now Balmbra's (rebuilt 1902), had a music hall at the rear. In Gateshead, the Metropole on High Street, 1896, vaguely Jacobean, had a (demolished) full theatre at one end [154].

Theatres proper had begun in Newcastle with *David Stephenson*'s Theatre Royal of 1787–8 in Mosley Street, demolished in 1835. *John & Benjamin Green*'s replacement Theatre Royal of 1836–7 is strikingly sited at the head of Grey Street's curve, an important element in the success of Grainger's new streets [113, 114]. In 1899 the interior was destroyed by fire and was rebuilt by *Frank Matcham* in his usual exuberant style (restored and rearranged in 1987). Newcastle's **Journal Tyne Theatre**, 1867 by *W. Parnell*, was the Tyne Theatre and Opera

18. Neville Hall (Institute of Mining and Mechanical Engineers), by A.M. Dunn, 1869–72

House, with an Italianate pale brick front [121]. Despite fire damage in 1985, its auditorium survives complete and its remarkable stage machinery has been restored.

In the commercial areas, lively **shopfronts** attracted customers' attention. A few especially good examples survive. Marks & Spencer opened a Penny Bazaar in 1896 in Grainger Market, with a long fascia with bold lettering and big lamps. *Simpson, Lawson & Rayne*'s Emerson Chambers [106] in Blackett Street, already mentioned, has shopfronts with elaborate glazing bars as part of the composition. This motif was echoed by *Benjamin Simpson* across the street in 1906, at Reids' the jewellers [126].

Local sandstones were supplemented by **building materials** from further afield. Strong sandstone from near Haydon Bridge in the Tyne Valley came by train, slabs three metres long forming the platform in front of *John Wardle Jun.*'s monumental Hancock Museum of 1880–4. This respects the Tyneside tradition of smooth ashlar with classical proportions and restrained decoration, but some buildings in the extension of Grainger Street introduce pink Shap granite or red Dumfries sandstone. The most complete interpretation of the poly-chromatic Ruskinian Gothic fashion is the North of England Institute of Mining and Mechanical Engineers (Neville Hall) in Westgate Road [18], 1869–72 by *A.M. Dunn*, with its richly carved foliage capitals and fine interior [18, 80]. *Waterhouse*'s Prudential Assurance in Mosley Street, of 1891–7, employs stripes of Dumfries sandstone and red brick

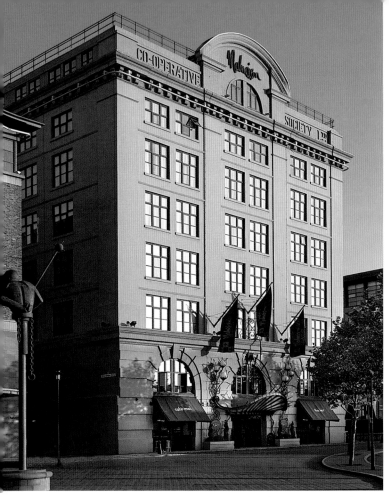

19. Former Co-operative Wholesale Society warehouse (now Malmaison Hotel), Quayside, by L.G. Mouchel with F.E.L. Harris, 1899–1900

above its red granite basement. The public office here was lined with *Burmantofts* tiles, revealed during restoration. Such **tiles** featured inside other buildings of *c.* 1900, notably *William Bell*'s refreshment room at the Central Station, 1893, also recently uncovered, and *J. Oswald & Son*'s Central Arcade of 1906, made within Grainger's fire-damaged Central Exchange Buildings [108].

 Reinforced concrete was another material much used from the late C19, in particular through *L.G. Mouchel*'s engineering firm licensing the *Hennebique* reinforcement method. One conspicuous example was the Co-operative Wholesale Society's Quayside warehouse [19] (1899–1900; now Malmaison Hotel), designed with *F.E.L. Harris* of the C.W.S. Architect's Office, where both frame and elevations are of concrete. At Cross House, Westgate Road (*Cackett & Burns Dick*, 1911) a *Hennebique* frame is clad in white Portland stone, a material introduced to Newcastle by *S.D. Robbins* at Scottish Provident House, Mosley Street, in 1906. This is iron- or steel-framed; Tyneside apparently had no iron-fronted buildings proper.

Earlier **warehouses** of the c18 and c19 were brick, and near the river. In Newcastle, of a large group built in Pandon in the early c19, one at Milk Market survives; others have been rebuilt in near-replica. Between the w end of The Close and Hanover Street, part survives of the long block of bonded warehouses built in 1841–4 by and for *Amor Spoor* [77]; restored and extended as flats in 2007–8. These are all relatively plain, but later c19 examples were sometimes highly elaborate, especially when combined with offices; e.g. the copper-domed C.W.S. building in Blandford Square (now the Discovery Museum [20], etc.), 1897–9 by *Oliver, Leeson & Wood*, and the same practice's Nos. 12–14 Dean Street, 1901, with mosaic figure friezes. Also conspicuous is the red brick printing works at Hanover Square later used as Turnbull's warehouses, a gabled complex of 1888 and 1896–8 by *F. W. Rich* [75].

20. Former Co-operative Wholesale Society warehouse (now the Discovery Museum), Blandford Square, by Oliver, Leeson & Wood, 1897–9

21. Swing Bridge, by W.G. Armstrong & Co., with the Tyne Improvement Commission, 1868–76 (foreground); photograph by Eric de Maré, *c.* 1965

Industrial buildings are otherwise no longer very conspicuous in central Newcastle and Gateshead. Notable survivals include parts of the locomotive works set up in the 1820s by George and Robert Stephenson in South Street, on the southern edge of Newcastle; the famous *Rocket* was built here [79]. Also still extant and in other uses are parts of the North Eastern Railway engine works at Gateshead, of the 1840s onwards. Another stronghold is the Ouseburn valley, where industrial activity included lime-burning and the manufacture of glass, lead and pottery. The most remarkable survivor here is *Dobson*'s majestic stone-built flax mill of 1847–8, now known as the Cluny warehouse.

Bridges multiplied, including several of innovative local design and manufacture. *John & Benjamin Green*'s Ouseburn railway viaduct of 1837–9 had laminated timber arches, later replaced in iron, on stone piers. The grandest railway bridge is *Robert Stephenson* and *T.E. Harrison*'s High Level Bridge of 1845–9 across the Tyne [22, 70, 71], with a lower deck to provide a second road crossing. Here the stone piers were combined from the outset with iron spans, using an ingenious combination of wrought and cast elements. The C18 Tyne Bridge was replaced by *W.G. Armstrong & Co.*'s Swing Bridge [21] of 1868–76, of iron with a pivoting central section, followed by a second high-level road bridge (1897–1901, rebuilt 1980–3) and a second railway bridge (1902–6), both placed upstream. Of other C19 bridges, the Byker road bridge of 1878–9 in the Ouseburn valley is a conventional brick viaduct, but further up the valley in Jesmond Dene is the elegant Armstrong Road Bridge of 1876–8, again by *Armstrong & Co.*, with lattice girder spans on box-section columns.

22. High Level Bridge, by Robert Stephenson, 1845–9, with T.E. Harrison, footway

23. St Matthew, Summerhill Street, by R.J. Johnson, 1878–80, and later

Outside the commercial centre, the expanding residential areas needed new churches and chapels, schools and colleges (as educational reforms demanded), and hospitals. For new **churches**, Gothic was preferred, mostly of c14–c15 type, and often with good furnishings by local craftsmen. *R.J. Johnson*'s St Matthew, Summerhill Street, 1878–80 with a tower of 1894–5 by *Hicks & Charlewood*, makes a striking contribution to the townscape of inner Newcastle [23]. Also in the Dec style is *W.L. Moffatt*'s St Michael (1862–3) in Byker; this was extended in the c20 using materials from *Dobson*'s St Peter, Oxford Street. In Gateshead, *A.M. Dunn*'s St Joseph (R.C.) was built in 1858–9, an imposing French Gothic group with presbytery and (demolished) school. **Nonconformist churches** turned to Gothic, e.g. for the Methodists in Gosforth (1877) and Jesmond (1900–2), but **synagogues** increasingly adopted free or non-Western styles, such as that which formerly served Jesmond, of 1914–15 by *M.K. Glass* [161].

New town centre churches were also built, and older ones restored. St Mary's R.C. Chapel (later Cathedral) in Newcastle is in the rich Decorated Gothic of *A.W.N. Pugin* [42, 43], 1842–4, with a later spire by *Dunn & Hansom*. At St Nicholas in Newcastle, in 1882 promoted to a cathedral, *R.J. Johnson* created a sanctuary with beautiful reredos and screens carved by *Ralph Hedley* [38]. Hedley's work also enriched new churches such as *T.R. Spence*'s lavish St George, Jesmond (1886–90) [165]. Restoration at St Mary, Gateshead, included work of 1874 by *Austin, Johnson & Hicks*.

The c19 and c20 produced excellent **stained glass** [41]. Of the most celebrated national firms, *Morris & Co.* glass may be seen at Jesmond Presbyterian Church (now United Reformed) and St Helen, Low Fell. *C.E. Kempe* and his successor firm are represented at St Nicholas's Cathedral, St Andrew and St Matthew in Newcastle, at St Nicholas, Gosforth, and at Jesmond Presbyterian Church. A high proportion of work was done by local makers: the prolific *William Wailes* (including early designs by *Pugin* at St Mary's R.C. Cathedral), succeeded by *Wailes & Strang*; *H.M. Barnett* (d.1888), an apprentice of Wailes; *Atkinson Bros*, who took over Barnett's practice; and *G.J. Baguley*. There is also the *Gateshead Stained Glass Co.*, represented by Arts and Crafts glass at St George, Jesmond (designer *John W. Brown*).

Schools built after the 1870 Education Act were no longer necessarily tied to churches or charities. Attractive examples include Gateshead's former Windmill Hills Industrial School, with big brick gables, 1879–80 by *Oliver & Leeson*, and Newcastle's wonderfully ornate Ouseburn Schools, Albion Row, 1891–3 by *F.W. Rich*. The Royal Grammar School in Jesmond, 1905–7 by *Sir Edwin Cooper*, is grander in scale and Anglo-Baroque in detail.

Buildings for **higher education** also proliferated (*see* topic box, p. 201). What is now the main Newcastle University site, at Barras Bridge, has *R.J. Johnson*'s monumental Armstrong Building (1887–8) at its heart, and the NW range and Armstrong Tower of 1904–6 by

W.H. Knowles. Knowles also designed the arched entrance to the quadrangle [141], the Fine Art building of 1911, and the (former) School of Agriculture of 1913. Mention should also be made here of *F.W. Rich*'s spacious reconstruction of the Literary and Philosophical Society interior [24] of 1893–4, after a fire.

Gateshead also preserves some other interesting buildings catering for cultural interests. A small workers' **reading room** and school of 1841 survives to the s in Low Fell. Of reading rooms for specific workforces, the most significant was the North Eastern Railway workers' club begun in 1887 in Hudson Street.

Hospitals expanded in the c19 outside the old town centres, as elsewhere. Newcastle's Infirmary, founded in 1751, moved to new buildings of 1900–6 on the Town Moor as the Royal Victoria Infirmary [142], and now incorporates the University's medical school. E of the moor, on land owned by the medieval St Mary Magdalene Hospital, the Fleming Memorial Hospital for Sick Children was built in 1887–8, and next to it, two orphanages of 1869 and 1873–6 (later combined as the Princess Mary Maternity Hospital; now flats). The borough lunatic asylum (St Nicholas' Hospital, 1866–9 etc.) was further N in Gosforth; later buildings there include a unique recreation hall with a tiled proscenium arch, dated 1896. Both towns had **dispensaries**: Newcastle's founded in 1777, later moving to Grainger's No. 14 Nelson Street; Gateshead's founded in 1832, from 1855 in a villa on West Street [150].

Tyneside Architects in the Nineteenth Century

By 1800 there were many pattern books to inspire builders who sometimes styled themselves 'architect'. In the early c19 the builder-architects *John & William Stokoe* produced very capable classical designs, notably the Newcastle Moot Hall [82]. *Thomas Oliver* published several excellent surveys of Newcastle, and was also the architect of Grainger's beautiful Leazes Terrace [144]. The engineer-architects *John* and *Benjamin Green* designed the Ouseburn viaduct and other works for the Newcastle & North Shields Railway (1837), the Literary and Philosophical Society building [81] (*John Green*, Greek Revival, of 1822–5), the present Theatre Royal [114] (1836–7), and Grey's Monument [15, 113] (*Benjamin Green*, 1838). Their near-contemporary *John Dobson*, supposedly Newcastle's first London-trained architect, brought new sophistication to the area with his ability to design in whatever style the client required.

Many local architectural offices worked in both Newcastle and Gateshead. As national businesses set up local offices later in the c19, bringing their own architects, and as architectural journals spread new ideas, Tyneside kept up with national standards. At the same time it did not lose its character, defined by the local sandstone and brick, and the simplicity of the local classical style.

24. Literary and Philosophical Society, library interior by F.W. Rich, 1893–4

Public sculpture includes impressive statues of Queen Victoria. Especially wonderful is the slender young woman depicted by *Frampton*, unveiled in 1906 in front of the Royal Victoria Infirmary [142]. By contrast, *Sir Alfred Gilbert*'s aged queen in St Nicholas Square [112], Newcastle, 1903, expresses power and responsibility with orb, sceptre and canopy. The local sculptor *J.G. Lough*'s commissions include the George Stephenson monument in Westgate Road, 1862, and the Lord Collingwood Monument at Tynemouth, on *Dobson*'s high pedestal, 1845. *Macklin*'s magnificent South African War memorial at Haymarket tells of virtue and heroism. Less complex are the confident figures of businessmen and benefactors: Joseph Cowen M.P. (*Tweed*, 1906) on Westgate Road, and Lord Armstrong (*Hamo Thornycroft*, 1905–6) at Barras Bridge.

Domestic architecture in the growing **suburbs** remained relatively sober. Exceptions include a few extremely large **villas** for industrialists, such as that which became Jesmond Towers (Tudor Gothic, with later c19 additions by *T.R. Spence* for Lord Armstrong's partner Charles Mitchell [166]), Jesmond Dene House (rebuilt in the 1890s from a *Dobson* house, with work by *Norman Shaw* and *F.W. Rich* for another Armstrong partner, and with its own real tennis court), and the glass manufacturer *William Wailes*'s self-designed Saltwell Towers [176], Gateshead, a castellated house built from 1862. The gatehouse (again by *Shaw*) and ruined banqueting house survive from Lord Armstrong's own house in Jesmond Dene.

It was some time before **working-class housing** reached an acceptable standard. Government investigations into the health of towns, and the ensuing Town Improvement acts, eventually led to careful regulation of new housing. None of the notoriously unsatisfactory back-to-back houses near the river now survive. Also near the river, at Garth Heads, the Newcastle upon Tyne Improved Industrial Dwellings Co. (formed by local business leaders) built a large brick block by *John Johnstone*, 1869 and 1878 [89]. Subsequent speculative housing, however, favoured long two-storey terraces of self-contained flats with paired front doors, the so-called Tyneside flats [25] (*see* topic box). In Gateshead, some flats of the 1870s in Shipcote had outside water closets, a tremendous improvement on the old ash closets. In Newcastle similar improvements were made, as terraces covered the fields of Benwell, Elswick, Byker, Heaton and eventually much of Jesmond. Tyneside flats continued as a c20 housing type: in Gateshead, there was no other available before 1914.

Nationally, the influence of Ebenezer Howard's Garden City movement, combined with government-granted powers to borrow funding for housing, led to council houses being built to the standards established from 1903 by Howard's Letchworth, Herts. Newcastle held a competition for (private) model cottages at Walkergate in 1908, and built its first council houses on Walker Road (dem.). For schemes of the 1910s–20s *see* below.

Tyneside Flats

The Tyneside flat was the dominant housing form of the C19 riverside. Unlike colliery houses these were not provided by the industrialist, but were built by speculators, mostly for rent. Typically one building two bays wide holds two distinct homes, with paired front doors. One door opens directly into the downstairs front room, the other to the stairs to the upper flat. (Sometimes there are groups of four doors, and the rear offshoots are joined.) The earliest and simplest flats stand directly on the street, but later versions have tiny front gardens and canted bay windows on one or both floors. Each pair has two back yards with small outhouses: usually a water closet (earth or ash closet in early days) and a coal house. The upper flats have enclosed rear stairs. A stone-surfaced 'back lane' allowed for coal deliveries and for night-time removal of soil from privies, through hatches in the high yard walls. Washing was pegged onto ropes in the yards, or strung across the lanes. A copper for boiling washing may have been in a washhouse or a rear scullery. In the kitchen/living room was a cast-iron cooking range, where flues from the open fire also heated an oven and a water boiler; the front bedroom had a fireplace. Larger flats had a smaller, unheated, third room. No bathrooms, but each house with complete privacy.

This housing type is almost exclusive to Tyneside (others are in Barrow-in-Furness, another shipbuilding area). While some of its characteristics can be found in the flats that Henry Roberts designed in London in the 1840s, there is no evidence of direct influence: both resulted from a need for solid, healthy housing at a time when many of the working class had to endure miserably crowded and unhealthy accommodation.

25. Typical Tyneside flats, Eastbourne Avenue, Gateshead, cutaway drawing

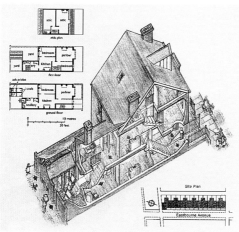

Parks were provided for both towns. In 1861 the freemen and borough-holders of Gateshead conveyed land to the Corporation to make Windmill Hills Park, probably Tyneside's first public park. Newcastle's first also originated in freemen's land, after the 1870 Town Moor Improvement Act: in 1873 part of Castle Leazes, the sw Town Moor, formed Leazes Park. The legislation also allowed the creation in 1878 of a park at the se corner of the Moor, renamed Exhibition Park after 1887 [159, 160]. Meanwhile in 1876 William Wailes sold Saltwell Towers to Gateshead Corporation, which continued to develop the grounds as a park. This was followed by the gift to Newcastle Corporation in 1880–3 of Jesmond Dene Park and other Ouseburn valley land by Sir W.G. (later Lord) Armstrong, part of the romantic grounds of his Jesmond house.

Between the Wars

New **civic buildings** moved away from the traditional centres after *c.* 1910. In Gateshead the Shipley Art Gallery by *Arthur Stockwell* opened in 1917 in Shipcote, some way s of the old town [174], followed in 1925–6 by the Public Library, designed by Stockwell and completed in modified form after his death. Newcastle acquired a City Hall off Northumberland Street (1928, with baths attached), and a grand classical building by *Cackett, Burns Dick & Mackellar* in Pilgrim Street housing Magistrates' Courts, Police Station and Fire Station (1931–3). A new town hall or Civic Centre was planned at Barras Bridge, but nothing was begun before the outbreak of war in 1939. Also in Barras Bridge is the best of the **First World War memorials**, the Northumberland Fusiliers, by *Sir W. Goscombe John* (1923) [136]. Close at hand is the most ambitious building for **higher education**, the present University's Students' Union of 1923–5, Neo-Jacobean by *Cackett, Burns Dick & Mackellar*. New **churches** of these years were mostly traditional in style, and placed in outer suburbs. One exception is the subdued but elegant and well-detailed Unitarian Church in Ellison Place [132], 1938–40, also by *Cackett, Burns Dick & Mackellar*.

The most significant single structure of the period, however, was the **New Tyne Bridge** [66, 68, 69], a giant single-span bridge designed by *Mott, Hay & Anderson* with *R. Burns Dick* as architect, and built in 1925–8. Its clean lines and *Moderne* styling were echoed by the 1929 pavilion by *W. & T.R. Milburn* of Sunderland in Exhibition Park [160], and by **commercial buildings** including Carliol House [26] in Pilgrim Street, stripped classical offices of 1924–8 by the local architects *L.J. Couves & Partners* and the national firm *Burnet, Tait & Lorne*. Of **cinemas**, Pilgrim Street retains the refurbished Tyneside Cinema [97] of 1937–8 by *George Bell*, built as a newsreel cinema, and the former Paramount of 1930–1 by *F. Verity* and *S. Beverly* (future uncertain). New shops, especially **department stores**, were also built despite the economic depression; low prices could be afforded by those in work. The big Art Deco premises in Northumberland Street do not survive;

26. Carliol House, Pilgrim Street, L.J. Couves & Partners with Burnet, Tait & Lorne, 1924–8

Fenwick's store there has an extension of 1937 in Blackett Street in a plain, strip-windowed style, by *Mauchlen & Weightman*. The most glamorous Art Deco department store was the Newcastle Co-operative Wholesale Society in Newgate Street [118], 1931–2 etc. by *L.G. Ekins* (future uncertain); another C.W.S. building of the 1930s survives as flats in Waterloo Street, with jazzy bricks and railings. Gateshead's extension of the Jackson Street Co-op, 1925, is Neo-Baroque.

The expansive Team Valley Trading Estate s of Gateshead, a pioneering industrial estate built from 1936 with government money in order to alleviate unemployment, falls outside the scope of this book. The same is true of the slum clearance schemes under the 1919 Housing Acts, which enabled Local Authorities to build well-laid-out garden estates. Of earlier **housing estates**, Sallyport Crescent survives on City Road: an especially well-planned block of flats, completed by 1916, with communal hot water, and rear balconies looking out to the river. The North Eastern Railway's Gosforth Garden Village (from 1921) follows the Garden Suburb model.

27. Vale House, Jesmond, by Douglass Wise & Partners with the City Housing Architect, 1966–8

From 1945 to *c.* 1985

Recovery after the Second World War was slow. Both towns were bombed, but the damage was mainly to industrial areas. One early priority was the need to accommodate returning members of the armed forces, which was met in part by **prefabricated houses**. Supposedly temporary, several types can still be found in excellent condition, e.g. in Gosforth and Bensham [169]. Permanent new Local Authority housing followed, including pitched-roofed flats in the pre-war tradition (e.g. Graham Court, Gosforth, 1948–52 [170]), and some high-density estates with slab blocks (e.g. Gateshead's Barn Close, 1955–6), replacing C19 terraces. From the 1960s these were joined by **tower blocks**, mostly in inner suburbs. A memorable one-off design is Vale House (1966–8), a tall slim system-built tower by *Douglass Wise & Partners* and the *City Housing Architect* [27], with abstract decoration. **Private housing** includes interesting 1960s terrace groups in Jesmond by *Brian Robson* and by *Cyril Winskell*.

28. The Byker Estate, by Ralph Erskine, perimeter and link blocks, 1972–5; low-rise housing (Grace Lee), 1974–6

The most significant housing development of this period, significant internationally, is at **Byker** [28, 155, 156]. The first stage here was preparation for a projected eight-lane E–W motorway, and consideration of ways to shelter the City Council's new houses from traffic noise. In 1969 *Ralph Erskine* was appointed architect. He designed the Byker Wall, an undulating wall of flats, almost blank to the new road, its windows and balconies facing S over the Tyne and over the low-rise housing that followed. Residents were, from the beginning, consulted about the designs for the streets and spaces, which are informal in plan and brightly coloured in materials. The appointment of a highly gifted architect and his team produced a superb estate, abandoned when nearly completed in 1981 and protected by official listing since 2007.

Both councils sought to supplement or replace their C19 **town halls**. Newcastle had held a design competition for the Barras Bridge site in 1939, but the outbreak of war halted the scheme. The present, Scandinavian-influenced Civic Centre [54–57], by the City Architect *George Kenyon*, was designed in 1950 and built 1958–68. It is a quadrangle with ranges of quite different characters and materials, including a Banqueting Hall, a projecting Council Chamber, a tower finished with heraldic seahorses' heads, a Rates Hall with *Victor Pasmore*'s murals, among several commissioned artworks that include sculpture by *David Wynne* [56], and furnishings and fittings of the highest quality. Gateshead's more modest plans began with the Borough Treasurer's Department [173] in 1954 at Shipcote, by the Borough Architect *A. Leslie Berry*, as 'Civic Centre First Stage'. However, the eventual Civic Centre (by Borough Architect, *D. W. Robson*) opened in 1987 nearer the heart of the old town [152]. It is of friendly vernacular materials – brick, with a red-tiled roof – planned in four courtyard blocks to maximize natural light.

The Metro

Construction of Tyne and Wear's Metro rapid transit system received Royal Assent in 1973. In 1980 the first section opened from Haymarket to Tynemouth, chiefly using existing suburban railways. By 1984 the full 'loop' was operating N of the Tyne, together with a line to Gateshead and South Shields. Some existing station buildings such as West Jesmond were adapted, others were new-built, including those on the tunnel that was dug through Newcastle and Gateshead. Other works included *Ove Arup & Partners*' elegant Byker viaduct and the Queen Elizabeth II Metro Bridge spanning the Tyne between the tunnel sections. Extensions include lines to Newcastle Airport, 1991, and to Sunderland, 2002.

Station design followed guidelines from the consultant architects, *Faulkner-Brown Hendy Watkinson Stonor*. They specified white and yellow enamel vitreous panels for interiors [29], with brown and red bricks and plastic-coated steel for standard exterior elements. Executive architects *L. J. Couves & Partners* designed the city-centre underground stations and that at Jesmond [158], with other work; *Ainsworth Spark Associates* the Control Centre at South Gosforth and the transport interchanges at Regent Centre (Gosforth), Gateshead and elsewhere; other stations and projects were by the *Waring & Netts Partnership*. Some stations are being redeveloped, starting in 2008 with Haymarket.

29. Monument Metro Station, artist's impression, 1979

30. Salvation Army (former Men's Hostel), City Road, by Ryder & Yates, 1976

Post-war **planning** in Newcastle began with proposals in 1945 for future development, prepared with the help of the City Engineer, *Percy Parr*.* The first Development Plan was approved in 1951. Little progress was made, principally because of restrictions on expenditure and materials, before T. Dan Smith was Leader of Council, and Chairman of Planning Committee, from 1958 to 1966.** *Wilfred* (later *Sir Wilfred*) *Burns* became Chief Planning Officer in 1960, and the two set about preparing for 'a strong and satisfying city'.

The resulting Development Plan was approved in 1963, including new N–S **motorways** on each side of the city centre and another E–W (*see* topic box, p. 190). Of these only the 'Central Motorway East' was built as planned, for which Dobson's Royal Arcade was sacrificed. Another essential element was lateral separation of traffic [130] and pedestrians, achieved by setting entrances to new buildings at first-floor level, linked by elevated walkways, above a ground-level road network for service traffic. A good example is M.E.A. House [131], completed 1974 by *Ryder & Yates* (the Salvation Army Men's Hostel [30] of 1976 is another good work of theirs). Also especially significant were the **Eldon Square shopping precinct**, opened in 1976 and since extended, for which two sides of the C19 Eldon Square were demolished, and two less popular blocks 'giving closure' to two medieval thoroughfares – Westgate House straddling Westgate Road (dem. 2006–7 under the Grainger Town project; *see* p. 41), and Commercial Union House over Pilgrim Street. More positive developments after 1965 included the **Metro**, an urban railway network implemented by the new Metropolitan County of Tyne and Wear (*see* topic box, facing).

*The Appendix 1, a 'list of new roads and widenings', strongly recalls pre-war proposals by the architect *Robert Burns Dick*.
**Subsequently forced to resign from office, and later imprisoned for corruption (1974).

31. Tynegate shopping precinct (dem. 2008–9), High Street West, Gateshead, by the Owen Luder Partnership, 1961–9. Photo *c.* 2003.

The post-war city plans also designated large areas N of the historic centre as an educational precinct, another proposal carried over from before the Second World War. The present **University** (King's College (Durham University) from 1937, Newcastle University from 1963) added several blocks under a short-lived masterplan in the 1950s. It then continued to grow in the 1960s, with slab blocks for sciences to the S, including *Sir Basil Spence & Partners'* physics building, and a large complex to the N by *Sheppard, Robson & Partners* [140], as well as *Sir William Whitfield*'s Student Union extensions and University theatre (both altered). Further expansion came with the brick-faced Robinson Library [139] of 1980–2 and later E of the Great North Road, by *Faulkner-Brown Hendy Watkinson Stonor*. E of the Civic Centre a new campus was made for the Rutherford College of Technology (later **Newcastle Polytechnic**; now University of Northumbria at Newcastle). The college and its buildings were a municipal responsibility, including the quadrangular Ellison Building by *George Kenyon*, 1949–65; they are now supplemented by adapted historic buildings nearby. There is also **Newcastle College** at Rye Hill in the inner West End, founded in 1956, likewise with a series of Modernist blocks augmented by recent additions.

Comprehensive planning had a similarly drastic effect on **Gateshead**. The borough continued to demolish C19 terraces, then the old town was cut through by the Felling by-pass (1960), Gateshead Highway (1961) and Western by-pass (1971), all with parts raised on piers above surrounding property. New houses and offices, such as the Barn Close flats of 1956 [151] and Tynegate precinct of the 1960s, replaced sub-standard houses and industrial premises. Gateshead also acquired a Technical College, relocated in 2008 from buildings of 1949–55 onwards at Shipcote to a new campus s of the Baltic Centre. The most striking change came with the construction in 1964–9 of Trinity Square [31]: shops and flats (dem. 2008-9) with a multi-storey car park towering over them, of exposed concrete, by the *Owen Luder Partnership*.

Tyneside since *c.* 1985

Notwithstanding the damage that followed, the 1963 Development Plan at least recognized that Grainger's town plan deserved protection as a coherent area. The last decades of the c20 saw renewed appreciation of the built heritage, reflecting enhanced protective legislation, expansion of the official lists of buildings of historic and architectural interest, and the designation of Conservation Areas, as well as more imaginative approaches to conversion and reuse. Early examples of **restoration** from the 1970s include Black Friars and Holy Jesus Hospital for the City of Newcastle, Alderman Fenwick's House in Pilgrim Street for the Tyne and Wear Buildings Preservation Trust ('Buttress'), and St Mary's church for Gateshead Council (then further damaged, but again restored).

Entire areas have since been transformed. The Grainger Town project of 1997–2003, by far the largest of Tyneside's regeneration schemes, covered some 90 acres containing 244 listed buildings. A masterplan was drawn up by *EDAW* for the City Council, English Heritage, and English Partnerships. Empty buildings were brought back into use, with upper floors often converted to flats. Also in Newcastle, the Ouseburn and Stephenson Quarter projects have brought near-derelict industrial areas back to life. In Gateshead a similar if more modest story is told by the restoration of Regent and Walker terraces and by the revived Old Town Hall.

A different approach was required for Newcastle's decaying Quayside, where the proportion of **new architecture** is much higher. Early examples include the *Napper Collerton Partnership*'s bold Law Courts of 1984–90, Postmodern-classical in character, and the same practice's Blue Anchor Court, 1987, one of the first instances of new private housing in central Newcastle for generations. Fresh impetus came from the newly formed Tyne and Wear Development Corporation, which commissioned a masterplan from *Terry Farrell & Partners* in 1991. The resulting buildings include residential, leisure and office developments in varied styles and materials, infilling within historic boundaries and redeveloping sites that had lain derelict, especially to the E. Designers include the local practices *Ryder Nicklin* and *Napper Architects*, and national firms such as *Arup Associates*, *CZWG Architects* and *Panter Hudspith* [93].

The Quayside works also include lavish provision of **public art**, including some very large sculptures, often in contexts of new pedestrian routes and hard landscaping [87, 92]. Provided with the help of various public funding bodies and private developers, public art has been a major component of many regeneration schemes since the late c20. Locally, the story begins in the 1980s with Gateshead's Rabbit Banks Sculpture Park on the s bank of the Tyne. Memorable works since 2000 in Newcastle include *Eduardo Paolozzi*'s great Vulcan [78] near Robert Stephenson's works in South Street, and *Thomas Heatherwick*'s Blue Carpet installation s of the extended Laing Gallery [32]. Standing above all, both literally and metaphorically, is *Anthony Gormley*'s Angel (1994–8), originally the Gateshead Angel but now the Angel of the North [183], embracing all comers with wide arms.

The Angel was closely followed by three no less spectacular projects that have transformed the Gateshead riverside and its relationship with the N bank. The **Millennium Footbridge** [66, 67], 1995–2001 by *Wilkinson Eyre Architects* and the engineers *Gifford & Partners*, is a

32. Laing Art Gallery, New Bridge Street, with Blue Carpet, by Thomas Heatherwick, 1996–2001

33. Sage Music Centre, Gateshead, by Foster & Partners, 1996–2004

tilting footbridge of innovative design, downstream of the older Tyne bridges. On the Gateshead side are two new **buildings for the arts**: the Baltic Centre for Contemporary Art [62, 63], converted by *Ellis Williams Architects* in 1998–2002 from the giant shell of former grain silos, and the Sage Music Centre by *Foster & Partners* [3, 33, 64, 65], 1996–2004, which groups concert halls and other facilities within an undulating shell of glass and stainless steel.

The early c21 has also left its mark on the **universities** and other **buildings for education**. Newcastle University has made some memorable additions, including *FaulknerBrowns*' Paul O'Gorman Building of 2003, and is implementing a master plan by *Terry Farrell & Partners* which will make a new 'gateway' building on Barras Bridge. The University also occupies part of the same architects' Centre for Life (1996–2000), an extrovert Lottery-funded design, sited off the main campus [124]. Plans have yet to be finalized (2008) for the

34. Newcastle College, Performance Academy, by RMJM, 2004

University's Science City beside St James's Boulevard. The University of Northumbria has spread E across the motorway to the shining new City Campus East by *Atkins* [134], 2007. Newcastle College is also swiftly developing on its 1960s site, with stunning new blocks by *RMJM* [34, 146]. Another colourful development is *Malcolm Fraser Architects'* Dance City, 2005, on St James Boulevard (laid out in the 1990s as the realisation of the western motorway planned in 1963). The city will in 2009 have a replacement Central Library, by *Ryder*.

Shopping remains a prime interest in the early C21. Eldon Square was remodelled in 2008 to add ground-level interest, throwing off the 1960s separation of levels. Gateshead will have new town-centre shops replacing Trinity Square. The conversion of industrial premises to **housing** continues, as at Turnbull's warehouses in Newcastle and Gateshead's Ochre Yards (the former North Eastern Railway works, with much new building in addition). New housing along the riverfront has varied in quality, but mention should be made of *Conran & Partners'* fine Quayside Lofts in The Close (2001–7). Other new build is less attractive, crowding small units into tall spaces, as behind the Baltic, but can work if carefully controlled, as at *Waring & Netts'* mixed-use Trinity Gardens development, Broad Chare.

Newcastle and Gateshead, having accommodated all of these changes, still have the feel of historic towns and are caring for their historic buildings and areas. Their medieval street plans are discernible among the motorways and flyovers, their old terraces are rejuvenated in the inner suburbs, and fine offices and public buildings in town centres are finding new uses. The river and its banks have emerged clean and shining after centuries of industry. If Sir William Brereton were to return he might repeat his comments of 1635: 'This is beyond all compare the fairest and richest towne in England . . . This towne, unto this countrye, serves in steade of London.'

Major Buildings

Cathedral Church of St Nicholas

St Nicholas Street and Mosley Street

Newcastle became a city in 1882. That same year, the diocese of Newcastle was carved out of the diocese of Durham, with the parish church of St Nicholas as its modest cathedral. St Nicholas is distinguished by its wonderful spire: William Grey, Newcastle's first historian (*Chorographia*, 1649), wrote 'it lifteth up a head of majesty high above the rest, as a cypresse tree above the low shrubs.' C21 planning policies endeavour to maintain its visibility.

The **site** is N of the Castle (*see* p. 62), and is bounded on the SE by the steep drop to the narrow street called The Side and on the E by the deep dene of the Lort Burn, now represented by Dean Street (*see* Walk 3). All sense of the original churchyard has been lost with the construction of St Nicholas Street at the W in the 1850s, and C19–C20 office blocks to the S and E. For the Queen Victoria statue, N, *see* Walk 4, p. 162.

Development

Around 1120 Henry I granted an unnamed church here to Carlisle cathedral priory, and in 1194 the church of St Nicholas was mentioned in a grant of tithes. In the early C13 there was an aisled cruciform church, with nave and crossing lower than the present. By *c.* 1370 a larger nave and transept were probably complete. The chapel E of the N transept (Chapel of St George) is documented, but appears to have been reconstructed in the later C15.* The heraldry of the medieval roof bosses belongs to the years 1390–1412. The continuous row of tomb recesses along the wall of the nave S aisle is broken by the Chapel of St Margaret, formerly called the Bewick chapel, established in 1394–5, so this S aisle wall was there before 1394. Shortly afterwards, clerestories were added round the whole building. The completion of the tower was next, and then the crown and tower vault in the later C15. The present building is therefore mostly C14 and C15, though with fragments of C12 and C13 fabric [37].

Post-medieval construction includes *James Gibbs's* rebuilding of the S vestry in 1736; reconstruction of parts of the transepts, aisles and chapels in the 1820s–70s variously by *John Dobson*, by *John Green* (who

---

*Payments from mayors of 1348, 1350, 1361 etc., indulgence of 1359 to donors to new chapel foundations, bequest for a chancel window 1369.

35. Cathedral Church of St Nicholas, from the north-west. Late C19 engraving

added the N and S tower porches) and *Benjamin Green*, and by *Sir George Gilbert Scott*; and the building of the NE hall and vestries in 1926 by *W.H. Wood*. Much repair and restoration has also been done. The early C19 work of the Greens and Dobson in particular has a recognizable character, in big blocks of pecked masonry.

Exterior

The **west tower** dominates because of its remarkable C15 spire (the whole is 193 ft 6 in., 59 metres, high) [35]. Its sturdy square base has chamfered and stepped diagonal buttresses. The C14 W doorway and large five-light window with panel tracery are renewed (as are all external windows). The belfry has tall paired openings separated by slender buttresses which continue as pinnacles above the pierced parapet; the corner buttresses reducing to narrow shafts which support statues in front of the turrets of the pinnacles. From these corners, the late C15 **crown** [36] rises: four flying buttresses lean against each other and hold up a tall square lantern, battlemented and pinnacled. On it rests a slender octagonal spire, its angles crocketed, on four smaller arcs. Crockets also adorn the ogees flowing up the crown to the lantern, and the spirelets on all the pinnacles. What began with solid lower stages ends as an extraordinarily airy confection with a flurry of gilded wind-vanes. A few other medieval instances of this form of crown occur in Britain: St Mary-le-Bow, London, *c*. 1357 or after (rebuilt before 1512); St Giles, Edinburgh, *c*. 1495; King's College, Aberdeen, *c*. 1500. The higher parts were rebuilt in 1608, and the crown repaired at least twice in the c18.

In the c19 there was much anxiety about the stability of the tower: the N and s porches of 1834 and 1832 were built by *John Green* to support it, the s one further braced by sloping courses of masonry at the w end of the s aisle. *John Dobson* repaired the foundations in 1833–4, and inserted iron bands at the level of the clerestory sills and in the ringing chamber, but problems remained. *Sir George Gilbert Scott* was more successful: in 1867 he re-underset the tower by 14 ft (4.3 metres) below the nave floor, with concrete foundations.

Church. The windows have renewed masonry, some copying the original, partly Dec with flowing tracery and partly Perp. The nave N aisle was partly rebuilt by *John & Benjamin Green*, 1834–6, perhaps copying the original windows, as was St Margaret's Chapel on the s side, to a changed design. Transepts, s aisle and clerestory all have c14 window designs, but *Dobson* rebuilt the N end of the N transept in 1824, and in 1859 the E gable, altering the windows and removing a high E roundel. *Scott* largely rebuilt the s transept in his restoration, completed 1877. There is cusped and intersecting early c14 tracery in the two easternmost windows of the nave s aisle, and one window reused in St George's Chapel (chancel N). The other windows of this chapel have tracery of the later, flowing type, as has the w window of the main part of the N transept. The upper windows of this transept are of a later type still, with three ogee-headed lights under one shallow segmental arch; the clerestory has similar windows; so has the s transept w aisle, where the transoms may be *Scott*'s (not shown in Horsley's 1715 engraving). The s transept E wall has one window with flowing tracery and one that is straight-headed with reticulated tracery. Other windows are all Perp.

The **Thomlinson Library** was added against the chancel s aisle in 1736 at the expense of Sir Walter Blackett of Wallington: a replacement vestry with a two-storey library above, for books Dr Robert Thomlinson had bequeathed to the parish [11]. Pure Palladian, the first such design in Newcastle; formerly attributed to Daniel Garrett, but now known to be by *James Gibbs*, and as such Newcastle's first known building by a national architect. Five bays, rusticated ground floor, giant Ionic pilasters above, alternating triangular and segmental window pediments on the first floor, the central one broken as though

36. Cathedral Church of St Nicholas, spire lantern and pinnacles, c14

for a missing inscription or bust. All windows have eared surrounds; the doorway, right, was formerly balanced by another, now become a window, left. Inside, a sturdy staircase with pedimented doorcases.

In 1926 the NE **hall**, **library** and **vestry** were added by *W.H. Wood*, entered by a stair from the chancel N aisle. Restrained Gothic. Stair and upper floor inserted at the w end by *R.R. Simms* to form offices *c.* 1980. To the E and SE, churchyard **railings** with Gothic-lettered Magnificat in the frieze, also of *c.* 1926.

Interior

There have been two big post-Reformation changes to the interior: the over-enthusiastic restoration of 1783–7 by *David Stephenson* and *William Newton*, who emptied it of most of its monuments and in the

37. Cathedral Church of St Nicholas, plan

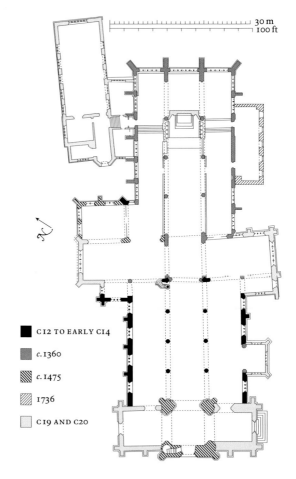

30 m
100 ft

C 12 TO EARLY C14

c. 1360

c. 1475

1736

C 19 AND C20

38. Cathedral Church of St Nicholas, interior

1880s, when it was made into a cathedral by *R. J. Johnson* with new stalls, reredos, chancel screen, etc., the altar brought forward, and the chancel floor raised.

The late C13 or C14 arcades and crossing, the C15 tower and the reordering of 1882 give the interior [38] its present character. Although not huge, the church is unified by the sweeps of arches which make it seem long; the arches in aisles and transepts, and wide nave aisles and chancel chapels reveal complexities of space. The nave and chancel have four bays each, the chancel E bay concealed by the richly carved reredos of 1882. All arches rise from octagonal piers without capitals, a continuous sweep of chamfers along the arcades to the crossing. Only hoodmoulds, headstopped in the nave, break the smooth walls. Triple-chamfered arches in the nave, the slightly lower chancel and the N transept; in the S transept, double-chamfered. The tower arch has sixfold chamfering. The tall, multi-moulded crossing piers and tower piers, the only element approaching cathedral scale, are triple-chamfered and without capitals. (C18 illustrations show a flèche over the crossing, but these piers look as though meant to support a much heavier structure.)

Details discovered during repair work and now revealed show an **earlier church**, of unknown length. In the wall above the N arcade near the NW crossing pier is a blocked late C12 round-headed window with roll-moulded surround. Early C13 are part of a square pier with semi-circular keeled shaft and moulded capital exposed within the NW crossing pier, and an E respond, also keeled and lower than the present one, in the S arcade. The corbels in the nave N aisle, and sawn-off corbels at the S, are relics of the earlier C13 aisles, which may in turn have replaced yet earlier aisles. The present lower nave walls of roughly shaped small square blocks also pre-date the taller arcades. The arcade walls were heightened in connection, and given clerestories with bigger masonry. Only the tower bay is vaulted, with liernes and the central octagonal bell-hole. The bosses have the arms of Robert Rhodes (d.1474), and around the bell-hole is the motto *Orate pro anima Roberti de Rodes* ('Pray for the soul of Robert Rhodes'). (The font heraldry is also his, *see* opposite.)

In the N transept E aisle (St George's Chapel) is the only unrestored medieval window, the little oculus with a wheel of five mouchettes low down in the W wall, typical of *c.* 1330–40. It allows borrowed light into an E–W **crypt** below the N end of the N transept, vaulted with five heavy, single-chamfered transverse arches; it has a triangular-headed piscina. The arches between transept and chapel are of late C15 type, suggesting a rebuilding of the C14 chapel then, with reuse of the original windows.

The timber **roofs** of sturdy Northern character are mostly late medieval, low-pitched, with arch-braced trusses on wall-posts; three rows of heraldic bosses on purlins and ridge are a mixture of medieval, C18 and later.

Furnishings

Tower. Late C15 **font** of dark grey limestone with many fossils, the bowl with eight slightly concave sides, some with shields of arms of Robert Rhodes [39]. The fine **cover**, *c.* 1500, is of wood, with elaborate tracery, gables, pinnacles, foliage and crockets. Inside, a tiny rib-vault, with a boss of the Coronation of the Virgin; brackets in the lower part are probably C17 repairs. – **Nave.** A brass eagle **lectern**, *c.* 1500, one of some twenty such in England. **Pews** of *c.* 1882 by *Johnson*, carved by *Ralph Hedley* with panels of blind tracery. – **N transept. Organ case**, until the late C19 at the E end of the nave, where it hid the chancel. Built 1676 for a *Renatus Harris* organ; enlarged 1891, modified 1932. Excellent classical carving, with replacement trumpeting angel over the centre. Additions of 1710 by *Harris*, with a case which now faces into St George's Chapel. – **St George's Chapel.** Sturdy **pews**, perhaps 1920s. – **S transept.** W wall, **royal arms** of Charles II, in high relief. – **Crossing and chancel.** Fittings sensitively designed in Gothic style *c.* 1882 by *Johnson*. **Reredos**, executed with great skill by *Robert Beall*, the figures by *J. S. Westmacott*; **pulpit**, also *Johnson* and *Beall*, like the reredos of Uttoxeter alabaster; **rood screen**, **bishop's throne** and **choir stalls** carved in the medieval spirit with varied poppyheads by *Hedley*, the **canons' stalls** with well-carved misericords. Behind the reredos, **sculpture** by *Stephen Cox*, 1997: eucharistic symbols, in alabaster and imperial porphyry.

40. Cathedral Church of St Nicholas, crypt stained glass, attributed to Basil Barber, *c.* 1932

Stained Glass

Excellent Victorian and C20 work, described clockwise from the W. W end: Tree of Jesse [41], 1866 by *Clayton & Bell*. – Nave N aisle: to Northumbrian volunteers of the Boer War, 1903 by *Bryans*; another by *Bryans*; third, Indian Mutiny memorial, 1859, vivid colours, by *William Wailes* of Newcastle; fourth, Northumberland Fusiliers memorial, delicate, 1921 by *P.C. Bacon*. – N transept: over the crypt porch, abstract by *S.M. Scott*, 1971; clerestory, two by *W.E. Tower* (*Kempe & Co.*), 1908. – St George's Chapel. Four superb memorial windows of 1934–5 by *A.K. Nicholson*: E, to Lord Grey of Fallodon, with SS Oswald and Cuthbert, and A.J. Bigge, 1st Lord Stamfordham, with SS Edmund and Edward; N, to the marine engineers Sir Charles Parsons and Andrew Laing. – Crypt: four charming small N lights to A.J.C. Ross, shipbuilder, d.1931, attributed to *Basil Barber* [40].

Choir N aisle: first, *c.* 1900, attributed to *Percy Bacon*; second, *Bryans*, 1902; third, a beautiful *Kempe* window, also 1902, to W.B. Wilkinson who in the 1860s developed an early reinforced concrete; fourth, by *Caroline Townshend*, 1907, another fine design with Northern saints; fifth, Danish seamen's Second World War memorial, with emblems set in clear glass, 2002 by *Mike Davis* (*see also* monuments, p. 56). – Chapel of the Resurrection (choir N aisle, E bay): N, by *L.C. Evetts*, 1958–9, also clear glass, Passion symbols inset; E, *Clayton & Bell*, 1901. – Chapel of the Incarnation: E, 1860 by *Wailes*, to the organist Thomas Ions. Crucifixion, Last Supper, the Four Evangelists. – Chapel of the Ascension (choir S aisle, E bay): E, *Evetts*, 1962–3; S, 1861 by *Wailes*. – Choir S aisle: first a half-window also by *Wailes*, commemorating Edward Spoor d.1856; then lights and windows blocked by the Thomlinson Library vestry of 1736; sixth, by *W.H. Atkinson* to the Rev. James Snape, d.1880, head of the Royal Grammar School; seventh,

41. Cathedral Church of St Nicholas, four lights from w end, by Clayton & Bell, 1886

Wailes's window to Joseph Garrett, chemist, d.1861, restored panels in clear glass. – Choir clerestory, *Kempe*, 1899–1903.

s transept: E, two by *Powell Bros*, Leeds (d.1870, and 1880); clerestory E, three by *Kempe & Co.*, 1908, prophets; s, four-light window by *Powell Bros*, and a wonderful smaller piece by *W.E. Tower* of *Kempe & Co.*; w, *Baguley*, in good colours.

Nave s aisle, first and second, 1889 by *E.R. Frampton*. – St Margaret's Chapel: E, a fine roundel with part of a C15 Virgin and Child, set in clear glass; s, by *Mayer & Co.* of Munich and London, late C19; w, by *A.E. Tombleson* for *Kempe & Co.*, 1896. – s aisle, continuing w, by *Kempe*, 1900. – s porch, 1870 by *Wailes*, with figures of SS John Baptist and Evangelist copied from C15 glass in All Saints, York.

A selection is given below, clockwise from the w end. Many medieval monuments were destroyed in the late C18.

Nave w end, s to N. R. Hopper Williamson d.1835, by *D. Dunbar*, life-size seated figure. – Sir Matthew White Ridley, d.1813, by *Flaxman*, toga-clad against an obelisk. – Admiral Lord Collingwood d.1810, and his widow Sarah, by *Rossi*, 1821. Bust on high, draped pedestal, Vitruvian scroll waves. Designed by *C.R. Cockerell.*

Nave N aisle, w wall. Calverley Bewicke of Close House, d.1815, by *E.H. Baily*, designed by *Theed*, exhibited at the Royal Academy 1819. White marble: a large, complex group surrounded by a Gothic frame. Bewicke, dying, his daughter supporting him, is seated, looking at a standing allegorical female originally holding a spade, while an angel hovers above, holding a scroll. – N wall, Hannah and Edward Mosley, d.1784 and 1798, obelisk and sarcophagus relief, by *Fisher* of York. – Several memorials and monuments to men killed in battle, mostly in India and South Africa. At the E end, large *Louis Raemaekers* cartoon of St George, with plaque to Brigadier-General J. Foster Riddell, d.1915.

N transept. Joseph Bainbridge, solicitor, d.1823 by *Baily*; marble portrait head. – William Peareth d.1775, who served as town clerk and as alderman nearly fifty years but always declined the office of mayor. By *Westmacott*. – St George's Chapel. w, William Hall d.1631 and his wife, Jane, d.1613, at prayer; a good Renaissance piece: two kneelers, six children below. – E, Robert Shafto d.1705. Cartouche, deeply carved frame with skulls, cherubs and coats of arms. – Thomas Surteis d.1629. Eroded, wide aedicule; mermaid and woodman supporters for coat of arms.

Chancel N aisle. s, Bishop Lloyd, 1908, designed by *Oliver & Leeson*; alabaster effigy by *F.W. Pomeroy* on canopied Gothic tomb-chest. – Brass to Ernest Wilberforce, first Bishop of Newcastle (1882–96) by *Singer* of Frome. – N, Major Robert Buggin d.1688, of London; cartouche, richly carved frame. – Patrick Crowe, d.1694. White marble, leaves-and-fruit-framed cartouche. – Memorial, 1983 by *R.G. Sims*, to Danish seamen killed 1939–45. Steel rods with slate panels. – E, Major George Anderson d.1831 (the sale of whose house, Anderson Place, made Grainger's new streets possible), sarcophagus.

E end, behind the reredos, the superb Thornton **brass**: Roger d.1429, his wife d.1411 (removed from All Saints). At 89 in. (2.25 metres) supposedly the largest in the country, and certainly one of the finest. Made before his death; probably North German. Two large figures, incised, not cut out and set in the stone. Framed by shafts with seven tiers of saints on buttresses, the outer ones with additional figures appearing in profile and only half visible, an early use of perspective. Seven sons and seven daughters below, and other narrative figures in canopies.

Chancel s aisle. John Collingwood Bruce d.1892, signed 1890 by *George Simonds,* erected 1894. Marble effigy on a sarcophagus, his feet resting on his *Handbook to the Roman Wall*, open at the acknowledgements. – Fine monument to Matthew Ridley d.1778 by *J. Bacon Sen.*, 1787. Seated Roman figure against a wide obelisk; a medallion on the base represents Newcastle as a woman crowned with turrets. – Henry Askew d.1796, and his wife d.1792; 1801 by *Henry Webber.* Josiah Wedgwood employed him, and had earlier sent him to Rome to study classical carvings and urns. A group of allegorical figures around an urn, on which are carved portrait heads. – Edward Collingwood of Chirton, 1790. Well-cut inscription supporting an urn, with enamel medallions. – Matthew Duane F.R.S., d.1785. Green and white marble, with obelisk and mourner.

s transept. E, the Rev. Hugh Moises (d.1806) by *Flaxman.* Scholar, and headmaster of the Royal Grammar School; portrait medallion on column which supports a plain urn, with a bored Religion beside it. – s, the only surviving medieval effigy, a c14 knight in armour. – NW, moved from a crossing pier, the most appealing of all the monuments, *c.* 1635 to the Maddison family. On a leafy bracket, painted and gilded, with six kneeling figures of Henry, Elizabeth and their parents, with their sixteen children below. The couple are at prayer, flanked by two fathers in armour facing front, two mothers half-hidden by Corinthian columns. Lively carving, shell-canopied niches in a projecting frame of deep base, jewelled panels; elaborate entablature with high broken pediment crested with arms, and figures of Faith, Hope and Charity. – w, Thomas Hedley, d.1877, who helped to endow the new bishopric.

Nave s, St Margaret's Chapel. Four medieval cross-slabs, all unfortunately painted white *c.* 1960; one of that rare type of a shroud with openings through which head and feet are revealed.

St Mary's Cathedral (R.C.)

Clayton Street West

The Cathedral and its auxiliary buildings are on a triangular site between Clayton Street West, Bewick Street and Neville Street. The church was built in local stone 1842–4 by *A.W.N. Pugin*, with 1,200 seats, as Newcastle's Catholic population grew rapidly; his contractor for building and for most furnishings was, as so often, *George Myers*. There had been a Catholic chapel in Newcastle for a long time: in the C17 a room in White Hart Yard, off Cloth Market, later in a house in Newgate Street; in the C18 in Father Worswick's Pilgrim Street house, and eventually in a chapel in his garden.* In 1850, when the Catholic hierarchy was restored, St Mary's became the cathedral for the new Catholic diocese of Hexham (from 1861, Hexham and Newcastle). Pugin's design for a spire was not executed, but 14 ft (4.3 metres) of the tower was built as a sw porch; the present tower and spire, 222 ft (68 metres) high, were completed in 1872 to a design by *A.M. Dunn & E.J. Hansom*, largely paid for by a £2,000 bequest of 1870. In 1901–2 a baptistery chapel was added to the (liturgical) w end of the s aisle, beside the tower, probably by *E. Goldie*. Beyond are courtyard ranges comprising presbytery, chapter house etc., s of the church. Restoration and redecoration after extensive repairs, 1980–8 by the *Napper Collerton Partnership*, included post-Vatican II reordering. From 1998 *Kevin Doonan Architects* closed the courtyard by adding the entrance screen and the bookshop on Clayton Street West, then began to redecorate the interior. They also reopened the s passage to the courtyard from Neville Street, and restored the boundary wall there to its original (lower) height.

Exterior [42]. The spire, dominating all points of view and an important element in the streetscape of this part of Newcastle, and in distant views, rises from the tower above the original sw porch, with corner spirelets, tall lucarnes and patterned bands. Aisles are full-length and gabled, the nave higher, so that the E end has a fine group of three-light windows flanking the great seven-light window, all with Dec tracery. The triple gables are steeply pitched, the central one without clerestory. The w end, rising dramatically from the pavement, has ballflower decoration to the s aisle window; a five-light central window over double doors, with elaborate hinges, in a multi-shafted surround. Niches flanking the central window hold statues of SS Bede and Cuthbert.

---

*Demolished for Worswick Street, and replaced with the present St Andrew of 1874 (p. 143).

42. St Mary's Cathedral, Neville Street front, by A.W.N. Pugin, 1842–4, spire by
A.M. Dunn & E.J. Hansom, 1872; library and chapter house by G. Goldie, 1851, left

Interior [43]. Arcades of six bays, a narrow chancel bay and a chancel slightly projecting beyond the N aisle. No clerestory; all light from
side and end windows. A vast space was created by the 1980s reordering,
which removed the choir screens, and repainted in a uniform pale
shade, after 1890s evidence (the Pugin interior was not recorded but was
known to be simple). *Kevin Doonan Architects*' redecoration of 1998
onwards uses colours and motifs from Pugin's palette elsewhere.

Furnishings. Carved **altars** of Caen stone, designed by *Pugin* and
made by *Hardman*. Restored in the 1980s to uncoloured stone, presumably original (they were described *c.* 1870 as 'barbarized' by paint). The
reredos and front of the old High Altar remain at the E end and the Lady
Chapel altar has become the forward altar. – Hardman also made
Pugin's Caen stone **font** (E end) and large **pulpit**, lowered and narrowed

to form the **ambo**. – Hanging **Crucifix**, recently restored to the sanctuary, from the (now removed) 1853 rood screen, and like it, designed by *George Goldie*. – The roof has **stencilling** of 1985 picking up the pattern of late C19 floor tiles. – Fine **tiled frieze** of 1901–2 below the window sills, painted by *Atkinson Bros*, with names of local saints and martyrs. – In the sanctuary, **brass** to James Worswick d.1842 by *Pugin*, made by *Hardman*. – **Screen**, Blessed Sacrament Chapel. By *Kevin Doonan Architects*, 2006.

Stained glass. Three richly coloured E windows designed by *Pugin* and made by *Wailes*, 1844: centre, Tree of Jesse; Blessed Sacrament Chapel, N, The Good Shepherd; Lady Chapel, s, Virgin and Child flanked by SS George and John. Many aisle windows were damaged in the Second World War, some of the glass being used to repair remaining windows. s aisle w (Baptism of Christ) by *Wailes*, installed by 1870, including a view of the church with unfinished tower. N aisle from E, first by *Wailes*, second by *Barnett*, w window to Elizabeth Dunn, d.1870, whose bequest largely paid for the spire (depicted). Fine recent windows, *Joseph A. Nuttgens*, 2005–6, three in the Blessed Sacrament Chapel, and one to Tyneside's pioneering industrialists and their workers, s aisle. Another, s aisle, by *Cate Watkinson*, 2005, a memorial to Private Adam Wakenshaw V.C.

Courtyard and presbytery. Entry to the courtyard from Clayton Street West is by *Doonan*'s glazed screen and porch of 2003 (the Cathedral's 1980s s door, in the polygonal baptistery chapel, opens off to the left). Across the courtyard at the Cathedral's SE, backing onto Neville Street, the ashlar **library** (later sacristy) and **chapter house** above it, added in 1851 by *G. Goldie*. The chapter house reuses C15 linenfold panelling from the old White Hart Inn chapel room. In 1869 *A.M. Dunn* ingeniously linked the block to the presbytery, right, by a polygonal stair-tower in the angle to an added bay facing Neville Street; formerly with open belfry and spirelet. The **presbytery** and associated buildings all brick, domestic in nature, Gothic in style: an interesting variety of window shape, a canted porch and a square stair-turret, steep roofs and polygonal chimneys. The first phase is of 1858 by *E.W. Pugin*. Originally symmetrical and free-standing, now with left front extension of 1884 by *Dunn & Hansom* and a canted porch and square stair-turret of 1938 by *R. Burke*. Burke's NW extension was brought forward into the courtyard and linked to the new entrance in 2003, when the new shop was also built, incorporating salvaged materials from the 1938 work. The whole forms a varied and successful group.

On Neville Street, below the E end of the Cathedral, on a round-edged stone platform, is *Nigel Boonham*'s memorial garden of 2002 to Cardinal Basil Hume. His larger than life-size bronze **statue** beckons from a sandstone outline of Holy Island (Lindisfarne). On a small boulder from Holy Island lines from the C7 Caedmon's Hymn are carved.

43. St Mary's Cathedral, by A.W.N. Pugin, 1842–4, interior

Castle

St Nicholas Street

Owing to the ruthlessness of the Victorian railways, Newcastle's chief medieval monument can be appreciated as a coherent castle only with effort. All there is to a significant height is a late C12 keep [44], a mid-C13 gatehouse to the NE (the Black Gate), the s postern, and much of the s curtain wall, bisected by the railway viaducts with their curtain of stone and iron.

The 'New Castle' was constructed by Robert, William the Conqueror's eldest son, in 1080. It was built on the site of the Roman fort (*see* p. 69), on a plateau overlooking the lowest bridging point on the river. The remains of this castle, of earth and timber, are only known from excavation. The stronghold was refortified after Henry II moved the seat of the sheriff from Bamburgh. Between 1168 and 1178 £1,144 was spent, and work was completed in the reign of John (1199–1216). This included the building of the present stone keep in the NW part of the castle, and of the North Gate, of which fragments survive. The gate was inserted into an earth rampart, on which a curtain wall was subsequently raised. This wall has mostly been levelled, but a stretch of Norman masonry with a Norman (tunnel-vaulted) **postern gate** can still be seen to the s in the remaining stretch of the C13 **curtain wall** sw of the Moot Hall, on Castle Stairs (*see also* Walk 1, p. 118). There was also an aisled stone Hall, foundations of which were excavated E of the keep in 1906, on the site of the future County Hall, now the Vermont Hotel (*see* p. 117).

The North Gate was superseded when a barbican or outer gateway – the present Black Gate [48] – was added to its NW by Henry III between 1247 and 1250. However, the later C13 brought the construction of a new Town Wall (*see* topic box, pp. 168–9), well beyond the castle bounds. After this the fabric was allowed to decay. Two storeys were added to the Black Gate in the C17, and more houses were built within the castle area, which became a refuge for those wishing to evade the town authorities' jurisdiction.* This decline was halted as antiquarian interest increased. After Newcastle Corporation bought the crumbling keep in 1809 it was given a roof and battlements, to make it look more presentable from the

*The former royal Castle, with the hall known as the Moot Hall, was not part of the historic town and county of Newcastle, but was until 1974 under the jurisdiction of the county of Northumberland.

44. Castle, keep, 1168–78

approach road to the new Moot Hall. In 1847 considerable restoration was carried out by *John Dobson* for the Society of Antiquaries of Newcastle who by then leased the keep, and in 1883 the Black Gate was restored for that Society by *R.J. Johnson*. But in 1849–50 the railway viaduct was built between the Black Gate and the keep, and doubled in width in the early 1890s. Because of C19 and C20 clearances, the railway now appears more like an overlay than an incursion.

The Keep

Newcastle is a late example of a tower keep [44, 45], built 1168–78. Its details are typical of the latest phase of the Norman style. It is roughly square, 62 ft by 56 ft (19 by 17 metres), with slight square projections at three angles and a bigger, irregularly polygonal one at the fourth (NW). The battlements are early C19 restoration, yet in conjunction with the broad areas of partly renewed golden sandstone they determine one's memory of the keep. On its E side is the restored forebuilding, an element not often surviving (cf. Castle Hedingham in Essex, and formerly also the White Tower, Tower of London). Here it is particularly elaborate and ingenious, containing a ground-floor chapel and a largely external staircase straight up to the room above it, with an intermediate landing to a short flight of stairs to the Great Hall doorway (left). A similar upper chamber occurs elsewhere only at the royal castle keep at Dover, a fact of considerable interest, because payment is recorded in 1174–5 to *Mauritius Caementarius* (i.e. mason) for work on our keep, while in 1181–2 a Mauritius Ingeniator (i.e. engineer) was paid in connection with Dover. In other respects Maurice's Newcastle work is very

45. Castle, keep, section from east to west. Engraving from Mackenzie, *A Descriptive and Historical Account of the Town and County of Newcastle upon Tyne, including the Borough of Gateshead*, 1827

46. Castle, keep, Great Hall door, restored *c.* 1847 by John Dobson, detail

different, including the detailing and the provision of an elaborately vaulted ground floor – a feature shared with the earlier northern castles of Carlisle, Bamburgh and Richmond.

Each floor within the keep proper has one principal room, with small rooms off it set in the thickness of the walls. Stairs, garderobes, a well room and galleries are also contained within the wall thickness. The present visitors' entry is to the first floor, but this description starts at ground level.

The **ground floor** has two distinct sections, originally unconnected: the principal room, popularly called the Garrison Room, and to its E the chapel, which takes up the narrow space in the forebuilding below the upper parts of the staircase. The **Garrison Room** is rectangular, with a circular central pier which has a many-scalloped capital. From this pier eight heavy single-chamfered ribs radiate to the corners and the middle of the sides – a concept clearly heralding the chapter houses of the C13. This room and the smaller, barrel-vaulted chamber to its E were originally accessible only from above, by a spiral stair in the SE corner, although now they are also reached from a doorway in the S wall. The **chapel** [47] was probably entered only from outside until an entrance was broken through from the chamber. It has a two-bay N–S nave and, at the N end, a one-bay E–W chancel, with a small W recess. The ribs of the oblong nave bays and nearly-square chancel are

47. Castle, keep, interior looking north, chapel, restored *c.* 1847 by John Dobson

decorated with chevron moulding in one bay, chains of beads in the others, and rest on corbels, not pilasters. The chancel arch has plain responds, but the two nave bays are separated by an arch with a chevron frieze. The obvious restoration is probably of the 1840s, by *Dobson*.

The **first floor** has the landing of the outer staircase, with a doorway with one order of (decayed) colonnettes, and a low-ceilinged hall and smaller chambers in the body of the keep. One small passage from the SE spiral stair leads to this hall (now museum), and another to a small barrel-vaulted chamber to the N. Modern doorways have been broken through from this chamber to the hall on its W side and the external stair to the E, creating a quite different pattern of access.

The hall is subdivided by means of a circular pier with plain octagonal capital and two single-chamfered arches. Off its N side, in the thickness of the wall, is the supposed **Queen's Chamber**. The small room off to the E was for observing the outer stair.

The external staircase reaches the **second** or **hall floor**, with steps to the left from the landing to the main entrance. The hall doorway, accurately restored in 1847 by *Dobson*, is unusually ornate, with an order of columns and voussoirs with lozenge and nailhead decoration [46]. The external stair continues to the N, to a room decorated with restored chevron moulding; it has been suggested that this was a second chapel (cf. a room in a similar position at Dover). To the s a little higher up is a shafted window in a broad shallow buttress projection. The middle buttresses on the N and s sides are narrower, that on the w side, where the C19 hall fireplace and its flue are, much broader. The **Great Hall** is not subdivided, i.e. there is no spine wall as at Dover or Bamburgh. To its s is a chamber some 22 ft by 8 ft (6.7 by 2.4 metres), perhaps identifiable as the **King's Chamber**. To the NE is a smaller room, the **Well Room**. At this level a straight stair opens off the SE spiral stair and climbs within the thickness of the E wall, passing through the window opening (allowing a view down into the hall), to a second spiral stair, NE. The NE and SE spirals lead first to a high wall passage which has openings looking down into the hall from all sides. The wall-sockets suggest that the hall roof was originally set below this wall passage, as formerly also at Dover and the White Tower (London). The present barrel-vault is of *c.* 1811. The spirals continue up to the roof platform, where the NW corner turret also dates from *c.* 1811.

The Black Gate

The **Black Gate** dates from 1247 onwards. It is a fortification of the improved C13 type, allowing flanking fire, and is set well forward from the earlier gate behind it. It is roughly oval in shape: a gateway between two semicircular guardrooms. On top of its two floors a house with mullioned-and-transomed windows was erected after 1618, and it is this which makes the building picturesque, especially with its brick rear additions of 1883 and their balustraded first-floor landing. Alexander Black was a C17 tenant.

The **gateway** [4, 48] is in three parts, an outer with a portcullis, a middle with a gate, and then a vaulted passage. In front was a draw-bridge; the slots in which the counter-weights swung can be seen below the roadway, sharp-edged piers forming three slots 13 ft (4 metres) long by 13 ft deep. Behind was another turning bridge, possibly of bascule type.

The clearance of old property *c.* 1850 to make St Nicholas Street caused the Black Gate to emerge from the huddle of houses which had surrounded it. Local opinion prevented not only its demolition but also the erecting of any other intrusive new building. After much campaigning it was restored with great skill in 1883 by *R.J. Johnson*.

48. Castle, Black Gate, west front, gatehouse, 1247; heightened after 1618 and restored 1883 by R.J. Johnson

A new staircase was also built, to replace the *ad hoc* arrangements of the many families who had been living in it. Much C13 detail survives in the ground floor, notably in the guardrooms with their ribbed vaults, and the trefoil-headed niches in the broad front pilasters flanking the arch. Of the C17 are the extra masonry in the front of the archway, the mullioned windows above and the moulded fire surrounds on first and second floors.*

Earlier Structures

The **Roman fort** of Pons Aelius lies under the Castle. It faced N, away from the bridge from which it took its name. The N defences seem to have been close to the Black Gate, overlooking the steep slopes down to what is now The Side; the river-cliff dictated the limit on the s. This fort, likely to have been polygonal on so awkward a site, was probably built in the late C2 or early C3, i.e. more than two generations after Hadrian's Wall. The w portion of the unusually small central head-quarters building, including the regimental shrine in the middle of the rear range, is outlined in setts immediately w of the keep (which over-lies the E side of the Roman building). Also marked out is a fragment of the commanding officer's house to the w. Below the railway arch and N of the keep, the setts delineate portions of two short granaries, with heavy buttresses and with axial sleeper walls supporting the floors.

The fort was occupied to the end of c4; in the Anglo-Saxon period the ruined buildings were robbed and levelled and the site became part of a cemetery. The square footings visible under the second railway arch have been interpreted as the tower of a Saxon church.

*Items from the collections of the Society of Antiquaries of Newcastle are to be shown at the Great North Museum (2009).

Guildhall

Sandhill

A complex building. The E end, rebuilt by *Dobson* in 1823–5, is Grecian; the main structure was built from 1655 by *Robert Trollope*, but was given a classical N front in 1794–6 by *David Stephenson* and *William Newton*, and a classical S front in 1809 by *John Stokoe*.

King John granted Newcastle Guild Merchant in 1216; a guildhall was mentioned in 1400. In 1425 Roger Thornton endowed the Hospital of St Catherine, later known as the Maison Dieu, which he built at the E end of the Guildhall. The town's accounts mention building a 'new house' in 1509. The **early Guildhall** had the court and council chamber on the first floor, and the exchange and weigh-house below. In 1639 it was described as standing next to the Maison Dieu, above which was the Merchant Venturers' Court. In 1655 the Town Council again ordered a new court to be built, on a longer site. *Robert Trollope*, a mason from York, won the contract; work was finished by 1658 [49]. The present plan was thus established: the Town Court running E–W at the W, with uses continuing as before, and the Merchant Venturers adjoining the E end. The Merchants' Court took the form of a crenellated tower, Trollope's Town Court that of a long hall with turrets at each end. On the Sandhill side, Trollope managed the junction with the old E part with an ingenious stair-tower projection. As illustrated for Brand (1789), it had twin flights of stairs with fat turned balusters set in classical arches, an upper large pointed arch, and round-arched loggias at the top. The tower rose between the loggias, to an octagonal turret and spire. Trollope's Town Court was more classical in composition than in detail, simply five bays and two storeys. The ground-level exchange and weigh-house had an open arcade to Sandhill with rusticated square piers, and closed arches towards the river, where most of the windows were round-headed. The principal first-floor window was pointed-arched, with balcony and wheel tracery (incorporating a sundial). The pilasters ended in picturesque spiral finials at the roof parapet. The Sandhill front was broken at the second bay to the right of the stairs by a much taller pointed arch with strange tracery. This arch, without tracery, can still be seen inside.

The outside of today's **Guildhall** is chiefly the result of alterations of 1794–1809 to the W parts, and of rebuilding by *Dobson* in 1823–5 of the old Maison Dieu and Merchants' Court at the E. To take the **W part** first: in 1794–6 *Stephenson* and *Newton* removed the stair-tower and rebuilt

49. Guildhall in the late c17, north side. Panel painting in the Mayor's Parlour

the entrance **forebuilding**, using an unfluted giant Ionic order with a pediment in a design closely resembling Newton's Assembly Rooms in Westgate Road (p. 178), with necking on the columns *à la* Adam [13]. w of the stair, they refaced the N front, replacing the mullioned windows with sashes, encasing the internal ground-floor pillars in sandstone and generally smoothing out the rustication to make a more refined and more fashionable building. They also made a hipped roof out of Trollope's gabled one, and the present cupola is probably theirs, replacing the eccentric flèche shown in engravings. (The present single-storey ground-floor addition, with vermiculated plinths to the pilasters, belongs to alterations of 1897–8 by *Armstrong & Knowles*, after a new Fish Market opened to the w. The less formal short w front is

50. Guildhall, by Robert Trollope, 1658; south front, 1809, by John Stokoe; east end, Fish Market by John Dobson, 1823

mostly of 1794–6. In 1807 it was decided that the **s front** should be similarly 'improved', so in 1809 it was refronted by *John Stokoe*, with pilasters along the upper storey, and a newsroom was made by walling off part of the ground floor. This caused the removal of all Trollope's jolly tracery and pilasters, leaving only four finials.

The ᴇ **end** was replaced in 1823–5 with one of *John Dobson*'s first buildings in Newcastle: a very satisfying solution, attractive from all angles [50] and allowing better passage from Quay to Sandhill. The plan is **D**-shaped. Dobson copied Stokoe's s front of 1809 for the two-bay Merchant Venturers' Hall, then turned Greek for the colonnade of the semicircular **Fish Market**. This has unfluted Doric columns with the stumpy proportions dear to the French architects of the 1790s,

51. Guildhall, by Robert Trollope, 1658, Town Court

supporting an entablature with triglyph frieze. Two floors above held the town offices. On the first floor, sashes in architrave surrounds; roof low-pitched and curved. Inside, Dobson reconstructed the Merchant Venturers' Court, with windows corresponding to those of the Town Court on the riverfront. In 1897–8 the Fish Market arcade was sensitively blocked in; the town offices moved in 1858 to the 'new town hall' in St Nicholas Square (since demolished).

Interior. Much of *Trollope*'s building survives inside but the **staircase** is a late C19 open-well replacement of that of 1794–6. On the inner wall a niche contains a C17 statue of Charles II in Roman tunic, from the gate on the old Tyne Bridge. At the top are paired doors to the **Town Court** [51], still occasionally used as a courtroom. The floor is of black-

and-white marble, the ceiling now plain but perhaps once painted. It retains its double-hammerbeam roof (the w bay altered for the hipped roof of 1796). The court fittings, which include balustrades, arcaded panelled benches, and spiky railings to the dock, seem to be mostly mid-c18, with early c19 additions. An odd-looking gallery high in the n wall has fat balusters set in rusticated pointed arches in the manner of the former stair-tower. It is probably Dobson's work of the 1840s, when the council decided to have a n gallery and improve ventilation. Below it, in the centre of the n wall, a **lobby** reveals the c17 pointed arch of Trollope's n front. From here, c17 panelled doors lead on the right to a cell with a small Tudor-arched window, and on the left to the **Mayor's Parlour** [52], the original Council Chamber. This has rare and interesting decoration: c17 chimneypiece with Corinthian pilasters and a high broken pediment bearing Newcastle's arms [53]; plaster ceiling with strapwork weaving round motifs of leaves and Tudor roses; panelling

52. Guildhall, Mayor's Parlour, c. 1658

53. Guildhall, Mayor's Parlour, c. 1658, arms of Newcastle in chimney pediment

with paintings, some depicting old buildings in Newcastle. One shows the Guildhall as it might have been when newly finished [49], with mullioned windows and the stair-tower described above; whether this is the source of later engravings, or copied from them, is not certain.

At the E end of the Town Court, a huge lugged doorcase leads to *Dobson*'s reconstructed **Merchant Venturers' Court** of 1823–5, now the hall of the Stewards of the Freemen of the City. A tall square room, of a quite different and astonishing scale. Dobson is said to have copied the C17 ceiling detail (the usual strapwork) but rather naughtily included the date 1620. The wooden chimneypiece he also copied, but incorporating rearranged carvings from the magnificent original overmantel dated 1636, now recognized as one of the finest examples of the C17 Newcastle school of woodcarving. The large reliefs show the Miraculous Draught and the Judgement of Solomon. Smaller representations of the planetary deities above. Anthony Wells-Cole has identified sources: biblical scenes from engravings by the Bolswert brothers after Rubens, deities and side figures from a suite designed by Maarten de Vos and engraved by Crispijn de Passe the elder (whose work was copied in plaster at No. 28 The Close, p. 109). The wall frieze is said to incorporate reused original carving. Much of Dobson's detail survives in the rooms above, now offices for the North-East Assembly.

The most altered part is the ground-floor **Exchange**. Used as a newspaper reading room in the C19, it became a club for those whose business took them to the river. The changes of 1897–8 also rearranged the spaces here. *Armstrong & Knowles* removed the stone pillars, lowered the floor, and inserted girders and stanchions. Departure of the Exchange Club in 1962 allowed further repairs by *Cordingly & McIntyre*. In 2004 part of the ground floor became a Tourist Information Office.

Civic Centre

Barras Bridge

This confident building by the City Architect, *G. W. Kenyon*, was begun in 1958 and opened in 1968 by King Olav V of Norway. It demonstrates both civic pride and a determination to move away to the light and space at the edge of the city centre.

The need for a bigger town hall was recognized by the early c20. *R. Burns Dick* of *Cackett, Burns Dick & Mackellar* published proposals in 1924 for a Town Moor site, then in 1933 for Market Street, to replace Johnstone's Town Hall of 1858–63 in St Nicholas Square. A competition was held in 1939, but progress was delayed by the outbreak of war. The 1945 City Plan proposed a civic precinct N of the centre, including the colleges of higher education. In 1950 the City Architect was asked to design a town hall here, on the site of early c19 terraces.

54. Civic Centre, plan

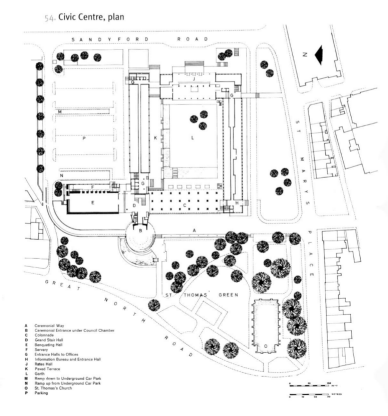

A Ceremonial Way
B Ceremonial Entrance under Council Chamber
C Colonnade
D Grand Stair Hall
E Banqueting Hall
F Servery
G Entrance Halls to Offices
H Information Bureau and Entrance Hall
J Rates Hall
K Paved Terrace
L Garth
M Ramp down to Underground Car Park
N Ramp up from Underground Car Park
O St. Thomas's Church
P Parking

55. Civic Centre, with Ceremonial Way, by George Kenyon, City Architect, 1956–69

Approval for construction came in 1956, delayed by Government controls on expenditure. The **plan** [54] is quasi-monastic: a square of grass ('the Garth'), offices on three sides, public rooms on the fourth, and Council Chamber off to one side, like a chapter house. Inspiration perhaps came from other town halls, possibly Dudok's Hilversum in Holland (1928–30) for its massing, a stark square tower at the corner of the square, and the rectilinear ranges of 1930s halls at Swansea and Norwich. The four-storey office blocks on the E and S were completed by 1959; the N block (twelve storeys) was built 1960–3. In 1965 work began on the W range: the main block of committee rooms, with metal fins to screen the glazing; at the NW angle the grand entrance hall and tall stair-tower; and E of that the Council Chamber, in line with the tallest office block. The W range extends N beyond the entrance hall with the Banqueting Hall and other civic suites; there is a large basement hall and underground car park. Cladding of the concrete structure is mostly stone: Portland (Whitbed, but with the more heavily pitted Roach Bed on the Banqueting Hall), Broughton Moor, Cornish granite and Norwegian Otta slate. The lower courtyard elevations have soft-toned hand-made bricks, with Rosso Levanto marble spandrels for the Rates Hall in the E range. Throughout, double-glazed bronze-framed windows. By November 1969 all was completed; total cost £4,855,000.

The formal approach is from the S and W, by the **Ceremonial Way** [55]. It passes committee rooms in the W range, above an arcade: granite-clad pilotis, shallow brick vaults, rising grilles between. These and the tall **flambeaux** are by *Charles Sansbury*. At the N end the ceremonial entrance with **glass screens** engraved by *John Hutton* with images of local history. On the left here, against a wall of riven Norwegian slate, water pours down the bronze 16-ft (4.8-metre) River God Tyne **fountain** by *David Wynne* [56]. Between the N range and the stair hall, the Portland-stone-clad stair- and lift-tower has a louvred carillon **turret** with seahorses' heads, supporters of Newcastle's arms, by *J.R.M. McCheyne*, and, high above, the arms' three golden castles. Hall and Council Chamber are great masses of stone: the hall with tall recessed slit windows leaving the wall as pylons between, the chamber a windowless elliptical drum with deep vertical grooves, raised on slender piers with graduated spacing. This forms a **porte cochère**, also opening to the ceremonial entrance. This has cast-aluminium portals and reveals by *Geoffrey Clarke*. Around the chamber a moat lined with granite setts. The drum has a shallow-vaulted soffit, its roof a shallow-pitched upturned funnel. In the quadrangle beyond, more water-washed sculpture by *Wynne*, **Swans in Flight**, rising from the W pool, and a wide terrace beside the N pool. On the tower, left of the office entrance, the 'Wren Stone', a stone supposedly selected by Wren for St Paul's Cathedral.

Artworks at the Civic Centre

The lavish provision of artworks is explained in the *Autobiography* (1970) of T. Dan Smith, Council Leader 1958–66 and chairman of the Planning Committee. For instance, Pasmore was 'let loose' in the Rates Hall because 'I wanted people to go there, albeit reluctantly, to pay their rates, and to come face to face with Pasmore's abstract art. . . . As they fingered their cheque books or opened their purses, I longed for them to snarl "This is the end. . .". I believe that this is what the relationship between the artist and the individual is all about.'

56. Civic Centre, River God Tyne fountain, by David Wynne, 1968

Interiors

The ceremonial range is richly furnished. The three-floor **Grand Stair Hall** [57], lined in English oak, has a wide, gentle stair to the first floor and concealed stairs to the upper gallery; eleven-tiered crystal chandelier by *A.B. Read*, floor of Portuguese Verde Viana marble. E wall of stone, with inscription by *David Dewey*. Inscriptions (naming mayors, etc.) continue around the **Banqueting Hall**, between the windows. Between the timber ceiling ribs, light red hide; on the ribs, bosses with the arms of the medieval guilds. Fine chandeliers. *John Piper*'s Aubusson tapestry adorns the N wall. At the E, deep arches to the servery, with retractable cast-aluminium grilles by *G. Clarke*. The **Council Chamber** is lined with cedar of Lebanon, and has natural light only from the funnel's eye in the ceiling, like the Pantheon. In the E range is the **Rates Hall**, where property-owners paid their dues beneath abstract murals by *Victor Pasmore* (*see* topic box, p. 79). Other fine pieces were **murals** by *Elizabeth Wise* in the Marriage Suite, and **lift door** motifs by *Sansbury*, which survive only in the SW lift shaft.

This remains a remarkable public building, dignified and well-judged, and perhaps ahead of its time in the extent to which it incorporates works of art. It invites the citizens in, and makes them proud of what they see there. Newcastle University's Bruce Allsopp must have the last word: 'the only building in Newcastle of the period 1940 to 1970 which will interest historians will be the new Civic Centre' (*Newcastle Journal*, 14 November 1968).

57. Civic Centre, Grand Stair Hall

Central Station

Neville Street

58. Central Station, porte cochère, by John Dobson, executed by Thomas Prosser, 1862–3

Newcastle alone amongst greater cities in the United Kingdom had only one large main-line **station**, a situation encouraged by Richard Grainger, who as early as 1836, when several companies were planning lines into Newcastle, argued for a 'Concentration of Termini'. The station was built between 1847 and 1851 for the York, Newcastle & Berwick Railway, allowing for use by the existing Newcastle & Carlisle Railway and the railway to North Shields and Tynemouth. *John*

Dobson's original design had a full-length porte cochère with paired columns marking the bays and a still deeper centre adorned with giant seated figures; its grandeur was diluted before construction began, probably because of financial difficulties. Moreover, the North Eastern Railway Co., formed by amalgamation in 1854, decided to accommodate its offices in the building. The porte cochère [58] was not built until 1862–3, executed by the NER's architect *Thomas Prosser* to a

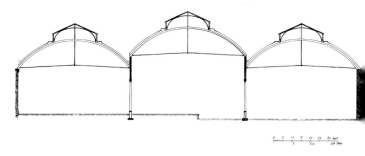

59. Central Station, train shed, section

revised design supplied by *Dobson*, his former master. The station is nevertheless a very fine, broad composition with its angle pavilions and deep central porte cochère of seven arches, measuring in all 590 ft (182 metres). The openings of the porte cochère and all windows are arched, the former with the original magnificent iron gates inside, the upper panels pierced. Emphasis is provided by Roman Doric pilasters, coupled at the angles of the pavilions and on the portico, and by heavy attics. Some of the detail is no longer of the purity of Dobson's earlier work. The pavilions have high plinths and attached Doric columns framing rusticated arches with coved and coffered heads under mask keystones. Lunette windows in the front light the upper-level offices.

Originally, the station offices included station-master's room, a waiters' room and bedroom, a bar sitting room, a smoking room, booking facilities, separate waiting, refreshment and washing rooms according to sex and class, and some hotel accommodation. The former first-class **refreshment room** has *Burmantofts* faience of 1893 (by *William Bell*, a later NER architect), revealed and restored when the present Centurion Bar was fitted out.

Train Shed*

Behind the portico, three high pillared archways lead to an astonishing **train shed** [59, 60, 61] constructed on a pronounced curve. The original train-shed roof comprises three parallel bays each 60 ft (18.3 metres) across, the central span springing from a slightly higher level. The whole covers an area of about 3 acres and is curved to a radius of 800 ft (243 metres). The roof is carried on a framework of tied, segmental wrought-iron ribs, formed from curved, built-up I-beams fishplated together. At the junction with the rear of the station offices (which are curved on the inside) every rib is sprung from pilasters set between the arcades; a masonry wall supports the outer end of the most

*Train shed and viaducts described by Stafford Linsley.

southerly span. Otherwise the ribs are supported on longitudinal timber trusses (hidden by simple wooden panelling), on plain slender cast-iron columns 23 ft (7 metres) high, located beneath every third rib. Each rib is tied across its ends by a wrought-iron rod [61]; a vertical hanger links the centre of the tie to the crown of the arch. The spans were roofed in longitudinal timber cladding from the springers to about two-thirds up the arc, and then glass for the roof-crown skylights and vents. The cladding was replaced by modern materials in the late 1970s, but the appearance of planking was retained.

Dobson's presidential address to the Northern Architectural Association in 1859 explained how he perceived that curved wrought-iron sections could be made by bevelled rollers, and that this innovation made his design a commercial possibility. It was *Thomas Charlton* of *Hawks Crawshay* of Gateshead who produced the necessary rolling mill, and although *John Abbot & Co.* of Gateshead won the tender for the ironwork it seems likely that the two firms collaborated in the

60. Central Station, train shed, by John Dobson, 1849, looking east

venture. (At about the same time Richard Turner produced curved ribs for the Palm House at Kew, but these were fabricated straight and then bent over templates.) This was the first train-shed roof constructed in this manner, a design much copied in modified form elsewhere.

The train shed was extended s with two less adventurous but still quite elegant arched roofs in 1892–4 under *William Bell*, his columns with long fluted brackets being somewhat more elaborate than Dobson's with their elegant clustered lotus-leaf capitals. New waiting and refreshment rooms were provided in this extension, while a bridge and a subway linked the old platforms with the new. At the same time an extended concourse with ridge-and-furrow glazing was made to the NE, for suburban platforms.

The glass and steel **travel centre** by *Nick Derbyshire* (*British Rail Architect's Department*), 1985, unashamedly of the 1980s, leaves the historic structure untouched. Small waiting rooms in similar style have been set on other platforms.

Extensions

The **Station Hotel** continues E along Neville Street. Dobson's planned hotel addition was not built until 1861–3, to designs by *Prosser* (ten bays plus a link bay, four storeys, the first-floor windows pedimented). This was extended eastward in 1888–90 by *W. Bell*, with a square entrance tower at the junction. Two storeys added later to the 1860s part. Much *Burmantofts* faience of *c.* 1890 remains inside, though, painted over.

To the W, No. 1 Neville Street, formerly the **Accountant's Office**, as reconstructed in 1883 by *Bell*. His is the grand frontage, with a French-looking roof. Behind it, the adapted former carriage shed of 1873, itself an enlarged reconstruction of the Newcastle & Carlisle Railway's goods station of 1852–4 removed from the other side of Forth Banks, s.

The Viaducts

The **railway viaducts** from the E end follow two great curves, one carrying the main line to Edinburgh and the other to the High Level Bridge (*see* p. 99), with which the station is integral. Engineering of great beauty. Incorporated into the first of these are two bridge structures of note. First the lines are carried over the N approach to the High Level Bridge, but not at a great height, on a cast-iron bridge, with open diamond-grid bracing in the spandrels, erected by *Abbot & Co.* in 1848–9; extended to N when the line was widened in 1894. Second, the lines are taken over a towering and finely constructed 80-ft (25-metre)-span elliptical arch in sandstone over The Side [16]. It too was widened to the N in 1894, in granite, and with a span of 106 ft (33 metres), to the design of *C.A. Harrison* [103].

61. Central Station, train shed, detail

Baltic Centre for Contemporary Art

Gateshead Quays

This, the first major modern development on the s side of the river, is where the renewal of Gateshead's Quayside really started. Converted in 1998–2002 by *Ellis Williams Architects* from former grain silos, it reflects three late c20 international trends: culture-led regeneration, reclamation of industrial sites especially on waterfronts, and the transformation of large industrial buildings into spaces for art. Earlier conversions of riverside or dockside buildings include the Arnolfini gallery in one of Bristol's Victorian warehouses, the Tate Liverpool in a warehouse beside the Albert Dock, and in London, Tate Modern, in Sir Giles Gilbert Scott's Bankside Power Station. Unlike some of these, the Baltic's original building was not considered of special architectural interest, and extensive redevelopment was possible. There is no permanent collection, but a programme of contemporary exhibitions, including light shows using the exterior as a screen. The conversion has been an architectural and artistic success, the structure providing a striking focal point where the river curves as it heads for the sea.

The Baltic owes its name to the custom of Joseph Rank Ltd of naming its mills after foreign seas. Built by *Mouchel & Partners* and opened in 1950, it worked only for some thirty years. It stands on the river's edge where imported grain was poured into its huge silos and then into a mill to be ground into flour; the mill was demolished in the 1980s. By the end of that decade Newcastle's East Quayside revitalization was under way (*see* p. 134), and Gateshead was looking towards renewal. By the 1990s Gateshead's patronage of the arts had gathered momentum, with successes including Anthony Gormley's Angel of the North (1994–8; *see* p. 280). At this point Northern Arts announced that it was seeking to establish new facilities for contemporary art in central Tyneside. The competition was held by the Borough of Gateshead, in conjunction with the Royal Institute of British Architects.

The red brick-clad concrete block [62], its long sides parallel with the river, has concrete towers at each corner, with stepped-back brick tops. High on the front the large letters BALTIC FLOUR MILLS above shallow pilasters, which reflect the former silo structure within. The inside

62. Baltic Centre for Contemporary Art, from the north-east. Flour silos by Mouchel & Partners, opened 1950, converted by Ellis Williams Architects, 1998–2002

63. Baltic Centre for Contemporary Art, from the south-west

was stripped of its silos and E and W walls, and the exterior restored, with a new stepped-back glazed top storey holding a restaurant. Empty ground to the W became Baltic Square, with the gallery entrance from a terraced piazza overlooking the water. The W wall has glazing between metal fins and a viewing box projecting at the top [63]. A low two-storey extension in front channels the public towards the ground floor (lightened by the fully glazed café to the right), and up steps to the main level. There are six floors and three mezzanines, providing galleries, studios, cinema and lecture theatre, library and archive. Public circulation is by steps and glazed lifts in the W end. None of the big gallery spaces is subdivided by permanent partitions; the central level is double-height so that the stair landings allow viewing down into the exhibition space and large objects can be displayed to advantage. The E wall was given full-height glazing behind a sliding screen.

Beside the entrance approach, the Millennium Bridge (*see* p. 95) links Baltic Square with Newcastle's Quayside.

Sage Music Centre

Oakwellgate, Gateshead

Concert halls, rehearsal spaces, community learning facilities – all are in the one place on the s bank of the Tyne, in the distinctive gleaming bulging form [3, 65] of the Arts-Council-funded Sage, named after its principal sponsor, the Newcastle-based software company. The project began in 1996 for Gateshead Council, and the building opened in 2004 after much preparation of the site. The competition-winning architects were *Foster & Partners*, with *Mott MacDonald* as structural and service engineers, *Buro Happold* as chief engineers for the roof, and *Arup* designing acoustics, communications and fire controls. Foster & Partners here demonstrated the changes brought by new materials and design tools, and created a free-form organic shape [64], following the contemporary movement away from hard-edged blocks.

The intricate roof has a maximum span of 260 ft (80 metres) formed by four primary arches, with beam segments of successively increasing radius giving a spiral profile. The result is a sheath undulating across a large strutted structure and wrapping round two small and one large reinforced-concrete halls, which sit on top of an education and conference centre. At the e and w ends enormous raking struts prop the glazed ends of the envelope to form high wide porches [33]; behind,

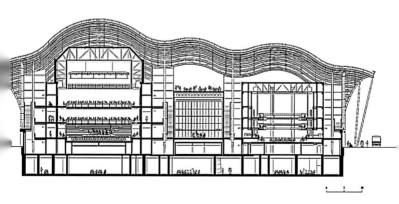

64. Sage Music Centre, longitudinal section, by Foster & Partners, 1996–2004

long steel stays seem to anchor it to higher ground. The shaped panels forming the sheath are stainless steel, except for the glass of three enormous stepped windows towards the river. Its curved profile aims to be sympathetic to the parabolic curves of the bridges either side of it, the near-contemporary Gateshead Millennium Footbridge and the 1920s Tyne Bridge. The relationship with the former is more than physical: the music centre joined Baltic in creating a highly significant cultural 'quartier' for the Tyne and for the region, and the new bridge united the two riversides.

The Sage provides a permanent home for the Northern Sinfonia orchestra and the Folkworks traditional music and dance organization. The largest auditorium holds 1,650 people, the second hall 450, with rehearsal rooms and exhibition space. At the higher level a wide piazza leads to the principal entrance on the w; inside, reception areas, café, restaurant and shop are on a serpentine-edged concourse which sits back from the skin of the building. Its balustrade is a curving glass screen by *Kate Maestri* with shifting tones of blue and green glass. Through the envelope is the panorama of the Newcastle skyline. The skin floats above and around, a multi-segmented sculpture of glass and steel. The smooth white exterior of the main hall rises inside, wrapped round by tiers of walkways. Throughout the building great attention has been paid to materials, finishes and details. The acoustics of the timber-lined auditoria have been highly praised.

This idiosyncratic construction does not please everyone with its quirky presence on the Quayside, but it does its job perfectly and its internal spaces are full of interest.

65. Sage Music Centre, from the north-west

Tyne Bridges

by Stafford Linsley

Newcastle developed as a defendable bridging point from Roman times on. The **Roman bridge**, perhaps near to the present Swing Bridge, was probably a wooden superstructure on stone piers. The first complete **stone bridge** was built by 1175; like the famous London Bridge, it had towers, houses, shops and workshops built on it, more on the Bishop of

66. Gateshead Millennium Bridge, by Wilkinson Eyre Architects, with Gifford & Partners, 1995–2001; behind, New Tyne Bridge and High Level Bridge

Durham's part, s, than on the Corporation of Newcastle's. It was severely damaged in the great flood of 1771 which destroyed every Tyne bridge except that at Corbridge; a ribbed arch of the medieval bridge is extant at the N end of the Swing Bridge, hidden in cellars (*see* Watergate Buildings, Walk 1, p. 108). A replacement nine-arched stone bridge was built in 1775–81 to a design by *Robert Mylne*. This remained the only bridge until the High Level Bridge of 1849, but the following century and a half would see a further five crossing points between Gateshead and Newcastle.

The bridges of central Tyneside are here described in topographical order, upstream from E to W.

Gateshead Millennium Bridge

A competition-winning design of 1995, opened to the public in 2001 [66]. The cost was £22 million. Designed by *Wilkinson Eyre Architects*,

67. Gateshead Millennium Bridge, by Wilkinson Eyre Architects with Gifford & Partners, 1995–2001, detail

with *Gifford & Partners*, consulting engineers, as a novel, cable-stayed, movable bridge ('the world's first and only tilting bridge'), intended to complement the Tyne Bridge visually, but only to be used by cyclists and pedestrians. This, the first large Tyne bridge built to serve leisure purposes, clearly reflects the *zeitgeist*. The bridge essentially comprises two large parabolic fabricated-steel structures, one forming a support-ing arch to 164 ft (50 metres) above high water, the other the deck slung from the former by steel cables [67], the pair being at about 90 degrees to each other and with common springing points. They span 345 ft (105 metres) between the quaysides and can be rotated through 40 degrees to provide 82-ft (25-metre) navigational clearance. As the arch lowers, the deck rises, each component counterbalancing the other; the move-ment is said to resemble a slowly opening eyelid. An elegant structure but somewhat disfigured by the piles sunk alongside into the river 'to protect the ships from the bridge and the bridge from the ships'.

68. New Tyne Bridge, by Mott, Hay & Anderson with R. Burns Dick, 1925–8, detail

New Tyne Bridge

Of 1925–8, designed by *Mott, Hay & Anderson*, with *R. Burns Dick* as architect and *Dorman Long* of Middlesbrough as contractors [68]. Newcastle's modern-day symbol was first proposed in 1921, to augment existing provision at high level and to provide a job creation scheme. The corporations of Newcastle and Gateshead, in anticipation of a 65 per cent government grant, obtained an Act of Parliament in 1924. Work commenced in 1925. Special construction techniques were need-ed, as the Tyne Improvement Commissioners insisted on full naviga-tional clearance, both height and width, throughout the work. This required a single-span bridge with level deck, and the designers came up with a reduced version of their bridge designed in 1916 for Sydney Harbour: a two-hinged steel arch of 531-ft (161-metre) span, with a suspended road deck at 84 ft (25.5 metres) above high water.

Massive concrete foundations support abutments for the hinges, and the huge Cornish granite-faced pylons above [69], which are of minimal structural significance, were designed to house warehouses (never used as such) and goods and passenger lifts. The Newcastle approach is carried on continuous girders supported by two pairs of octagonal columns, each pair being skewed to accommodate the street plan below. Cast-iron balustrades and lanterns by *MacFarlane & Co.* of Glasgow. The largest single-span bridge in Britain at the time of opening.

69. New Tyne Bridge, north pylon

Swing Bridge

1868–76 by *W.G. Armstrong & Co.*, with the *Tyne Improvement Commission* [21]. At the time of its opening, the largest such bridge in the world. A necessary development to allow for upriver navigation by seagoing vessels, by the replacement of Mylne's bridge of 1775–81. Armstrong's firm constructed the superstructure, the Commissioners the foundations and abutments. Work commenced in 1864–5 with the building of a 592-ft (180-metre) temporary bridge to provide access and continuity of passage. The wrought-iron superstructure of the Swing Bridge, which is 281 ft (85.6 metres) long and weighs 1,450 tons, is supported centrally on cast-iron rollers and provides two 95-ft (29-metre) river openings. The whole is driven by the original Armstrong hydraulic engines, but the steam-powered pumps which once charged the hydraulic accumulators (sunk into the river bed) were replaced by small electric pumps in 1959. The bridge, which swings only rarely now, is controlled from the attractive cupola above the superstructure. All services, water, once gas and now electricity, are brought down the central pier of the High Level Bridge. Since 1876, nearly half a million ships have passed through.

High Level Bridge

By *Robert Stephenson*, 1845–9, with *T.E. Harrison* [22, 70]. A superb example of Stephenson's use of materials appropriate to their function. Its design followed at least nineteen different proposals by such as *Samuel Brown, John Green, John Dobson* and *I.K. Brunel*, for both high and low level bridges to augment Mylne's c18 bridge. The final impetus was the need to link the railway from Darlington to Gateshead with Newcastle (*see* topic box, p. 228), necessarily at high level. In 1845 the

70. High Level Bridge, by Robert Stephenson with T.E. Harrison, 1845–9. Drawing by Robert Hodgson, 1858–9, detail

decision was taken to build a combined road and rail bridge giving 120-ft (36.5-metre) clearance above low water.

In its overall length of 1,400 ft (425.6 metres), the High Level Bridge approached the scale of Stephenson's near-contemporary Britannia tubular bridge in North Wales, but long spans were not essential here, hence the design with six main spans of 125 ft (38 metres), with narrower land arches. Masonry piers on massive timber piles (first use of Nasmyth's steam hammer for piling) support the main spans, each of which consists of four cast-iron ribs of I-section tied with wrought-iron chains [70]; the main ribs were cast by *Hawks Crawshay* of Gateshead. The rail deck above is supported by cast-iron box columns rising from the main ribs, while the road deck is suspended from the rail deck by wrought-iron hangers encased in the box sections above the

71. High Level Bridge, from the south-west

ribs and in matching columns below. There have been a few changes since the bridge opened, e.g. the addition of road suspension rods strengthening the structure to take tramcars in 1922. Restored in 2001–8, the ironwork painted the original cream colour.

Queen Elizabeth II Metro Bridge

1976–80 by *W.A. Fairhurst & Partners* with *Cementation Construction Ltd* and *Cleveland Bridge & Engineering Co.* as contractors. A rather inelegant (but, at £4.9 million, presumably cheap) through-steel-truss construction with fabricated box chords. Three unequal spans with a total length of 1,184 ft (360 metres). In 2006–7 painted blue and white, with night lighting changing with the tide, devised by the artist *Nayan Kulkarni.*

King Edward VII Rail Bridge

By *Charles A. Harrison* for the North Eastern Railway, with *Cleveland Bridge & Engineering Co.* as contractors, 1902–6. The original plan was for two lattice-girder spans with land approach arches, until old coal workings were discovered at both ends. Consequently the bridge was built with four massive steel lattice-girder spans carrying four rail tracks, each 28 ft (8.5 metres) deep and up to 300 ft (91 metres) long, supported on solid stone piers. It cost just over £500,000 and is very much a workaday design.

Redheugh Road Bridge

By *Mott, Hay & Anderson* in association with *Tyne and Wear County Council*, built in 1980–3 by *Nuttall/HBM* to replace a bridge of 1897–1901. A good example of modern medium-span bridge design. A post-tensioned concrete box construction with four traffic lanes and one footpath over three spans totalling 1,184 ft (360 metres) in length, the main span being 526 ft (160 metres), with a 1,161-ft (353-metre) approach viaduct on the N side. Internal ducts within the box sections carry gas, water, electricity and telephone services, with portholes to prevent possible explosions; piers fluted to suggest lightness. Contract value was £15.35 million.

Central Newcastle and Gateshead

Walk 1.

Sandhill and the Western River Banks

The first walk looks at many of the buildings which survive from Newcastle's mercantile and maritime past (others in Walk 2). It starts at Sandhill, goes w along the riverside, uphill to the Stephenson Quarter and the Castle, and down back to Sandhill.

72. Walk 1

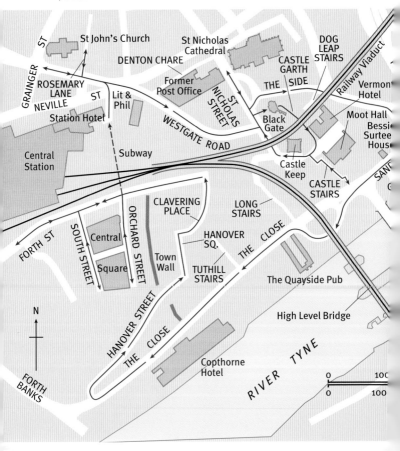

Sandhill and the Riverside

Sandhill, the triangular area beside the Swing Bridge (*see* p. 99), embodies much of Newcastle's history. Mentioned as early as 1310, Sandhill was the hinge of all routes into Newcastle from the s, over the bridge from Gateshead. The Romans built a bridge somewhere nearby, guarded by the fort on the hill above; the medieval bridge was where the Swing Bridge is now, guarded by the Norman Castle built on top of the Roman fort. Upstream, w, was The Close; downstream, Quayside, where ships tied up beside the town quay (Walk 2, pp. 121–2). The Lort Burn's deep valley meets the Tyne here, the stream now underground. The fine stone Guildhall (p. 70) by the river was the seat of the town's government until 1858; merchants, traders and ship-owners also met to conduct business there.

Sandhill retains the finest group of **timber-framed houses** in Northumberland and Durham. In his *Chorographia* (1649) William Grey, Newcastle's first historian, mentioned 'many shops and stately houses for merchants' here. Some of these, now restaurants, pubs and offices, are opposite the Guildhall, against the cliff of the castle hill: a handsome mixture of C17 construction, mostly from the 1650s when the Guildhall was also rebuilt, and C18 brick, some replacing timber-framed fronts (an engineering problem for restorers). The houses are four or five storeys tall, the street range one room deep, any extra rooms in rear wings. The timber fronts have expanses of glass, indicating great wealth, alternating with render. Full-width mullion-and-transom windows with small panes, most with broad ovolo mouldings, and narrow scroll corbels. The left group also has posts treated as shallow fluted Doric pilasters, contrasting with sturdy beam-ends of the floors above; classical influence also in spear-like beading on the pilasters, carved acanthus brackets to the ground floor, and rope-like mouldings. This decorative treatment is apparently without parallel elsewhere.

The widest of these fronts is part of **Bessie Surtees' House** (Nos. 41–44), so called because of Bessie's elopement in 1772 from No. 41 with John Scott, the future Lord Eldon, Chancellor of England. Its interiors are described below. The present No. 44 also incorporates an older and lower timber frame with stone party walls. Around 1741 this was given a brick front (left) with sashes and a high parapet; thc frame, with brick-nogging, appears in the left gable. Fine late C18 pedimented doorway, right, opening onto stairs up to a rear yard. Nos. 39–40 (right) have pilasters only at the ends of each floor, and formerly had a tall central projecting bay, indicated by more robust joist ends. Inside, plain pan-elling with fluted pilasters, and a carved overmantel dated 1658. Nos. 36–38, C18 brick with altered windows, again hiding C17 timber framing. Next, Nos. 33–34 (now **Derwentwater Chambers**), a wide timber-framed house with thin balusters instead of pilasters. Inside, on the first floor a wide Tudor-arched chimneypiece under a brick relieving arch, and at the rear a chamfered Tudor-arched stone doorway, with another on the floor above, as if to a former stair wing. No. 32 also timber-framed: early C18 brick front with floor strings, and sashes in old, wide boxes under lintels carved like rusticated voussoirs. The E side of Sandhill's triangle differs in character, as described in Walk 2 (p. 122).

Bessie Surtees' House was acquired by the City, then restored by the *Napper Collerton Partnership c.* 1982–9. **English Heritage** opens some rooms to the public. Not all is as it seems: in 1931 the Hon. S.R.G.P. Vereker, later 7th Viscount Gort, bought Nos. 41–44 and 'restored' them with help from a retired engineer, *R.F. Wilkinson,* who scoured the country for old material. *C.I. Greenhow,* an architect who worked for Northumberland County Council, was also involved, but whether recording or designing is not clear. Open-well staircase, with slim waisted balusters. Initials and heraldry suggest that the carved first-floor

73. Sandhill, N side, Nos. 32−46, with five-storey Bessie Surtees' House, towards left

chimneypiece of 1657 in No. 41 was made for that house, and the C17 panelling in the room has fluted pilasters with details matching those on the front. But the strapwork ceiling is of 1931, reputedly copying one from another Newcastle house. Linenfold panelling in the rear wing came from Broad Chare, and the ground-floor fireplace backing onto the party wall with No. 44 is Vereker's device to strengthen that wall. Around the yard, most is also the creation of Vereker, who demolished rear outbuildings and made a new wing from old materials.

Houses w (left) of Bessie Surtees' are simpler. No. 46 is early C18, with greater floor heights, and tumbled-in brickwork in the left gable. Nos. 47–52 have C20 shopfronts in late C18 façades; next to Castle Stairs, a brick building of 1991 in late C18 style.

Across the road, w of Guildhall, **Watergate Buildings**, shops and offices of 1830 by *John Dobson*, extended SE in the same style 1890 (No. 57). The same ashlar front, floor band and cornice, and sashes in plain reveals as in the simpler of Richard Grainger's buildings of 1835–9 up the hill (*see* Walk 4). It replaced the medieval bridge chapel of St Thomas the Martyr, removed because it obstructed traffic.* The river used to be much wider: the N arch of the medieval bridge survives in cellars below. The small stone building on the Swing Bridge approach is a former **coroner's court**, late C19. w of the bridge the single-storey former **Fish Market** (now **Neptune House**), red brick, 1878–80 by *A.M. Fowler*. Baroque in details and rhythm, with splendid iron grilles. Over the riverside entrance *George Burn*'s Neptune statue, flanked by fishwives.

Castle Stairs opposite divide Sandhill from **The Close**, to the w. Now a wide street; merchants' houses used to face each other across a narrow roadway. The name derives from the early C14 enclosure of ground between Castle and river. One pier of the High Level Bridge of 1849 (*see* p. 99) stands isolated on a large roundabout, towering over what buildings remain.

The only surviving riverfront **warehouse** is No. 35, now **The Quayside** pub [74]. U-plan, the courtyard opening N (here truncated for road-widening, with C19 gables flanking C20 gates). Facing E, the long wall of the E range and the exposed timber-framed gable of the s range. The L-shaped SE corner is the oldest, with a roof with kingposts set into arched tie-beams and a ridge set square in the side of jowls in the kingposts and braced lengthwise; trees felled 1514. This local roof type is also in Nos. 14–16 Cloth Market (p. 140) and at Trinity House (p. 126).

*Dobson also designed the replacement church, at Barras Bridge (p. 196).

74. The Quayside pub, early C16 and later

75. Turnbull's warehouses, by F.W. Rich, 1888 and 1896–8

Facing the courtyard, the E range has two builds, the S part older, both of brick but with some stone below or behind; the S range is rendered, timber framing above stone, and sashes with broad glazing bars in the first-floor Venetian window, an early C18 alteration; w range of reused stone with early ground-floor openings to the yard, and two stacks of loading bays. The ventilation 'dormers' are of 1989. The w range projects at the S, and still has loading doors: at high tide goods could be transferred from boats. Now separated from the water by the promenade made in 1984–5.

From the courtyard of No. 35, a good view of **Turnbull's** bright red brick warehouses [75], originally a printing works, on Hanover Square to the N, towering over The Close: 1888 and 1896–8 by *F.W. Rich*. Converted to flats by *Hopper Howe Sadler*, 2005.

Across The Close, Nos. 28–30, plain C18 with C19 ground-floor alterations, but medieval in origin (the left flank shows the ends of some big floor beams). The interior tells the true story. Plain ground floor, latterly used for warehousing, with early C19 cast-iron piers. Overhead, three types of floor joists (including at sw a dragon beam) show that there were three medieval plots here; one fireplace now, of uncertain date, at the rear of the E room. On upper floors, close-set medieval beams with sophisticated Renaissance plaster decoration, the sources identified by Anthony Wells-Cole as engravings published in Antwerp, 1580, and Nuremberg, 1601. Repeated motifs, with pairs of herons, flowers and arabesque patterns, and a small cartouche showing Man's position in the Cosmos according to Plato. The whole scheme demonstrates the high status of the owners, Claverings of Whitehouse

76. No. 32 The Close, The Cooperage, after 1543, and later

and later of Axwell, near Gateshead. Like Nos. 41–44 Sandhill, the house later belonged to the Hon. S.R.G.P. Vereker. Behind can be seen the upper-cruck trusses of the wing added in the 1980s by *Simpson & Brown*, architects for the Tyne and Wear Building Preservation Trust, to replace a stair wing added by Vereker. At the rear a fragment of a possibly medieval stone building.

Across Long Stairs, the less sophisticated No. 32 (**The Cooperage**) [76]. The timber structure was added in four phases, after 1543 and up to the C17, to the ruins of a stone house. Ground floor of large stone blocks; front-gabled and jettied timber frame with diagonal corner bracing; rendered infill in the upper floors. Wall to Long Stairs with brick-nog-ging, and carpenters' marks of two periods. In the exposed front truss of the roof, curved principals tenoned into the tie-beam; the internal trusses have similar principals, but some are truncated, with a collar at the apex.

AMOR SPOOR'S GENERAL BOND WAREHOUSES, N? 50.
Close, Newcastle upon Tyne.

77. Warehouses in The Close, perhaps by Thomas Oliver, 1841–4. c19 engraving

Across the street, w of No. 35, **Bridge Court**, undistinguished 1990s offices for British Telecom. Opposite are **Tuthill Stairs** where **Quayside Lofts**, three blocks of flats with shops below, by *Conran & Partners*, 2001–7, climb up to Hanover Square. The framing is mostly clad with red brick, with timber and rendering for the less formal elevations. Hard landscaping by *Ian White*. A fine group, but in a new idiom.

The s side next has the **Copthorne Hotel** by *Arup Associates*, 1991–3, partly on the site of the town's brick-built Mansion House (1691, burnt down 1895). Two blocks face the river, with tall windows and arcades over the promenade, separated by a tower designed to straddle the remains of the late c13–c14 **Town Wall** (*see* topic box, pp. 168–9). N front, clearly the service side, made a porte cochère by projecting the car parking over the entrance; but the lack of coherence is disappointing. The Wall extended to the water's edge from the Close Gate; N of The Close it can still be seen in the stretch called **Breakneck Stairs**, with steps alongside, climbing steeply up the hillside (cleared and landscaped up to 1991 in the 'Hanging Gardens' project for Tyne and Wear Development Corporation). Beyond, dramatic **bonded warehouses** of brick [77], built in 1841–4 by and for *Amor Spoor* and perhaps designed by *Thomas Oliver*. Spoor also made Hanover Street which climbs from w to e along the rear, demolishing White Friars Tower in the Town Wall. The warehouses filled the space between, forming a composition of almost Piranesian grandeur, with the curve and fall of the street accentuating the rhythm of the gables. Stone plinth, with tall, wide, rusticated arched entrances on The Close, and immensely thick walls in Flemish bond, unusual for Newcastle until much later in the c19. An arched brick canyon covers stairs between the streets. Three major fires destroyed the w part and the e interior; flats on the site by *Napper Architects* (2008) are part restoration and part new build. Beyond the Metro bridge on Forth Banks, a large mixed-use development also by *Napper*, with a half-round tower of apartments; 2007–8.

Up **Hanover Street**, with two lines of smooth Shap granite to take the wheels of the carts (cobbles between, to help horses to get purchase), passing on the left an **arch** to a street (houses – a whole row and warehouse) by *Spoor* let into the hill, to **Hanover Square**. The first square to be developed in Newcastle, named in the 1720s in homage to the dynasty – except that it wasn't completed, and most of what was built has been demolished. One badly preserved house, No. 1, s corner – old brickwork, sashes; Tuscan doorcase perhaps later. The chapel intended for the Unitarians (1726) was swallowed up by a late C19 brick warehouse (recently demolished). Round the E corner in **Clavering Place**, two large brick houses of the 1780s (right), reminders that this was a fashionable development before the railway came with viaduct, smoke and noise. Each has a central doorway; the first, of five bays, stands in front of the former Turnbull's Warehouses, already seen from The Close. **Clavering House** beside the viaduct has a pedimented doorcase with narrow side windows, echoed above by a pseudo-Venetian window with a blind head and blind side windows, between full-height canted bays. Opposite, the former **Presbyterian Chapel** of 1822 by *John Green* for the United Secession Church, with Tudor-arched windows with Gothic intersecting glazing bars. Used as a warehouse for many years but intended to become part of a housing development.

Walk w along **Forth Street** by the railway viaduct, in what the City now calls **Stephenson Quarter**, past a full-height stretch of the Town Wall. The former **Royal Mail Sorting Office** here, Neo-Georgian red

78. Vulcan, Central Square, by Eduardo Paolozzi, 2002

79. Former Stephenson Locomotive Works, South Street, *c.* 1849 onwards, interior

brick of 1935, was transformed in 1998–2000 into **Central Square** by *Carey Jones*, who added a storey and created an impressive atrium, and built a s block in 2000–1. **Sculpture**: in a paved area next to Forth Street, *Eduardo Paolozzi*'s impressive bronze figure of Vulcan [78]; between the blocks, a large sculpture by *Kenneth Armitage* called Reaching for the Stars, both of 2002 and commissioned by Parabola Estates (Peter Millican).

The choice of Vulcan is explained by the history of the site: the birth of the *Rocket* at the former **Stephenson Locomotive Works** [79] established in 1823 by George and Robert Stephenson in **South Street**, to the w. On the w side the works of 1867 onwards, with twenty-four intact tall round-headed windows. Next to it (N) the boiler shop of *c.* 1849–59; the present frontage, with its iron lintel reused from a beam engine and eight-bay offices to the right, is of the later date. Preserved by the Robert Stephenson Trust. On the E side, the much-altered works where *Rocket* was completed in 1829. N of Forth Street, the Central Station extensions of the 1890s, including a big water tank dated 1891 on plain stone offices, w.

Walk back E and turn left, up Orchard Street under the railway viaduct, to **Westgate Road** (the medieval 'Westgate'), on the line of Hadrian's Wall. In the roadway the **Stephenson Monument** by *J.G. Lough*, 1862, a bronze statue on a big plinth; four heroic corner figures: platelayer with a piece of George Stephenson's rail, miner with his patent safety lamp, blacksmith with anvil, and locomotive engineer resting on a model engine. The Station Hotel (s side, w) is described with the Central Station, p. 87. w of the Stephenson Monument a **gatepier** from the Virgin Mary Hospital, demolished in the 1840s when Neville Street was constructed. The medieval hospital building became Newcastle Grammar School for a time; other piers were reset at the present Royal Grammar School in Jesmond (p. 239). To the NW across Neville Street the **Church of St John**. (Walk 4 covers Grainger Street, to the w.) Mostly C14 and C15, of rough and decayed masonry; originally a chapel of St Nicholas's parish church (p. 46). Cruciform, the aisles clasping a stumpy but dominant w tower, with pinnacles and battlements. A donation by Robert Rhodes, d.1474, is recorded on a boss in the tower vault, and his arms (renewed) also on the s transept gable. Gabled s porch. N aisle with C14 windows with triple ogee-headed lights. N transept also C14, with the distinction of a w aisle, not usual in the C14 in the North. Of the C15 the s transept, without an aisle, and the low clerestory. Chancel restored 1848–50s by *John Dobson* with a new E window, other repairs 1862–76. Church hall, N, 1954. A Norman window head on the chancel N side is visible internally. Inside, double-chamfered arcades in local C14 style, i.e. without capitals (except in the N transept); octagonal piers. Shields as hoodmould stops over the N arcade. Single-chamfered tower arch, higher than the vault behind it, and hollow-chamfered N and s arches. – Delicate **communion rails** and **chancel screen**, part of reordering by *S.E. Dykes Bower*, 1965–73. – Beautiful C17 **font cover** with canopies and pinnacles, and **pulpit** with Corinthian columns. – **Stained glass**: N chancel, medieval fragments, including the arms of Newcastle. Other chancel windows, s transept s, and N transept N (two) by *Wailes*. N transept, two, E, signed *G.E.R. Smith, c.* 1926; w, unsigned St George and St Barbara; war memorials. – **Monuments**. J. Taylor by *Dunbar*, 1835, with bust. – Gothic plaque, 1888, to Richard Grainger d.1861: 'A citizen of Newcastle . . . does not need to be reminded of the genius . . . a stranger is referred to the principal streets in the centre of the city.'

E of the church, **Rosemary Lane** has a C17 house in brick, the original shaped gable, E, copied at the w. Next to it **Parish View**, flats, 2004 by *David Ash Partnership*.

Next E on Westgate Road, the former **Union Club**: a splendid French château, 1877 by *M.P. Manning*, brought back to life as a pub after years of neglect. Next to it a new block is proposed, partly on the site of Westgate House of 1965–71 by *Cartwright Woollatt & Partners*; this straddled Westgate Road, overshadowing all and blocking long views. To the E is Collingwood Street (*see* Walk 4, p. 161).

On the s side, E corner of Orchard Street, the full-blooded Ruskinian Gothic building is another manifestation of the region's prominence in engineering: **Neville Hall**, 1869–72 by *Archibald M. Dunn*, for the North of England Institute of Mining and Mechanical Engineers [18]. Prudham sandstone with red bands, pointed arches, nook-shafts with foliage capitals, carved and inscribed frieze, eaves dormers originally decorated with griffins, and a corner turret with the Neville emblem (bear and ragged staff) as finial. Inside, the Wood Memorial Hall [80] is redolent of the power of coal and its engineers, double-height with top lights and traceried end windows, and a canopied statue of Nicholas Wood, the pioneering colliery railway

80. Neville Hall, Wood Memorial Hall, by Archibald M. Dunn, 1872

engineer, by *E.W. Wyon*. Balconies inserted 1902 by *Cackett & Burns Dick* who also created the lecture theatre underneath the library, with splendid fittings. Fine iron railings to Westgate Road, where red concrete marks the line of Hadrian's Wall.

81. Literary and Philosophical Society, Westgate Road, by John Green, 1822–5

Next a contrast: the **Literary and Philosophical Society** (Lit & Phil),
1822–5 by *John Green*, a pedimented Greek Revival front of excellent
ashlar [81]. Big steps up to the entrance of fluted Doric columns *in antis*.
Imperial stair inside, with copies of the Parthenon frieze sculptures;
on the landing, a standing figure of the Radical barrister James Losh,

1836 by *Lough*. Green's simple rectangular plan, with galleried library upstairs, was extended to an L-plan in 1888–9 by *A.B. Gibson*, copying the honeysuckle frieze; present interior with glass-domed roof by *F.W. Rich*, 1893–4, after a fire [23]. Next door, the **Bolbec Hall**, cheerful Baroque with garlands and Gibbs surrounds, 1907–9 by *Rich*, a speculative development for the Lit & Phil. Next, two North Eastern Railway buildings, backing onto the railway viaduct: **Irving House** of 1910 by *William Bell*, Baroque, and further on the former **Central Station Parcel Office** of 1906, three wide, weatherboarded gables (demolition proposed).

Opposite, the medieval Denton Chare, then the rear of the 1890s extension to the Post Office on St Nicholas Street (*see* below), offices since 2001, with the jagged outlines of the added penthouse flats. Then the former **Cooper's Auction Yard**: originally blank brick front to a horse auction mart, with ramps to stabling on two levels, of 1896 by *T. Dawson*; remodelling by *Percy L. Browne & Son* with garage, car lift and showrooms, 1925–6. In 2008–9 converted to offices by *Ryder*.

Westgate Road ends at St Nicholas Street, constructed *c.* 1850 to approach the High Level Bridge. By 1863 **St Nicholas Buildings** on the corner, by *William Parnell*, was in use. One of Newcastle's earliest office blocks. Stately, with two-storey round-arched entrance bays (now with a new central entrance under a Paris-Métro-style canopy). A long central courtyard provided natural light; replaced with a glazed atrium in *Alan J. Smith Partnership*'s rebuilding, 1993–7. To the N, a narrow repeat of the design. Between the two, set back opposite the Cathedral (*see* p. 46), the former **Post Office** of 1873–6 by *James Williams*. A splendid tall composition with superimposed giant orders, Roman Doric below (the porch *in antis*), Corinthian above. Between the Corinthian pilasters, the second-floor windows have alternating pediments, the central one segmental on Ionic columns. Converted 1998–2001 by the *Alan J. Smith Partnership*, later *Red Box Design Group*, to architect's office, art gallery, flats etc., extending W through to Westgate Road as already seen.

To the S, E of St Nicholas Street, the plateau with the Castle (*see* p. 62), bounded on the S by the cliff of the Tyne Gorge and on the N and E by The Side, and crossed by the 1849 viaduct which skims the NW corner of the castle keep. Beyond the railway arch and beside the High Level Bridge, the **Bridge Hotel**, a bright brick and sandstone pub of 1901 by *Cackett & Burns Dick*. Free Style. Tuscan columns frame the windows and pedimented doors; bowed oriel; corner turret with tall finial. Interior altered, but windows still with lovely stained-glass top lights.

The former **Northumberland County Hall** stands on the E edge of the plateau, the Moot Hall on the S. When county councils were created in 1889 the Northumberland offices were set up first in the Moot Hall, then in a new building facing it. That four-storey-and-basement nucleus of 1910 by *J.A. Bain* was extended backwards, upwards and downwards in 1929–34, in stripped classical style, by *Cackett, Burns Dick & Mackellar*, starting at ground level on The Side [17]. In 1988–93 it was converted for the **Vermont Hotel**, after the creation of the new county of Tyne and Wear in 1974 made it redundant. Bain's restrained classicism (Ionic half-columns, Doric porch) respected the Moot Hall opposite; the enlargement has shallow pilasters at the centre, and prominent cornices, and impressively solves problems of changing levels. Six storeys face the Moot Hall, ten on the right return tower over The Side, of which the fourth is the double-height Council Chamber with stained glass and inlaid hardwood dado.

The **Moot Hall** [82] was built in 1810–12 for the County of Northumberland. Designed by *William Stokoe* as County Court and Prisons, but called the Moot Hall because it replaced a medieval one in the Castle. The first local government building of the C19 in Newcastle is also its most severe example of Greek Revival, the style adopted for major buildings until Grainger introduced a wider repertoire in the 1830s. The high quality of the sandstone ashlar is comparable with that at Sir Charles Monck's no less severely Grecian Belsay Hall, Northumberland (1807–17). Eleven bays, two storeys. Pedimented Doric porticoes N and S, the latter blocked when *W. Crozier* of Durham re-ordered the interior in 1877, reducing the power of the view from the Gateshead side. He inserted extra windows, recognizable by narrow-margined sashes, and made full-width steps across the N side (original steps restored in the 1980s when the *Napper Collerton Partnership* converted the building to a Crown Court).

A quick return to Sandhill is possible down **Castle Stairs** [7], an ancient pedestrian route W of the Moot Hall, past a restored medieval well (right), and under the postern arch in the Castle's S wall. Below, a path to Long Stairs (right), an C18 house (left), and mid-C19 fluted cast-iron handrail posts on the last wide flight.

The main Walk continues back from the plateau through the Black Gate, towards the cathedral, then right down the steep, narrow, cobbled Side (*see* p. 150), or else by a short cut down **Dog Leap Stairs**, alongside the **railway viaduct**. This is of 1849, doubled in the 1890s (when the stairs were re-sited). Beyond its high ashlar arch, right, **The Side** has the rear courtyard of the former County Hall (good **railings**), with the double-height Council Chamber visible. The left side is dominated by **Cale Cross House**, of 1972–8 by *Hubbard Ford & Partners*, a square tower, set back (re-clad *c.* 2000 by *Ove Arup & Partners*). In front, a lower wing of brick, with shops. No. 35 (on the right-hand side) has a late C18 brick front. At Nos. 31–33 the **Crown Posada** pub, 1880 by *W.L. Newcombe*, grey granite and sandstone. Pre-Raphaelite stained-glass windows by *Baguley*; fine, traditionally partitioned interior. Then **Proctor House**, shops and offices dated 1906 and 1926, brick and ashlar on a red granite ground floor, and Nos. 1–13, Italianate, *c.* 1855, after street widening. The varied street surfaces of *c.* 2003 here were designed by the sculptor *John Maine* to indicate the Lort Burn beneath. The Side continues to curve towards the river, and Sandhill is reached.

82. Moot Hall, Castle Garth, by William Stokoe, 1810–12

Quayside and East Quayside

This walk follows Quayside downstream, E from Sandhill (*see* Walk 1, p. 104), with slight digressions away from the river. While the immediate post-war period saw great changes in the town centre, the riverside remained unaltered until Byker was redeveloped in the 1970s (*see* p. 232). Quayside regeneration gathered pace under the Tyne and Wear Development Corporation from 1987 to 1998 and continues as buildings in the Ousebourn valley are cleared or restored. These former commercial and industrial areas have been enriched by sculpture and designed streetscapes, fitting settings for the present mix of business, residential and leisure uses.

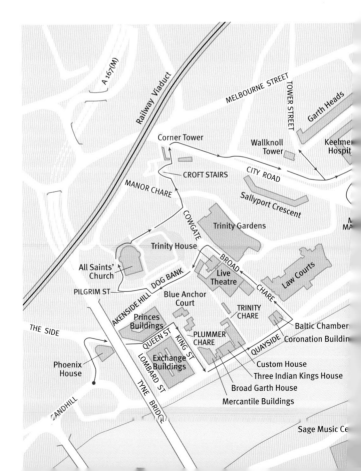

Quayside and to the North

The dramatic oversail of the Tyne Bridge (p. 97) emphasizes the topography of this riverside area, the flat valley bottom enclosed by steep banks. Historically, **Quayside** was the street running E from Sandhill to Sandgate, with chares (alleys) between the houses for access to the long burgage plots; steps at the heads of some chares led to the higher ground. The land was reclaimed from the river in the C14, timber piers becoming chares when houses were built between them. The Town Quay and a stretch of Town Wall lay E of the medieval bridge; the street called Quayside ran behind the wall (removed 1763), with houses on its N side. Quay wall and bollards remain, but no longer do hundreds of ships tie up here, nor porters carry cargoes to and fro.*

*As the use has changed, so has the sense of what the name means, with 'Quayside' now often used for anywhere near the river, although it is strictly this block between Sandhill and Sandgate.

83. Walk 2

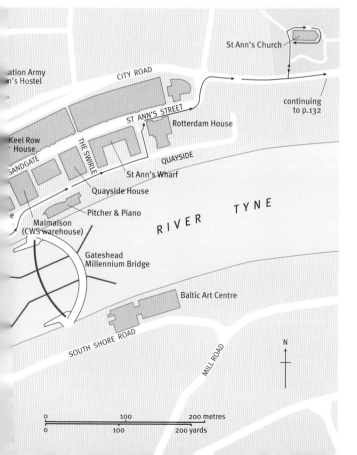

In 1854 blazing débris from a fire in Gateshead destroyed many Quayside buildings and six chares. The Town Council laid out new wide streets (Queen Street, Lombard Street, King Street), to a plan of *John Dobson*'s, from a full scheme which was not otherwise adopted; the buildings were by *William Parnell*. Only the NE part of **Sandhill** was affected, but after the Swing Bridge opened in 1876 stone-built banks and shipping and insurance offices replaced timber-framed and brick houses along the E side; these are now bars and restaurants. From the s corner: No. 13, 1879 by *Edward Shewbrooks*, free Baroque; No. 15, 1880–1 by *John Burnup & Sons* for Lambton & Co.'s bank, ground floor remodelled 1909 by *Waller & Sons*, Gloucester, for Lloyds Bank; No. 17 of 1885 by *A.B. Gibson*, Renaissance, with superimposed Corinthian columns and lozenge decoration. Then *Parnell*'s classical work on the curve to **Queen Street**: No. 18 for the Royal Insurance Co., 1863, now flats and called **Phoenix House**; company arms over the door, Tuscan pilasters on the ground floor, giant Corinthian above, round-arched on the top floor. The block between Queen Street and **Akenside Hill**, oversailed by Tyne Bridge, is *Parnell*'s **Princes Buildings**, *c.* 1863. On Queen Street s side beyond, *Parnell*'s **Exchange Buildings**, Italianate offices of *c.* 1861–2, filling the rectangle of new streets; its other fronts on Lombard Street, King Street and Quayside. Central courtyard for natural light, as at Parnell's St Nicholas Buildings (p. 117). Converted to a hotel etc., *c.* 2001.

On the N side of Queen Street, E of the steps to All Saints (p. 129), No. 29, 1871 by *Matthew Thompson*, with Corinthian detail. At the E end of the street is **Blue Anchor Court**, 1987, the first post-1945 housing in the Quayside area, infill by the *Napper Collerton Partnership*. Down **King Street** to No. 25, 1875 by *R.J. Johnson* for the Tyne Steam Shipping Co., with fine mouldings and a hierarchy of orders, Tuscan, Ionic (twice) and Corinthian, with pulvinated friezes, leaded lights in stone-mullioned windows, and an old noticeboard naming shipping destinations. The slender front to Quayside keeps the pre-1854 plan, with the very narrow **Plummer Chare** to the E. Next Nos. 15–23 Quayside, **Mercantile Buildings**, 1883 by *J.C. Parsons*, also with entablatures above each floor, and wreath-carved pediments over paired central windows; less ornate is Nos. 25–27, **Broad Garth House**, 1869 by *John Wardle Jun..* **Three Indian Kings House**, 1987 by *Napper Collerton Partnership*, is stone-clad with three full-height oriel windows.

Custom House Entry passes under No. 39, the former **Custom House** [84], now barristers' chambers. After demolition of the Quayside stretch of Town Wall in 1763, Newcastle's Customs moved here from near Sandhill in 1766. Its brick was re-fronted in Palladian ashlar by *Sydney Smirke* in 1833, with a rusticated ground floor, first-floor windows with pedimented surrounds, smaller second-floor windows, dentil cornice and blocked parapet; fine royal arms over the shallow porch. Then Trinity Chare, leading to Trinity House (*see* p. 124). At the river's edge here, the great engineering work of the C19 **Quay**, with bollards for

84. Former
Custom House,
Quayside,
1766; front
by Sydney
Smirke, 1833

moorings, and fine views of the bridges, the Gateshead riverside, and
ahead, the first glimpse of the Byker Estate on its steep site. Beyond, a
development is proposed by *Ryder*; then No. 63, a plain house, *c.* 1800
(now a bar). No. 65 is **Coronation Buildings,** former shipping offices of
1902, the rear demolished. **Baltic Chambers**, *c.* 1900, extended 1991 by
its owner *Ralph Tarr* with *Ryder Nicklin*, with a corner turret to Broad
Chare. *Napper Collerton's* **Law Courts** of 1986–90 on the E corner was
the first major building of the Quayside revival. A new material for the
riverside, red sandstone from Dumfriesshire. Full-height piers support
a high gallery; brick sides and rear, with nautical portholes.

Broad Chare was the only chare wide enough for a cart: even wider
now, incorporating Spicer Chare, E. On the left, brick former warehouses of the mid C19: Nos. 11–21, then three belonging to the Trinity
House of Newcastle upon Tyne, now holding **Live Theatre** (conversion
begun 1990 by *David Ash & Partners*, extended 2007 by *Waring & Netts*),
with windows in the loading bays. Three houses with nine small gables
here, built by Trinity House *c.* 1678, were rebuilt in 1841 by a Mr *Oliver*
– either Andrew or Thomas; plans were approved and tenders considered by Dobson, the architect adviser to Trinity House.

85. Trinity House, Broad Chare, medieval to c19, entrance by John or William Stokoe, 1800, and Banqueting Hall, 1721, right

Where the chare is pedestrianized, a gatehouse leads to the secluded court of **Trinity House** [85, 86], a complete change of building type and era. The medieval site, with a complex of buildings that began as a courtyard house, has been home to the Newcastle Company of Mariners since 1505. In that year they signed an agreement to build a chapel, meeting house and almshouses on the site 'of old time called Dalton Place', which they had acquired from 'Rauff Hebburne squyer'. Further almshouses, meeting rooms and offices were added. The present buildings are a medieval house, the chapel, c18 meeting hall and almshouses, and c19 gatehouse, almshouses and office, some now leased out, all incorporating parts of earlier structures, especially at ground level. A full analysis has yet to be made, but each new investigation adds to the jigsaw.

The Tudor-style two-storey **gatehouse** on Broad Chare is dated 1841, and is by *Oliver*. To the right, the E wall of the **chapel** has old masonry, of varying sizes and golden hues, with a four-light window renewed in

1841. The small round-headed niches flanking it, and the asymmetrical gable peak above, are shown in a margin picture on Corbridge's 1723 survey of Newcastle.

The passage leads to **Trinity Yard**, the most important of three yards. It passes the **undercroft** of the chapel, with one door and c16-style windows restored by *Dobson* and at the w a genuine c14 doorway. Inside, a Samson post supporting the chapel floor has been tree-ring-dated *c.* 1183, calling for further research. The medieval house had a chapel, location unknown.

Trinity House

'The Fellowship of Masters and Mariners of ships of the town of Newcastle upon Tyne' is a private corporation, which by Henry VIII's 1536 charter had responsibility for high and low lighthouses at the mouth of the Tyne at Shields, and permission to levy a toll on ships entering the river. The House also looked after buoys and beacons between Whitby and Holy Island, trained and examined river and deep-sea pilots, and advised Newcastle Corporation on the management of the port, until its powers were reduced by the Act of Parliament which established the Port of Tyne Authority in 1850. Trinity House's dues were collected when ships' captains reported to the Custom House, from the 1760s reached via Trinity Chare. The main courtyard of Trinity House is at the time of writing, open during office hours; appointments may be made to visit some of the buildings.

86. Trinity House Chapel, with fittings of 1635

The intermingling of work of different centuries in the yard beyond is part of the building's charm. All the high-status spaces are at first-floor level. The three-storey stone building on the N side is a medieval house, perhaps C14.* The Masters and Mariners probably obtained the ground floor as part of the 1505 deal, and certainly acquired the upper floors in 1524. In the C17–C18 it was used as a **rigging loft**, in the C19 as the hospital. A stumpy buttress between bays 3 and 4; a wide garderobe projection at the E reaching to the eaves (was there a water-collecting device?); left of it a first-floor medieval doorway has been blocked and its arch is just visible over a window. Blocked small square windows on the top floor. The present windows are twelve-pane sashes; door and window architraves are recent additions. The steep-pitched roof has even steeper protruding gables of an earlier roof. The sundial dated 1721 was probably moved from the S wall of the Banqueting Hall when its light was blocked by the new school in 1753 (*see* below). In the C19 the external staircase was replaced with an internal one. Inside a first-floor garderobe door with a shouldered lintel, and pointed and chamfered ground- and first-floor rere-arches.

The **entrance hall**, E, has a sweeping flight of steps to a pedimented Doric doorcase in the new front approved in 1800; the mason was *Mr Reed*, and *Mr Stokoe* (*John* or *William)* was paid for 'his trouble respecting the new entrance'. Next to it, N, the former **Secretary's Office** of 1849–50. The w side of the yard has brick **almshouses**, a big plaque recording their rebuilding in 1787. Two storeys to the yard but one behind, facing a raised yard (**High Yard**), where there was formerly another almshouse block further w. (The steps up to that yard are S of the 1787 almshouses; the lower, stone, part of their wall much older, C16 or early C17 on the evidence of the flat Tudor-arched doorhead and small square window. Brick-vaulted cellars run underneath High Yard.)

The brick **Banqueting Hall** on the s side has a fine plaque giving the date, 1721, and naming the officers at the time. Elliptical-headed windows with original sashes with wide glazing bars, ovolo-moulded inside. The gutter cornice is nearly matched along the almshouses of 1787 on the w side (see the dated rainwater head in the angle).

The **entrance hall** is separated from the present **chapel** by a carved screen, with glazed two-light openings. Roof trusses were renewed in 1651 with moulded tie-beams; in 1656 ceiling boards were added. Excellent Jacobean-style box pews of 1635, a two-decker pulpit, a desk and the reader's desk facing one another – a complete, attractive ensemble, with much lively detail. *Richard Newlove* was paid one penny for each cherub's head he carved on the pew ends. Early C20 panelling above the dado. The vestry was the little room to the s, now the **Master's Room**, above the gateway; the door from the chapel has a pointed arch.

*But with tree-ring-dates of 1183–1209 for some first-floor beams, and 1436 for one. 1524 for the earliest surviving roof trusses, i.e. the year Trinity House acquired the upper floors.

A bridge links the entrance hall with the s group of buildings; *William Newton* designed its 1790s covering. At right angles, a passage to the Master's Room (E) and to the Election Room, now **Board Room**, of 1791 by *John Stokoe*, s. Simply decorated, though dignified with dado and modillion cornice; lit partly by a Venetian window (C20 glass) onto a small yard.

w of here, the passage has windows of 1721; double doors open to the **Banqueting Hall**. Bolection-moulded panelling, stucco ceiling decoration with central compass (*see* topic box, p. 11). The fireplace has an older carved overmantel, its central panel, trimmed to fit, the Stuart arms with CR for Charles I. Two windows on the s blocked when the school (*see* below) was rebuilt in 1753, 'beautified' with naval scenes on canvas in 1768.

The **Low Yard** (s) is reached by a passage from Trinity Yard, under the Banqueting Hall, to a narrow alley between that and the blank wall of the former **school** of 1753 to the s. Passing w under the school's stair wing, which abuts the Banqueting House, the alley leads to **Trinity Chare**. Here are C18 railings to the **Low Yard**, in the C17 the Brethren's bowling green. On its N is the school, partly buried by the new yard surface when **almshouses** were built on the E side in 1782 (now also occupied by Live Theatre). On the s side, the gable-end of a modest almshouse block dated 1820, and beside it a little **outbuilding** provided in 1782 for the convenience of the old men on their return from the Three Indian Kings hostelry next door. All these buildings are of brick, some painted white.

Opposite and beyond Trinity House, **Trinity Gardens**, 2005: a big development by *Waring & Netts* around the head of Broad Chare. Mixed use, cheerful design, yellowish and whitish materials. Landscaping by *SouthernGreen*, 2008. A central low amphitheatre with pale granite steps holds a **sculpture** called **Give and Take** [87], by

87. Give and Take, sculpture by Peter Randall-Page, 2008

Peter Randall-Page, a glacial boulder carved in bulbous hexagons and pentagons. It marks the now-buried Pandon Burn which flowed into the Tyne just E of Broad Chare.

N of Trinity House, turn left along the cliff, up the steep, narrow **Dog Bank**. In the C19 the Quayside was a congested area, old houses split into many dwellings. The Broad Chare/Dog Bank corner was the subject of a public clearance order in the 1930s; a sculpture to commemorate Admiral Collingwood is planned here. Next to it, the N side of the former rigging loft of Trinity House, set into the cliff.

Dog Bank leads w to **All Saints' Church** [88], rebuilt 1786–96 after a competition won by the first Newcastle man to study architecture in London, *David Stephenson*. This medieval church began to collapse in the 1770s. An C18 drawing shows it with a C12 doorway and C14–C15 windows; a boss with the arms of Robert Rhodes proves that it received a new tower vault in the C15. The C18 church was deconsecrated in 1961, and converted into offices and auditorium by *Pearce Howe Murray*, 1981–4. Now used for worship by the Old Catholic Church as St Willibrord with All Saints.

This is an extraordinarily satisfying building, original and sophisticated in its oval plan and classical elevations. It rises above the chares from the edge of the virtual cliff of the river valley. Before the building of the new Tyne Bridge in the 1920s its s tower and superb spire, detailed throughout with uncommon sensitivity, dominated the Quayside. Stephenson's first design, for a church with a domed attic storey above a coupled Ionic colonnade, was quickly superseded by one with no attic storey and with a s tower and octagonal spire rising 143 ft (44 metres). In 1790 that spire was abandoned for what we see now – 202 ft (62 metres) high. The problem of combining a tower with a church front, solved by James Gibbs at St Martin-in-the-Fields in London with middling success in the 1720s by setting the spire behind a wide portico, is here handled far more satisfactorily. The entrance is marked by a further detached portico in front of the tower. This portico is of four slender Doric columns, Greek in form (i.e. fluted and without a base) though Roman in their capitals and their slender proportions, carrying a pediment. A flight of stairs leads up to the portico. The tower has rusticated masonry, then one storey with one broad shallow-arched tripartite window and a pediment, a second with only a semicircular bell-louvre, then the clock stage, square with diagonally projecting bases for the coupled Tuscan columns standing well away on the diagonals of the next, octagonal, stage. Then an intermediate stage and openwork balustrading and a final smaller octagon with single Tuscan columns and the slender ball-finialled octagonal spire. The whole is as much a filigree of transparent forms as any Italian

88. All Saints, by David Stephenson, 1786–96

Baroque spire. Flanking the tower base, subsidiary rooms with Ionic pilasters and shallow-arched tripartite windows. Behind these and the circular domed lobby inside the tower, to the N, the church itself curves round, an oval with Ionic-pilastered shallow apse projections to W and E, their upper parts carved with delicate paterae and swags [10]. The design was probably inspired by Gibbs's proposal for a centrally planned St Martin-in-the-Fields (published 1728).

Much of the magnificent **interior** survives. Stephenson had not resolved the confusing sudden change of axis on leaving the lobby and expecting to find the altar ahead, for the change of axis remains, all the more odd as the box pews and curved gallery faced E. So one arrives inconspicuously below one side of the gallery, expecting at least a balancing entrance of equal weight opposite, on the N. In the 1980s the church floor was adapted so that the central pews could be sunk, the woodwork restored and the ceiling repainted in a lively C18 style. One cunning alteration is barely visible: N of the apse, a wall section slides out to form a fire escape. All the C18 **woodwork** is mahogany. The apse, with tall Corinthian columns, is Stephenson's; the present **reredos** is of 1904. Originally there was painted glass in the three windows here. The **galleries** rest on iron piers in fluted Doric casings. Below the organ, W, paired doors and a curved **screen**. – **Boards** with painted Lord's Prayer, Creed and Commandments. – **Fonts**. One of c. 1900, of stone, a copy of the medieval original. Another of *Coade* stone, c. 1790, with Gothic panels. Now in the lobby; originally in the SW (Morning) chapel. – Also in the lobby, some of the better **monuments**. Edward Moses, son of the master of the Grammar School, d.1813, obelisk with Latin and Greek inscriptions, and a plaque commemorating David Stephenson, architect, d.1819: both by *R.G. Davies*.

W of the church, the narrow curved path is the S end of old Pilgrim Street, isolated by the Tyne Bridge approach and further by 1970s office developments. These blocks, which include one just N of the railway viaduct, were meant as parts of the **All Saints Office Precinct** (planned by *Sir Basil Spence* from 1969, with *T.P. Bennett & Son*), which was to have spread in terraces all the way down to Quayside. They have canted corners and concrete elevations.

N from All Saints' churchyard, steps down to **Manor Chare**; then E back to Trinity Gardens. The renewed **Croft Stairs** lead NE to the Town Wall's **Corner Tower**. Not a true tower, but a turret, where the wall survives to some 9 ft (3 metres) high, running S then turning E towards the medieval vill of Pandon, the change of direction the result of Newcastle's acquisition of Pandon in 1298. N a few yards to **City Road**, then downhill to the right, **Sallyport Crescent** (completed 1916), excellent municipal housing by *F.H. Holford*, City Surveyor. Brick and render (casements removed); two levels, the rear with balconies and river views. Along City Road, reached up steps from its N side, **Sallyport** or **Wallknoll Tower**. In 1716 the council gave this Town Wall gate tower to the Ships' Carpenters' Company, and on top of the old gate they built this bold ashlar meeting hall. Architect unknown; comparisons have been drawn with Vanbrugh's work. Pilasters and big eaves cornice; two windows in each long side in rusticated keyed round-headed surrounds, another window in a bow on the short side to the w. On the E, steps lead to the hall door: round overlight in a rusticated corniced panel; above, a relief of a ship's hull. Square corner turrets, with small round-headed openings (blind), pyramid tops and ball finials.

To the NE is **Garth Heads**: workers' dwellings of 1869 and 1878 by *John Johnstone* for the Newcastle upon Tyne Improved Industrial Dwellings Co. [89]. A big unpretentious block: polychrome brick, painted ashlar dressings, fire-proof concrete stairwells; good plaque on the E side naming the Board.

On **City Road**, further E and with its back towards Garth Heads, the **Keelmen's Hospital** [91] (architect unknown): a plain brick quadrangle of 1701–4. It was paid for by levying a penny a tide on the keelmen, who lived in crowded chares in the Sandgate area below. Their keels carried goods between ship and shore. In the centre of the s range

89. Garth Heads, Tower Street, by John Johnstone, 1869 and 1878

a square, domed tower with sundial and clock face [91]. Pilasters in three primitive orders flanking the pedimented plain doorcase and at the angles of the tower, which has a commemorative panel. Dormers with shaped gables, slightly clumsy scroll decoration and central lozenges, all brick. The whole has been much repaired and restored: no visible evidence of the rear tower of C18 illustrations. The former **Salvation Army Men's Hostel** [30], now Social Centre (1976; *Ryder & Yates*), respects the height of the older neighbour and its relationship to the road, sweeping back in an asymmetrical angle of brick, with narrow windows.

Turn s towards the river. Here was a group of brick **warehouses** of *c.* 1830 on stone plinths. After 1989, one facing **Milk Market** became flats; two were damaged by fires, one now rebuilt as flats, one replaced with a hotel, partly re-creating scale, rhythm and grouping. Here the Town Wall crossed Quayside at Sandgate.

90. Walk 2, Ouseburn valley, *see* p. 136

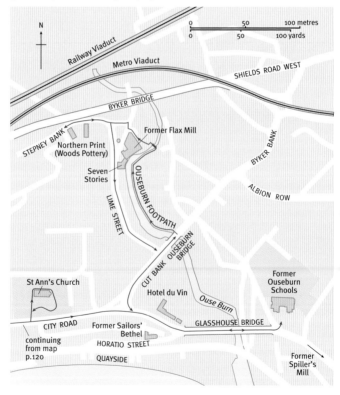

91. Keelmen's Hospital, 1701–4, tower

The Keelmen's Hospital
Built at their own Charge
Anno Domini 1701

Mr MATTHIAS WHITE Esqr Govenor
Mr EDWARD GREY } Stewards
Mr EDWARD CARR
Of the KEELMEN'S Company
for the time being
AND
Trustees for the Hospital

East Quayside and Ouseburn

The riverside from Milk Market westwards to the Ouseburn is **East Quayside**, designed under the Tyne and Wear Development Corporation, which commissioned works of art commemorating the history of the Quayside and gave buildings and spaces old Quayside place names ('Square' was applied to spaces not necessarily square). *Terry Farrell & Partners* drew up the masterplan in 1991 (adopted 1992, completed 1998) for offices, pubs/restaurants and leisure uses, by several architects and not to a uniform style, but using traditional brick and sandstone. Hard landscaping was designed by *Branson McGuckin Associates*, with *Insite Environments* as landscape subconsultants.

Start at **Sandgate**, which John Wesley in 1742 said was 'the poorest and most contemptible part of the town': **Wesley Square** has a resited granite obelisk memorial to him of 1891; also, on posts around the square, bronze **Siren**, 1995, and **River God**, 1996, by *André Wallace*. *Neil Talbot*'s **River Tyne**, 1996, is carved into the long retaining wall. To the E, No. 100 Quayside, plain, with bowed w window, E oriel and porch facing **Sandgate Square**. At the NW, **Sandgate Steps,** 1996, elaborate railings by *Alan Dawson* [92]; carvings by *Neil Talbot* and *Graciela Ainsworth*, with the Tyneside song 'Weel may the keel row that ma

92. Sandgate Steps, East Quayside, railings by Alan Dawson, 1996

93. Pitcher and Piano, East Quayside, by Panter Hudspith, 1995–7

laddie's in . . .' Beyond the steps, the tall, curved **Sandgate House** by *Ryder Nicklin*, wave roof rising westwards. At the NW angle a tall drum matching that on *Ryder Co.*'s **Keel Row House** behind, forming a gateway to **Sandgate**, which runs parallel to the Quayside. Next, the only building remaining from the old waterfront, the **Co-operative Wholesale Society warehouse** [19], 1899–1900: now the **Malmaison Hotel** (conversion by *Gordon Farrier*). Early reinforced concrete by *T.G. Gueritte* of *L.G. Mouchel*, with *F.E.L. Harris* of the C.W.S. Architect's Office, using the *Hennebique* method; supposedly the earliest surviving Hennebique building in England. Bare concrete structure, eight storeys including the basement, and an attic storey added in 1910. The three-bay giant order of plain pilasters without frieze but with block cornice stands on a triple-arched corniced podium; the canopy and flambeaux are hotel additions. In front, the **Gateshead Millennium Bridge** (p. 95).

Then **Keelman Square**, with sculptures **Column and Steps**, steel and stone, and bronze **Rudder**, both by *Andrew Burton*, 1996. Behind and in front, a simple masonry block with glazed front behind curved loggia, by *Red Box*, and sitting nicely beside the river, the **Pitcher & Piano** [93], 1995–7 by *Panter Hudspith*, with wave-form roof and glass front walls. **Quayside House** on the E side of the square, *c.* 1995, pale brick with recessed glazed attic under wide eaves, balances the proportions of the Malmaison hotel.

Next, **The Swirle** follows the line of the historic street and stream, marked by *Raf Fulcher*'s **Swirle Pavilion,** 1998. A colonnaded circle enclosing a globe, referring to the destinations of ships from the Tyne. The striking U-plan block next is **St Ann's Wharf,** by *CZWG Architects*: two high central stone arches; stone top storey with long brackets supporting extended eaves. On the promenade, the **Blacksmith's Needle** – a six-section cone: central bell and surrounding objects representing the senses, 1997 by members of the *British Artist Blacksmiths Association*. **Rotterdam House** next, 1999–2000 by *Ryder Co.*, T-plan red brick, render, glass walling and part-wave roof. Behind, two attractive **car parks** on Sandgate and St Ann's Street by *Napper, c.* 1995, and beside **City Road**, a glass-clad office block by *Ryder Co.*, N. To the NE, **St Ann's church**, rebuilt in 1764–8 by *William Newton* (using stone from the recently demolished quayside stretch of Town Wall). An elegant preaching box with pedimented Doric portico below a pedimented W gable carrying a tower and steeple; corner urns but no balustrades. On Quayside, evenly spaced blocks of flats by *Napper Architects* at **Mariners' Wharf**, *c.* 1997. Between City Road and the quay, the tall flèche of the brick and sandstone **Sailors' Bethel** in Horatio Street; now offices: 1877 by *Thomas Oliver*, Gothic, with schoolroom added 1900 by *Oliver, Leeson & Wood*. On the N side of City Road, the **Hotel du Vin**, converted in 2007–8 from the Tyne-Tees Steam Shipping Co. offices. A new rear wing has been added to *J. W. Taylor*'s building of 1908, with its sparse English Baroque detail.

To the E lies the **Ouseburn valley**. Once full of industries – lead and flax were processed, pottery and toffee made – this is being revitalized, and is now home to cultural companies and organizations. The approach from City Road is NE along Cut Bank and Byker Bank, then up the E bank of the stream to see the E fronts of buildings on **Lime Street**. *Dobson*'s **flax mill** of 1847–8 for Messrs Plummer and Cooke is massive stone, twelve bays, four storeys and attic, with access for goods from the water, left. Now artists' studios, etc. s of it, an important part of the revival [94]: **Seven Stories**, a centre for children's literature, a conversion completed 2005 by *GWK Architects*, Newcastle, of a C19 brick flour mill. Cross the footbridge to see the fascinating extension on the landward side, evoking the turning pages of a book. Further N are **bridges**: the high railway viaduct of 1837–9 by *John & Benjamin Green*, its laminated timber arches replaced with iron in 1869 (widened 1887), and the elegant **Metro viaduct**, 1979, consultant engineers *Ove Arup & Partners*; parabolic reinforced-concrete trusses. In front of these, **Byker (road) Bridge**, a commercial toll bridge, opened in 1878 for pedestrians, 1879 for road traffic. Between the road and Metro bridges, **Crawford's Bridge**, a small C18 stone arch. Head w up **Stepney Bank** to see the mix of old and new buildings, with skilful conversions such as that of Woods Pottery by *Mosedale Gillatt Architects*, 2004–5.

94. Lime Street, C19 warehouse, with extension for Seven Stories by GWK Architects, 2005, left

Visible E of the Ouse Burn, the riverfront has the remaining part of *Oscar Faber & Partners'* majestic **Spiller's Flour Mill** of 1935–8 – a white, ship-like monument. Inland, the end of the Quayside and the beginning of Byker is marked by the wonderfully ornate **Ouseburn Schools,** Albion Row: 1891–3 by *F. W. Rich*. Tall square towers with elaborate tiered ogee-hipped roofs. Beyond, the Byker Estate fills the hillside (p. 232).

Walk 3.

The Historic Centre

This walk explores the upper part of medieval Newcastle with the Castle and St Nicholas's Cathedral at its heart (pp. 62 and 46). **Markets** grew beside the church and roads to it, and two bridges were built across the Lort Burn's deep valley. Two routes led N: one (now Cloth and Groat markets, Bigg Market and Newgate Street) on the burn's w bank, skirting the convent of St Bartholomew; another, now Pilgrim Street, on the E bank. This walk follows those routes and the links between them, finishing with the C18 formation of Dean Street which improved communication between riverside and upper town.

95. Walk 3

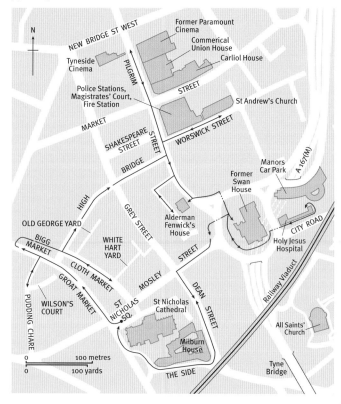

The start is at **St Nicholas Square** of 1842, N of the Cathedral, at the base of the market triangle (for Queen Victoria's statue, *see* Walk 4, p. 162, for Collingwood Street, W, *see* p. 161). On the N side, instead of medieval stalls, the solid mass of No. 2 **Cathedral Square**, built as Sun Alliance House, 1974–6 by *Hadfield Cawkwell Davidson & Partners*; glass entrance *c.* 2005. It replaced *John Johnstone*'s ornately classical Town Hall of 1858–63, which incorporated *John & Benjamin Green*'s classical Corn Exchange of 1838–9.

Into Groat Market, and NW. By the C19 the merchants' houses here had become inns, shops, offices, workshops and warehouses. After a tall Edwardian building, a much lower C18 house, then (twenty-eight windows long), **Thomson House** (NCJ Media), *c.* 1964, printing works and offices for the *Newcastle Journal* and *Evening Chronicle* by *Cackett, Burns Dick & Mackellar*. Portland stone, grey mosaic, grid structure; not sympathetic to the surroundings, but the rhythm of floor levels and bay divisions was intended to echo the C19 Town Hall, framing the view of Cathedral and Castle. Nos. 31–41 show how complicated town houses become as they change, the gardens of the burgage plots filling up with outbuildings. No. 31, *c.* 1800, wide, painted brick with stone sills and lintels. Nos. 33 and 35–37, mid-C18 fronts with rendering imitating rusticated ashlar, lintels imitating voussoirs. No. 33 has aprons, Nos. 35–37 (five bays) early C18 splat balusters in the upper staircase, and delicate C18 plasterwork beside the stair and on the ceiling of the long first-floor room. Under No. 35 a passage to **Wilson's Court**, perhaps the only complete survivor of the warren of yards and courts which once filled this neighbourhood. Here a C17 rubbed brick arch, showing parts of an earlier house within the later. Then No. 41, a painted brick early C19 front; gables perhaps C17.

After C20 office blocks Groat Market ends and **Bigg Market** begins, NW to Grainger Street (Walk 4, p. 158). First a detour, left down **Pudding Chare**, a medieval lane to Westgate Road. Here at the other end of Wilson's Court is a charming four-bay building of *c.* 1790, Nos. 24 and 26: two upper floors with Venetian windows, on the first floor in arched recesses on a sill band; (restored) sashes with intersecting glazing bars. At the head of Bigg Market, a domed **drinking fountain** by the Newcastle architect *Charles E. Errington*, commemorating J.H. Rutherford, Presbyterian minister and Temperance campaigner. Red Corsehill sandstone, granite basin. Lions'-head spouts on the eight-sided column; Quattrocento arches round arms of Gateshead and Newcastle, '1894', 'WATER IS BEST', and BOHU [Band of Hope Union]. Built in St Nicholas Square 1894, then moved to the foot of the Bigg Market in 1902 to make way for Queen Victoria; councillors joked that people who passed St Nicholas Square were not those seeking a water fountain.* Moved uphill 1998 during refurbishing of the market area.

---

*Bigg Market in its turn now has both fountain and reputation; and a C19 gents' **urinal** survives below ground, with conical glass roof.

On the N side, after dull 1990s rebuilding, Nos. 10–16, **Half Moon Chambers**, a pub and offices of 1903–5 by *Simpson, Lawson & Rayne*. Lively elevation with Art Nouveau lettering, Ionic columns, bombé balconies; roof turrets with fish-scale tiles, spike finials. No. 8, right, C18, with more voussoired lintels; the right gable with tumbled-in brick-work. (Upper staircase with ramped handrail and fat turned balusters.) No. 6, slightly later, has similar voussoirs. Both with early C19 incised render. The left corner with High Bridge is **Sunlight Chambers**, beau-tiful Neo-Baroque, 1901–2 for Lever Bros by *W. & S. Owen*, who designed many buildings for them – especially at Port Sunlight. Tall and vigorous: strongly rusticated windows, broad mosaic frieze depicting harvest and industry.

Across High Bridge, the **Beehive Hotel** (No. 54 **Cloth Market**), 1902 by *J. Oswald & Son*. Strong corner turret, ground-floor extravaganza in faience [96]; upper floors now student accommodation. Nos. 44–48, **Cloth Market Buildings**, 1869–70 by *R. Fairbairn* for Pumphrey and Carrick Watson as café and shop. White brick and sandstone, sober, but a fine mansard roof, its high centre hipped with iron crestings. On the first floor elements survive of the 1897 coffee rooms by *Oliver & Leeson* in a mixed Arts and Crafts/Moorish style: fretwork screen downstands, slatted seats below net parcel racks; panelled stairwell with bullseye glass screen. Oak Room, 1914, panelled. Disused in 2008. The shopfronts flank the entrance to **Old George Yard**. Here a former coaching inn, partly C17 or earlier; C18 and C19 changes. The main block (left) stuccoed; inside, a wide segmental fire-arch and C18 joinery. Later stables, stores and (probably) brewhouse, brick with some late C18 sashes. Nos. 28–42 Cloth Market, a bar and offices, 1978–80 by *Clifford Culpin & Partners*, imitating historic proportions and introducing an irregular building line. No. 26 (1899), brick and stone with a gable, and an old entry, Heywood's Court. Three altered C19 buildings, then Nos. 14–16: one of Newcastle's most important houses, its timber frame dis-guised by an C18 brick front and C20 shopfronts flanking a passageway to White Hart Yard. Above, the timber jetty has been cut back and the brick-faced front leans forward. First-floor rear wall with two C16 fire-places, one rearranged; a Tudor stone arch to the S rear wing. Second-floor closet with old wallpaper. Main roof of a local type (cf. No. 35 The Close and Trinity House rigging loft, pp. 108 and 126), tree-ring-dated to the 1520s. Kingpost construction, the ridge with mortices for longi-tudinal bracing; sturdy tie-beams on curved braces. Brick-nogged gables. A wide plot, with ranges on both sides of the yard: left, an early C18 front with one cross-window surviving, then a C19 range incorporating a Tudor-arched door; right, C19 warehouses and offices. At the end, an alley (closed to the public) to Grey Street (Walk 4), which sliced the medieval plots in 1835. No. 10 Cloth Market, narrow, red brick and sandstone, dated 1908, but in its gated alley older buildings: one C17/C18, late timber-framed, one early C18 brick, both with mullion-and-transom windows, and one early C19, belonging with Grey Street

96. Beehive Hotel, Cloth Market and High Bridge, by J. Oswald & Son, 1902

behind. Nos. 6–8, 1902 by *A. Stockwell*, replaced the Wheatsheaf pub, famous as Balmbra's Music Hall, celebrated in the song 'The Blaydon Races': curved-glass pub front, shaped gable.

Back uphill and NE into **High Bridge**: narrow, mixing C19 and C20. A dip indicates the buried medieval bridge; the cobbled yard (right) formerly led to the 1808 'Butcher Market', dem. 1835. Nos. 31–37 (left), Wards Buildings, 1903 by *Cackett & Burns Dick*, skilfully designed for the narrow street. Bright red brick, sandstone top floor and full-height bays, slate-hung mansard; some original shopfronts. Nos. 41–51, 1901–2, also *Cackett & Burns Dick*, a three-storey extension of Grey Street's former Turk's Head Hotel (p. 166).

High Bridge continues beyond Grey Street (the S side rebuilt), to **Pilgrim Street**. A medieval street from All Saints' church, S to Pilgrim Street Gate in the Town Wall, N. Many changes since. The gate was removed in 1811 to ease traffic; in 1835 Grainger partly redeveloped the w side; the railway viaduct cut across in 1849, Worswick Street broke into the E side *c.* 1870, and Tyne Bridge of 1925–8 needed widened approach roads. Post-war town planning took traffic from the bridge to the deeply trenched Central Motorway East, bypassing the old town. For that scheme, Dobson's Royal Arcade was sacrificed (*see* topic box, p. 146).

At the N corner with High Bridge, replacing part of a *Grainger* block on Pilgrim Street, **Moor's Buildings** (Nos. 54–56). Completed 1894 by *John Johnson* of London (plaque, right of the door) as a Freemasons'

97. Tyneside Cinema, by George Bell, 1937–8, interior

Hall and temple; later the Moor shipping line offices; now a club. Tall, elaborate, with superimposed pilasters and pilastered attic, mixing Jacobean and classical; tall arched doorway. (Former Grand Central Lodge, Ionic; Upper Lodge with Corinthian pilasters; domed second-floor 'Knight Templars' Encampment'.) *Grainger*'s work starts at Nos. 46–50, *c.* 1836. Perhaps by his architects *Wardle* and *Walker*: giant Corinthian order on the Shakespeare Street corner, big second-floor cornice, low attic storey.

Next N, between Shakespeare Street and Market Street (N), *Grainger* again, in his general style but part of *John & Benjamin Green*'s Theatre Royal block.* Recessed five-bay centre, end pavilions with paired giant pilasters framing pedimented first-floor and smaller second-floor windows, tripartite on the right. A plainer Grainger block, *c.* 1838, between Market and Hood streets (Nos. 22–28), simply articulated by bands and a bold second-floor cornice, the corners curved and recessed.

After another Grainger block, the **Tyneside Cinema** (Nos. 10–12), N corner of High Friar Lane. Built as the Bijou News-Reel Theatre, 1937–8 by *George Bell*. Late for a news theatre, but supposedly the last working newsreel cinema in Britain; later a specialist cinema (restoration and polycarbonate-clad rooftop extension 2006–8 by *Fletcher Priest*, consultant conservation architect *Cyril Winskell*). Fine Art Deco/Persian interior [97]; later **mural** by the Newcastle architect *Peter Yates*. For the Blackett Street corner, *see* Walk 6, p. 185.

*Their drawings (Metropolitan Museum, New York) show plan and section, but not the elevation of this front.

Back s down Pilgrim Street. The E side was partly set back for the Tyne Bridge approach. Here the former **Paramount Cinema**, the last complete Paramount in Britain; latterly the **Odeon** (future uncertain). A striking building, with the former Gaumont on Westgate Road/Clayton Street, one of only two big pre-war cinemas surviving in the centre. 1930–1 by *Frank Verity* and *Samuel Beverly*. Cream brick with ashlar ground floor, cornice and details; Art Deco interior by *Charles Fox*. Its neighbour is the horrendous **Commercial Union House** by *Howell Brooks Tucker & Partners*, completed 1971, astride the road on pilotis. Like its late unlamented contemporary Westgate House (*see* p. 114), intended to 'give a sense of enclosure'. Their sheer ugliness and inappropriate scale galvanized support for the conservation of the city centre in the late 1960s–70s.

The street block is completed by **Carliol House** [26], 1924–8 by *Burnet, Tait & Lorne* with *L.J. Couves & Partners* of Newcastle, for the pioneering Newcastle upon Tyne Electric Supply Co. (N.E.S.C.O.). Steel frame, fashionable Portland stone cladding (not its first appearance in Newcastle: *see* e.g. Scottish Provident House, 1906, p. 163). A strong composition with a low-domed corner turret incorporating showroom entrances. Bronze **plaque** by *Richard A. Ray*, 1931, to Sir Joseph Wilson Swan, 'inventor of the electric incandescent lamp and a pioneer in the science of photography'. The long, sleek Market Street front curves downhill; at its centre, the Greek-derived office entrance of granite with fat Doric columns of grey fossil-flecked limestone.

Its companion across Market Street is more monumental than elegant: **Magistrates' Courts, Police Station and Fire Station**, 1931–3 by *Cackett, Burns Dick & Mackellar*. Steel-framed, Portland-stone-clad, with brick for staff flats on Worswick Street; the third police station here since 1840. Upper floors with recessed giant Corinthian columns, characteristic also of interwar architecture in the City of London. Sculpture is confined to flattened griffins terminating the colonnades. Garage doors with granite surrounds. Police Station entrance on the corner, Courts entrance in Market Street. Brick fire tower.

Worswick Street, of the 1870s, is named after the C18 Catholic priest who built a chapel in his garden; house and garden were demolished for the street. On the left the replacement **St Andrew's church (R.C.)** and **presbytery**, an imposing group: the presbytery with shouldered lintels; the church C14 English Gothic, rock-faced, with buttressed bays, traceried windows and tall apse. Designed 1874 by *Thomas Gibson* of Newcastle; linking vestry by *Dunn, Hansom & Fenwick*, 1897. The porch holds a spiral organ stair. Wide N aisle. Front-facing **altar** made from the original pulpit. The street slopes E to the submerged course of the Erick Burn, the boundary of Pilgrim Street's burgage plots.

Opposite, **Worswick Chambers**, with Nos. 85–91 Pilgrim Street: 1891–9 in two builds by *W.L. Newcombe*. Red brick and ashlar, subdued Gothic, with central galleried auction room. Stone band over the first-floor windows with arched panels with heads sculpted by *J. Rogers* from

98. Nos. 98–100 Pilgrim Street, Alderman Fenwick's House, late C17

family photographs. Then Nos. 93–101, three Late Georgian brick houses, each four storeys and two or three bays, with shopfronts. House door with ogee arch. Transverse stairs behind the shops; good plaster decoration survives in some rooms, Greek in No. 101 where the Stokoes lived (cf. the Moot Hall, p. 118): so did they design the group? (Awaiting restoration.)

Opposite, downhill from High Bridge, more reminders of pre-Victorian Newcastle. First, Nos. 60–64: typical early C19 brick, with stone lintels and sills. Then the **Market Lane** pub, once a fine town house of *c.* 1740: symmetrical front with tapered pilasters (now truncated) and sash windows (renewed), grouped 2+1+2. Pastiche C18 pub front. The left gable shows many periods: two storeys of coursed rubble, old brick above, apparently a retained party wall, with a shaped gable of *c.* 1700 partly outlined; C18 offshoot with tumbled-in brick. w of the yard, remains of an C18 **banqueting house** (restoration awaited).

Nos. 98–100, **Alderman Fenwick's House** [98], is the best and most complete historic house in Newcastle. Of many periods: medieval site,

99. Alderman Fenwick's House, staircase

later C17 main structure. James Corbridge's 1723 map marked its present name, but the Fenwick owners were merchants; perhaps their alderman cousin lived there. As at Schomberg House (1698) in London's Pall Mall, the end bays project, but this house is more severe, with rusticated stone piers under the end bays (with the yard entrance, right), heavily moulded and plastered brick cornices on each floor, and a parapet. The rear, visible from a 1980s service road, is archaic by contrast, with a cogged brick string and plain gabled wings. Between them a stair-tower, with renewed windows, weathervane and cupola reinstated after Corbridge's illustration. Renewed s gable.

Inside, an open-well staircase [99] with wide grip handrail on fat turned balusters. It opens onto the roof, with passage through the steep-pitched front roof to the parapet walk. New wind indicator and cloud-painting inside the dome. Full-width first-floor room with fine bolection-moulded early C18 panelling; C17 strapwork ceiling with pendants and a plaster motif seen elsewhere in Newcastle (*see* topic box, p. 11). Restored fireplaces. The house became the Queen's Head

The Royal Arcade

The Royal Arcade was a fine classical composition opposite Mosley Street, complementing Stephenson's smart shops and houses there. When the Town Council would not agree to build a corn exchange on this Pilgrim Street site, Grainger chose *Dobson* to design the arcade, begun June 1831 and completed May 1832.

In London, the Royal Opera Arcade of 1816–18 by John Nash had shown how to combine shops in one building by using glazed domes to light the central space. Other arcades followed, including London's Lowther Arcade of 1830. In engravings this could be mistaken for Newcastle's Royal Arcade, so alike were they, with giant pilasters, transverse arches, glass domes and two levels of dignified shops on each side. Dobson's elevation had a Doric ground floor and a giant Corinthian order above, surmounted by a sculptural group by *David Dunbar Jun.*; the E end had steps down to Manor Chare.

Away from the shops of Dean and Mosley streets, and then overtaken in terms of fashion and convenience by Grainger's own new streets, the Royal Arcade unfortunately did not succeed. After the C19 it became a refuge of non-mainstream activities: printers, bookbinders, left-wing groups, a jazz club, etc. When it stood in the way of the grand

vision offered by the Central Motorway East, the council obtained permission to remove the arcade, the Royal Fine Art Commission recommending reconstruction nearby. The stones were marked, but the dismantled masonry was never reassembled; most of it was buried, and much scattered around Byker and in Armstrong Park. This was the most serious of Newcastle's architectural losses in the 1960s.

100. Royal Arcade, by John Dobson, 1831–2, demolished late 1960s. Engraving after T. Allom, 1833

101. Swan House (now 55° North), by Robert Matthew, Johnson-Marshall & Partners, 1963–9

coaching inn, in 1783 'now fitted in a genteel manner', probably incorporating the plainer, new-built No. 100 (left). In 1883 the houses became the Liberal Club; from 1962 empty; restored 1982–97 by *Simpson & Brown* for Buttress (Tyne and Wear Building Preservation Trust). Nos. 112–118, attractive Free Baroque offices of *c.* 1902 by *C.E. Oliver* for the Consett Iron Co. Nine Bays. For Nos. 128–130 *see* Mosley Street (p. 149).

Diagonally opposite Alderman Fenwick's, Nos. 107–109, *c.* 1920, a Manchester warehouse by *Marshall & Tweedy* for J. & G. Cooper (future uncertain). Grey faience on a steel frame; French late C18 detailing. The 1960s **roundabout** and submerged Central Motorway East, ahead, truncated Pilgrim Street. Meeting the roundabout corner, the former **Bank of England**, 1968–71 by *Fitzroy Robinson & Partners*. Strikingly monumental, with big vertical square bays, clad in roach-bed Portland stone, stepped back to ascend the newly curved street: a vigorous building (future uncertain).

On the roundabout (or Pilgrim Street), soaring overhead, is **Swan House** [101] (now called **55° North**), designed in 1961 (like the pedestrian traffic routes) by *Robert Matthew, Johnson-Marshall & Partners* and built 1963–9; refurbished 2004 as a ground-floor bar and offices, flats and penthouses by *Ryder HKS*. A slab block cantilevered over the roundabout and roadway. Long concrete elevations punctured by a grid of openings. Originally with low stone-clad blocks facing s and w; partly replaced with a 'wave' screen, pink-rendered, and a fountain. Within the ground floor was originally a sorry imitation of the interior of *Dobson's* **Royal Arcade** (*see* topic box).

102. Former Holy Jesus Hospital, 1681 for the Newcastle Corporation

The **Holy Jesus Hospital** [102] lies SE, reached by underpass from the roundabout. The site was an Augustinian friary, occasionally used after the Dissolution by Henry VIII's Council of the North. Acquired in the C17 by Newcastle Corporation, who built the hospital in 1681 for a master and thirty-nine poor freemen or their widows. In 1971–93 it housed the John George Joicey Museum; now the National Trust and other tenants. A simple brick building, given grandeur by the arcade. This loggia has thirty moulded arches on square pillars; behind, doors to the ground-floor rooms, and in the centre the (originally open) stair. The front has moulded floor strings and small three-light windows, on the first floor with alternating segmental and flat brick arches. Central (replica) inscription in a carved frame, below a segmental pediment on grotesque masks, typical of the provincial North in the later C17. Two shaped W gables of C17 type but of 1880, when the soup kitchen was added behind and the adjoining gable probably rebuilt. E gable plain, perhaps rebuilt. Restoration *c.* 1969 retained the original arrangement of small rooms opening off long corridors. Sturdy stair, straight flights with fat turned balusters (cf. Alderman Fenwick's House). In front, large C17 stone **conduit** or pant. At the rear, E, the **Tower of the Manors**, often misnamed Austin Friars' Tower but mostly later C16. Its s wall incorporates a pointed window arch of the friary church choir's N wall (inside the hospital). Excavation showed that the lower part of the w wall was a surviving fragment of the friary sacristy; the tower's other walls could only have been built after the Dissolution.* Behind is **Manors Car Park**, 1971 (*D. T. Bradshaw*, City Engineer), another part of the motorway scheme.

Back across the roundabout to Newcastle's first post-medieval street: **Mosley Street**, with Dean Street planned and built for the Corporation by the architect *David Stephenson,* by Act of Parliament of 1784. These wide T-plan streets filled the Lort Burn dene, Dean Street connecting Sandhill to the higher ground, and Mosley Street linking Pilgrim Street to the Flesh or Cloth Market. In the late C19 this became the business area of Newcastle, and was much redeveloped, so little remains of Stephenson here (more in Dean Street). The NE corner is Nos. 128–130 Pilgrim Street, 1899 by *Benjamin Simpson*. An interesting office-and-shop, iron-framed internally, with a big stair oriel to Mosley Street. Stephenson's original scale at Nos. 3–5, seemingly an C18 house refurbished, window surrounds added *c.* 1900. Nos. 7–19, the retained façade of an 1870 building by *Alfred Swan*, nephew of Sir J.W. Swan, for Mawson & Swan (in 1990 rebuilt as **Kelburn House**). Swan's early experiments with incandescent electric light bulbs were done here.

Rounding the SE corner, Nos. 2–4 Mosley Street, classical, 1908 by *Newcombe & Newcombe* for the Alliance Assurance Co. Common but attractive combination of sandstone ashlar walls and granite plinth. No. 8, narrow, of bright red brick and red sandstone with a second-floor balcony: 1906 by *W.H. Knowles*, as his office; lively use of the orders. At the sw corner with Dean Street, No. 12, free Northern Renaissance style, with mullion-and-transom windows: 1891–7, for the Prudential Assurance Co. By their usual architect *Alfred Waterhouse*, in his usual red materials, here sandstone and brick, with a granite plinth. Corner entrance to the public office, now a restaurant, with *Burmantofts* green and yellow tile lining, uncovered in 1990s restoration. No. 21, N side, six-storey offices by *Fred T. Walker* for the Edinburgh Life Assurance Co., 1906: red granite ground floor, ashlar above; giant Corinthian order through floors two and three. Rear link to No. 10 Grey Street, 1908, where the same materials are easily recognized. Overdoor company arms between figures of Plenty and Security by *C. Neuper* of Eldon Square. Wrapped round by this building is Grainger's final work in Grey Street, treated in Walk 4, with the w part of Mosley Street (p. 164).

*A fine medieval effigy of a knight found during excavation is now in the Discovery Museum.

Dean Street, joining Mosley Street here, has a fascinating mixture of buildings [103], dominated by the railway viaduct to its s (*see* p. 87). On the E, after Waterhouse's corner, *Stephenson*'s late C18 houses step downhill: red brick, three storeys, two bays wide; some C18 Westmorland slate roofs and small segment-headed dormers. Nos. 50–52 were extensively remodelled in 1902 by *Benjamin Simpson*, the Art Nouveau shop with exaggerated Ionic half-columns. Then mock-Georgian infill of 1989 fronting a car park with wide, high entrance (on the site of old Low Bridge, the lower of the two Lort Burn crossings).

On the w side, **Cathedral Buildings**, 1901 by *Oliver, Leeson & Wood*, big and beautiful. Five or six storeys and mezzanine, seven gabled bays of tall narrow oriels; free Jacobean style. Shop windows behind cast metal columns with Renaissance decoration. Tiled stairwell behind a central tetrastyle porch. s of **Cathedral Stairs** (on the line of the old street, Low Bridge) the former verger's house, 1902, also *Oliver, Leeson & Wood*, with original shop, the house above facing the churchyard behind. A clever design for a two-level site. Red brick with stone quoins; tall balconied oriel window with strapwork panels; shaped parapet with ball finials. Nos. 17–21, 1897 by *Marshall & Dick* for the Manchester Fire Assurance Co. Baroque terracotta-clad public office below, prominent central gable.

Nos. 16–18 and 20 opposite, two more 1780s houses with *c.* 1900 shops. Nos. 12–14, offices and warehouse of 1901, now a hotel; again *Oliver, Leeson & Wood*. Brick dressed with stone, cladding a steel frame. On the front panels of mullioned windows with mosaic friezes, homage to Sandhill's timber frames (p. 105). No. 10, ashlar, 1888 by *Stockwell & Spicer*; simple Italianate; narrowed in 1895 for the viaduct.

Back on the w side, a large office block, **Milburn House**, 1902–5. More *Oliver, Leeson & Wood*, for J.D. Milburn, a shipping owner. Steeply sloping triangular site, the rear on The Side, redeveloped after fire. Brick with stone dressings, free Baroque detail, with entrances on several levels. An effective composition with floors marked by cornices; big attic gables. Two-storey basement with a shop entrance on the lowest level, the rounded s corner. Interior – light wells, stairwells and corridors, glazed screens, armorial glass, panelled walls – handled in masterly fashion, with an especially impressive entrance from Dean Street. Extensive use of tiles in the public areas, an early example of the work of *H. & R. Johnson*, successfully restored by them in 1990–1.

Follow Milburn House round to **The Side**, climbing alongside the Castle's NE boundary. On the left, two houses survive of an early C19 development, perhaps by *David Stephenson*. One retains sashes of Georgian type; the other has a 1980s stair-tower by *Bill Hopper*. On the NW angle of Milburn House a **bust** of Admiral Lord Collingwood, born 1748 in a house on this site. Here, by the Black Gate, we meet the course of Walk 1 (p. 118).

103. Dean Street, including (left to right): Nos. 16–18, by David Stephenson, 1780s; Nos. 12–14, by Oliver, Leeson & Wood, 1901; No. 10, by Stockwell & Spicer, 1888

Walk 4.

Grainger Town

This walk looks at *Richard Grainger*'s transformation of central Newcastle. The process began in the 1820s with Blackett Street and Eldon Square, as described below. Then in 1834 Grainger persuaded the Corporation to buy the C17 mansion, Anderson Place, and its grounds w of Pilgrim Street, where the Franciscan friary had occupied a large site just s of the Town Wall. He proposed a grid of new streets linking N and s, E and w parts of the old town, with ashlar-fronted houses and hotels, shops, theatre and market. By 1840 Grainger's grid thus linked all strands of the medieval web of Newcastle.

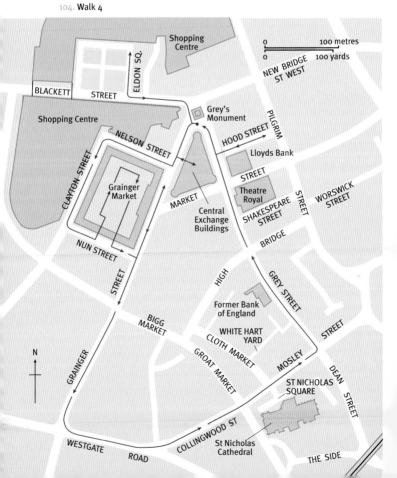

A new market (now Grainger Market) was needed first, because the meat market of 1808 had to be demolished to build the key N–S street between Mosley Street and Blackett Street. This 'Upper Dean Street', later Grey Street in honour of Earl Grey, continued the late C18 alignment of Dean Street (*see* p. 150), and made, for the first time, a wide route from Tyne Bridge to the upper town. Grey Street was crossed E–W by Market Street, from Pilgrim Street to the new market on what is now Grainger Street. The shorter Hood Street and Shakespeare Street, from Grey Street to Pilgrim Street, provided houses with offices rather than shops; Nun Street and Nelson Street, N and S of the Grainger Market, joined Clayton Street to the W, a third new street running approximately N–S. Less elaborate architecturally, Clayton Street touched Blackett Street at the N and crossed medieval Newgate Street to reach Westgate Road. From here Clayton Street West continued SW to the line of Neville Street, with houses and offices, including that of Grainger himself. In 1868–70 Grainger Street, originally ending at the Bigg Market, was extended S to the Central Station.

Despite Margaret Dobson's statement in *A Memoir of John Dobson*, 1885, her father was not Grainger's principal architect, although he was the most eminent. He designed the market, the elevations of Thomas Oliver's Eldon Square, and, said correspondence in 1860s newspapers, Grey Street's E side between Mosley and Shakespeare streets. *John & Benjamin Green* designed the adjacent Theatre Royal block, and – so far as is known – *John Wardle* and *George Walker*, of Grainger's office, all the other streets.

Grey's Monument [14] is the focus of Grainger's developments: from it radiate his streets. Grainger Street runs SW; Blackett Street to E and W, never grand and much rebuilt, but with part of the elegant Eldon Square surviving on its N side; and famous Grey Street curves downhill to the SE. (The other main street, Clayton Street, began opposite the square but is now blocked by the 1970s shopping centre.) All these were planned and mostly executed some years before the column appeared, in 1838. Designed by *Benjamin Green*, it is Roman Doric, 135 ft (41.5 metres) high, on a tall pedestal. A balcony above the capital, then a square pedestal supports *E.H. Baily*'s statue of Earl Grey [105]. A long inscription extols Grey as 'champion of civil and religious liberty' under whom the 'great measure of parliamentary reform was . . . safely and triumphantly attained'. Amazingly, first proposals for the column were opposed because it would spoil the buildings; the Town Moor was suggested as the site instead. The stone platform belongs to refurbishment *c.* 1982, following Metro engineering works.

Blackett Street originated in *Dobson*'s 1815 survey for a street to replace a lane outside the Town Wall between Pilgrim Street Gate and the New Gate. In 1823 that stretch of wall was demolished; in 1824 *Grainger* built Blackett Street, with terraces of brick houses by either *Thomas Oliver* or *Dobson*. None survive, but on the N side, W of the Monument, Grainger's **Eldon Square** (1825–31) is still a green space. First plans were by *Thomas Oliver*; then, according to Oliver in 1831, elevations were designed by *Dobson*. The ashlar-fronted houses in their spacious square staked a claim to formality and monumentality that was new to the town [14]. The three ranges were treated with Greek simplicity, the N range planned with a central projection with Ionic columns (not executed; instead, a slight projection had plain giant pilasters), and the W range like the surviving one opposite, with giant plain antae or pilasters framing five-bay end pavilions, with prominent cornice and lower attic storey. A Grecian honeysuckle-pattern cast-iron balcony linked the pavilions at first-floor level. On the surviving side, steps lead to doors above basements protected by (renewed) area railings. No. 5 is now a mere façade to Metro ventilation shafts; No. 1, s, has some original interior detail, including ceiling stucco. In the square the town's **First World War memorial**, a fine equestrian St George and dragon, 1923 by *C. L. Hartwell*, the pedestal designed by *Cackett & Burns Dick*, the space around restored 2007.

Blackett Street is at present largely a traffic route flanked by the two original blocks of the confusingly named **Eldon Square shopping centre**, 1969–76 by *Chapman Taylor & Partners*, in conjunction with the City Planning Officer, *Wilfred Burns*. To build it, the N and W ranges of Eldon Square were demolished. A contemporary booklet justified the decision: 'Their architectural quality [had] been . . . impaired . . . it was found impossible to incorporate them in the two-level shopping centre without such drastic further alterations as would defeat the purpose of the retention.' In their place, blank-panelled brick elevations faced the square, the upper level recessed behind a walkway; the height of the new build was kept to that of the surroundings (*Arne Jacobsen*'s proposed multi-storey hotel on the W side, clad in bronze anodized aluminium, was not built). First-floor pedestrian circulation was planned, with ground-floor traffic and service roads, and a recreation centre within the top floor. Originally covering 7–8 acres, increasing to 13 (and still expanding), the centre set new standards for such developments by retaining some original façades rather than imposing a bulky mass upon the whole area. Grainger's elevations to Nelson Street and the N end of Grainger Street remained, with inevitably awkward junctions.

106. Emerson Chambers, by Simpson, Lawson & Rayne, 1903–4

The s side of Blackett Street is mostly dull blank brick, the ground floor a colonnaded footpath, except for mirror-glazing near the Monument. To the w, the shopping-centre bridge over Blackett Street, widened and given a bright blue glass gable in 1988. In Percy Street to some extent and in 'Old' Eldon Square, forbidding blank brick walls have been enclosed in glass-fronted additions, 2006–8 by *Comprehensive Design* of Edinburgh. The work includes remodelling the old bus station (behind the N side) as retail space, and building a new bus station facing Percy Street. Other enlargements, with the rest of the centre, are dealt with in the Walks as they come up.

The N side of **Blackett Street** to the E has a sleek brick-and-glass rebuilding of 1937 by *Mauchlen & Weightman* of part of Fenwick's department store in Northumberland Street. Opposite Grey's Monument, **Emerson Chambers** [106], wonderfully inventive Free Style of 1903–4 by *Simpson, Lawson & Rayne*, built as restaurant, shops and offices: a

107. Central Exchange Buildings, Grey, Grainger and Market streets, by John Wardle and George Walker, 1837–8

glorious confection of canted oriels, strapwork and friezes, balconies and domed turrets, dormers and little roof-lights with high pyramidal roofs, and high corniced chimneys. Fat Ionic columns of granite with bronze decoration and capitals at the central ground-floor projection, and fine (restored) Art Nouveau glazing bars. Lost except for its ceiling is the entrance and grand staircase, s, to the former basement restaurant.

For the commercial remainder of Blackett Street to the E, *see* Walk 6; for the upper parts of Grey Street on this side *see* p. 166.

The triangle between Grey Street, Market Street and Grainger Street is **Central Exchange Buildings** [107], by *John Wardle,* assisted by *George Walker,* in Grainger's office. Main ranges 1837–8: rounded corners with giant Corinthian columns on the upper floors, ribbed domes and ostrich-feather finials. Nash's London schemes were perhaps the inspiration for composition (West Strand Improvements, 1830–2) and finials (Sussex Place, 1822). Some original ground-floor detail, including rustication at the corners, survives; upper floors restored as flats. Grainger had intended the interior to be the town's corn market, but a rival bid for the Groat/Cloth Market site prevailed. Instead, in 1839 he opened a colonnaded newsroom ('of unspeakable splendour') which became successively art gallery, concert hall and vaudeville theatre. The timber roof, described in 1838 as being built 'on principles of ecclesiastical architecture', was perhaps a factor in the intense fire which destroyed the interior in 1901. The central space reopened in 1906 as the **Central Arcade** [108], by *J. Oswald & Son,* with entrances from

108. Central Arcade, Central Exchange Buildings, by J. Oswald & Son, 1906

Grainger, Grey and Market streets. (On Market Street, the lower-level trades entrance to the former Central Exchange Hotel has its painted glass nameplate.) It has beautiful Renaissance decoration in yellow and brown faience by *Burmantofts* of Leeds, possibly their last interior; the fine floor by *Rust's Vitreous Mosaics* of Battersea renewed rather garishly in 1990 in *American Olean* mosaics.

Grainger Street starts at the shopping-centre entrance with a retained façade (with altered shops). The blocks that follow are organized with pavilions punctuating long plainer stretches, as in some of Grainger's other streets; decoration is kept to a minimum, and the effect relies upon well-judged proportions and details. But first **Nelson Street** opens off on the right, with smaller retained façades, some with inscriptions, on the shopping-centre side. No. 8, now the **Café Royal**, and No. 14, originally the Dispensary, later Fruit Exchange, are matching pavilions, less severe than most of Grainger's work, with ornamented window surrounds and a balustraded parapet. No. 14 still has its rusticated ground floor; No. 8 a good shopfront with pink granite columns, c. 1890. Nos. 10–12, 1838, housed a music hall with lecture room below; round-headed openings. At No. 12a a warehouse, c. 1899 by *Marshall & Tweedy*, free Baroque with quasi-Ionic pilasters below. The plainer Nos. 16–22, **Cordwainers' Hall**, 1838, balances the Grainger Street end of the block. The left bay, curved to the former High Friar Lane, now meets the shopping precinct. Where Clayton Street now begins, the vista is closed by a double-bow-fronted pub, the **Lord Collingwood**. **Clayton Street** was Grainger's last street, still under construction in the mid 1840s, with plain façades and much less ordering into symmetrical compositions. Its sw extension is described in Walk 5, p. 180.

The **Grainger Market** [109], the commercial hub of the scheme, occupies the block bounded also by Clayton Street (behind) and Nelson and Nun Streets (N and S).* 1835, by *John Dobson*. Plain external walls – forty-six bays on the long sides, thirty-four on the short ones – articulated, like all Grainger's scheme, by pavilions. At the ends on Grainger Street these have giant simplified Corinthian pilasters; tripartite windows on Nelson and Nun streets. The ground floor has plain pilasters to the shops, their fronts all altered; most run through to the interior. Most sashes small-paned: fifteen panes on the first floor, nine on the less important second floor, six on the top storey on pavilions and SE front; many restorations, some inaccurate. The **interior** has four arched E–W passages crossing four clerestory-lit alleys, originally for butchers' stalls. Original detail includes big numbers on fascias, and shopfronts with iron ventilation grilles above; some restored. The third alley from the E, N end, has the **Marks & Spencer Penny Bazaar** – a

---

*In the 1970s Grainger's market was left intact. On Clayton Street, the later vegetable hall known as the Green Market was replaced with a hall in the new development, itself demolished 2006–7.

109. Grainger Market, by John Dobson, 1835, interior

delightful survivor: opened 1896, extended 1906, with painted glass
fascias. A wider top-lit w alley runs N–S. This, the **Vegetable Market**,
originally had Dobson's impressive timber-and-glass aisled roof:
queenpost trusses, their pendants imitating hammerbeam structure, on
curved braces set on tall slender iron columns; perhaps the first such
market-hall roof. (Dobson and Carmichael's watercolour shows the
space without columns; presumably a proposal only.) By 1898 'very
defective . . . needing annual repairs', the roof was replaced in 1901 with
a glass-covered elliptical span 56 ft (17 metres) wide. **Nun Street**, s, has
one late C19 shopfront with slender pilasters (No. 26, s side), and is closed
by another double-bow-fronted pub, the **Duke of Northumberland**.

110. Collingwood Buildings, Collingwood Street, by Oliver & Leeson, begun 1897–9

Facing the market across **Grainger Street** is an eighty-bay-long range with giant fluted Ionic columns or pilasters at ends, centre and sub-centres, turning the obtuse angle with Market Street by a gentle curve (Nos. 112–118). Damaged in the past by shop canopies, but recently restoration has been attempted. Between, the usual rows of plain windows, prominent cornice, and low top storey with smaller cornice. The w side between Nun Street and Newgate Street is plainer, the only accent being three-bay end pavilions.

Grainger Street s of the Bigg Market is an improvement of 1869–70 of the old St John's Lane, to reach the Central Station. By that time fashions had changed. Classical simplicity was abandoned; Gothic and Renaissance styles, with an abundance of carved decoration, fervently embraced. On the E side, some way after Bigg Market, **Victoria Buildings**, Nos. 42–50, 1874 by *Matthew Thompson* in Northern Renaissance style. Superimposed pilasters, big eaves brackets, garlanded pedimented dormers. Nos. 34–40, also of 1874, Jacobean with shaped gable; No. 30, 1884–6 by *John Johnstone* for the Newcastle and Gateshead Gas Co., now a pub, rich French Renaissance with oriels, superimposed pilasters, big gable and interesting roof. On the w side, Nos. 53–61, **Chaucer Buildings,** full-blooded Gothic incorporating a Freemasons' Hall. Dated 1870, perhaps by *Gibson Kyle*. The corner with Westgate Road is the former **Trustee Savings Bank**, 1862–3 by *J.E. Watson*. Classical, the centre of each front with engaged Ionic columns supporting carved pediments (façades only, after collapse during renovation). Across Westgate Road (for which *see* Walk 5, p. 179), the eclectic **County Hotel**, 1874 by *John Johnstone*, extended in 1897 by *M.H. Graham* (the three s bays, and along Neville Street).

111. Sun Insurance Building, by Oliver, Leeson & Wood, 1902–4

In the Grainger Street/Neville Street/Westgate Road triangle **Baron House**, a 1970s block replacing the old Douglas Hotel and its famous long bar, does not enhance the area. In front, **sculpture**, Man with Potential Selves, an arresting sequence of three painted bronze figures, 2003, by *Sean Henry*.

Now E past St John's church, following the route of Walk 1 (*see* pp. 113–15) until **Collingwood Street**. Formed 1809–10 and named after the local Trafalgar hero, Nelson's admiral, it completed the new E–W route begun by Mosley Street (p. 149). Its original brick houses have been replaced with banks and offices, many now pubs and clubs. On the N corner, **Collingwood Buildings** [110] (Nos. 28–62), begun 1897–9 by *Oliver & Leeson* as shops, offices and a hotel. Big arched windows, giant Corinthian order. Marble-lined banking hall, inserted 1903 by *Cackett & Burns Dick* for Barclays Bank, with mahogany fittings to the architects' designs by *Waring & Gillow,* and stucco ceiling by *G.G. Laidler*. Opposite, the **Sun Insurance Building** by *Oliver, Leeson & Wood*, 1902–4. French C18 style, with a copper roof. Atlantes hold up the entrance canopy; iron first-floor balustrades; large sunburst in a pediment [111] to Westgate Road. Further E, Nos. 9–17, 1888–91 by *R.J. Johnson,* for Hodgkin, Barnett, Pease, Spence & Co.'s bank. Italian Renaissance, with a red granite plinth and portal, pedimented first-floor Gibbs surrounds and garlanded frieze. No. 7, late C19 brick, resembles the original domestic scale, then No. 5, by *J.W. Taylor* for J.C. Eno, manufacturer of health salts, 1898. On the N side, E corner, **Northern Assurance Buildings** (No. 2), 1878 with 1890s extension to Groat Market (NE), by *Austin, Johnson & Hicks*. An elaborate classical front, with rusticated ground floor and pedimented *piano nobile*

112. Queen Victoria
Monument, St Nicholas
Square, by Alfred
Gilbert, unveiled 1903

windows with frivolous serpentine balconies; giant pilasters, big
cornice, pedimented dormers. On the s corner **Collingwood House**,
formerly Bank of Chicago, 1971–4 by *Mauchlen, Weightman & Elphick*.
Might the full-height oriels be homage to the bank's Chicago sky-
scraper? The two-storey mansard fails to reduce the bulk. From here a
fine view of the Cathedral of St Nicholas (p. 46); the market streets on
the N side belong with Walk 3 (pp. 139–40).

The Walk continues E along **Mosley Street** (for its easternmost
section *see* Walk 3, p. 149). N of the cathedral, in the paved **St Nicholas
Square**, the **Queen Victoria Monument** [112] by *Alfred Gilbert*, given by
W.H. Stephenson and unveiled in 1903. A modified version of Gilbert's
Jubilee Monument of 1888 in Winchester Castle. The figure sits under a
domical wrought-iron canopy; the ornamental detail shows all the
sculptor's exuberant mannerisms. On the E side of the square, the former **Newcastle Joint Stock Bank**, *c.* 1845, possibly by *Benjamin Green*.
An Italian palazzo, with rusticated ground floor, round-arched
windows on the lower floors, balconies and giant Ionic columns above,
and a big bracket cornice. On the N side, No. 31 Mosley Street is **Scottish
Provident House**, by *S.D. Robbins*, 1906, described then as the
first (American-type) 'gridiron' structure in Newcastle. Portland stone,
giant order, corner entrance with Doric columns in grey granite.

113. Grey Street, east side by John Dobson, 1834–7, watercolour by J.W. Carmichael, 1830s

Good wrought-iron window guards. No. 27, by *W.L. Newcombe* for the **North British and Mercantile Assurance Co.**, was completed in 1890. Rusticated ground floor, pedimented first-floor window surrounds, long brackets between the attic storey windows.* Further E on the S side, Nos. 32–34 of English-bond brick are an important survival, although altered, of *Stephenson*'s houses of the 1780s in the new street. Nos. 28–30 (1894 by *Armstrong & Knowles*, with shop of 1902 by *Watson & Curry*, left) meets the challenge of a tall narrow frontage by enclosing first and second floors in a giant Ionic order, with squat blocked columns framing arched top-floor windows. At the Dean Street corner the former **National Provincial Bank**, 1870–2, by the bank's architect *John Gibson*. Italian High Renaissance, with giant pilasters on rusticated ground floor, upper windows in aedicules. Informative inscriptions on the friezes below big eaves.

Grey Street, the finest of *Grainger*'s streets [113], begins at this crossing. Planned in 1834, it was almost complete by 1837. Ascending from here the gentle rising curve is best appreciated, the portico of the Theatre Royal at its head, Grey's Monument the climax. 'The proportion and correspondence of every part in the whole, and the admirably grand effect produced by the perspective view from Mosley Street, are calculated to impress the beholder with indelible surprise.' (M.A. Richardson, *Descriptive Companion through Newcastle upon Tyne and*

*Between No. 31 and No. 2 Grey Street, the narrow **Drury Lane** reminds us that *David Stephenson*'s Theatre Royal of 1787–8 was demolished for Grey Street. Its S and W walls were reused by Grainger (*see* the blocked door and windows in Grey Street's rear wall).

Gateshead, 1838). The chief ranges are not completely symmetrical, but both sides are so well balanced that the alternation of plain and adorned sections comes off perfectly. End and intermediate pavilions, of three storeys with attics and some balustraded parapets, are enriched mostly with the Corinthian order, either as attached columns or as pilasters, above rusticated ground floors. These points of emphasis are linked by plainer blocks with less prominent cornices and lower attics. Low plinths step gently round the street's curve.

A typical three-bay property originally had a central shop door with house door at one side. Cast-iron columns within the shop windows supported the upper floors. Some of these survive, unlike the original shopfronts: the present examples are in many styles, some aggressive, others more polite. In other places only façades survive, with plinths gone, and clashes between windows and floor levels. Of numerous other changes, some arrogant and insensitive, several have been reversed.

Now individual buildings. First the E **side**. The SE corner with Mosley Street, Nos. 2–8, was completed only in 1842, perhaps a rebuild of an C18 house, aided by a Corporation grant to Grainger. *Dobson* signed one of three surviving drawings, *Grainger* another. Restored after years of neglect; now a hotel. Big brackets over the round-arched first-floor windows support stone shelves, originally balustraded balconies. Curved corner. No. 10, tall, thin and elaborate, is an extension of 1908 of No. 21 Mosley Street (*see* p. 149). Nos. 12–16, a fussily modelled four-bay elevation by *Johnson & Hicks*, *c.* 1879, plus two altered earlier C19 bays. After these incursions, the rest of the E side up to Shakespeare Street is attributed to *Dobson*. Nos. 18–26, pavilion by Dobson, shops and embellishments *c.* 1890 by *W.L. Newcombe*. Nos. 26–32 are a six-bay link, Nos. 34–40 a five-bay pavilion, recessed centre, Corinthian pilasters, almost unspoilt upper floors; insensitive late C20 ground floor. Linking two pavilions, Nos. 42–50: a steel-framed building of 1969 by *L.J. Couves & Partners* for Midland Bank, the façade a reinstatement of Dobson's centrepiece of *c.* 1836, most of which had been rebuilt differently in 1910. Eight bays, with giant attached Corinthian columns. Urns on the attic storey. Un-Grainger-like ground floor without plinth. Nos. 52–78, again pavilion-link-pavilion, but the further pavilion narrow and with tripartite windows. Dobson's pavilions along this whole section are marked by pilasters advancing from half-pilasters. From High Bridge to Shakespeare Street Nos. 80–96, corner pavilions, with simplified acanthus capitals of Hellenistic type.

At the highest point of the curve *John & Benjamin Green*'s **Theatre Royal** [114], 1836–7. The monumental classical tradition combining with English Picturesque. Corinthian portico of six columns, the outer ones paired on tall heavily moulded plinths, royal arms by *Christopher Tate* in the pediment. Corinthian pilasters frame the projecting outer bays. Aedicule surrounds to the upper windows; roof balustrades, urns. After fire in 1899, entrance and interior were vigorously remodelled by *Frank Matcham*. Refurbishment by the *Renton Howard Wood Levin*

114. Theatre Royal, Grey Street, by John & Benjamin Green, 1836–7

Partnership in 1987 kept Matcham's balconies and boxes and inserted a second foyer staircase. Further refurbishment by *Napper Architects*, 2006, taking space in buildings in Market Street (behind).

Wardle and *Walker*'s w **side** has fewer pavilions, but a strikingly rich Corinthian order and longer, plainer links. The Mosley Street corner is curved, echoing the E side, with giant columns and a grand Baroque doorway of *c.* 1900. Nos. 5–13 plainer; renewed ground floor. Nos. 15–17 a pavilion, originally a hotel, with keyed elliptical arch, left, to a lane and stabling behind; originally a route via White Hart Yard to Cloth Market. This can be read as the s part of a forty-four-bay composition up to High Bridge, with pavilions and a boldly modelled ten-bay centrepiece, Nos. 33–41, a palazzo built *c.* 1835 for the **Bank of England** (removed to Pilgrim Street, 1968) and the Northumberland and District Banking Co. Giant Corinthian order *in antis*, the wall behind more heavily emphasized than Dobson's opposite, with pedimented first-floor windows, and attic completely behind the balustrade. (*Cockerell* was then the Bank's architect – did he contribute at all?) Now a restaurant; windows lowered on the left. Nos. 43–51, a façade screening 1990 offices. The corner pavilion is No. 53 with ground floor of *c.* 1900.

N of High Bridge, Nos. 55–59, an Ionic pavilion with pilasters, Nos. 61–67, a nine-window link, and the centrepiece Nos. 69–73, formerly the Turk's Head Hotel (extended behind in 1991 as **Barclay House**). Four bays of giant Ionic columns *in antis*, flanked by narrow pilastered bays. Nos. 77–85 (**Earl Grey House**) make the corner to Market Street: mansard added *c.* 1900; rebuilt 1982, with atrium, behind the altered façade. Then again the triangular-plan Central Exchange Buildings.

Finally the E **side** beyond Market Street. Neighbour to the Theatre Royal is **Lloyds Bank**, originally Northumberland and District Bank, *c.* 1839. In 1851 'considered one of the most chaste and neatly decorated buildings in the town'. It took the last empty plot, where Grainger had schemed unsuccessfully to build Town and County Courts, Town Clerk's and other offices, and a Judges' residence. Perhaps a design for this project by *Wardle & Walker* was adapted for the bank. Attached Corinthian columns *in antis*; pilasters on the outer bays, formerly private houses. First-floor windows pedimented. Ground floor with round-headed openings between Tuscan pilasters; elaborate entablature with dentilled and modillioned cornice. Interior reconstructed with atrium in 1987. In **Hood Street**, right, a nine-bay house of 1839, now the **Northern Counties Club**. Greek Doric porch. Nos. 104–108 Grey Street, 1904, *W.H. Knowles* and *T.R. Milburn* for Messrs Mawson, Swan & Morgan: Edwardian Mannerist variation on the rest of the street. Giant Corinthian order and ornate windows. Elaborate second-floor pediments from Rossi's *Studio d'Architectura Civile di Roma* (1702). Stained-glass shop friezes. Nos. 112–116, a former music hall, was refronted as a cinema in 1914. Also classical, but without a giant order. Now **HSBC**. At the top of the street, Grey's Monument.

The Town Wall and Western Centre

Starting at St Andrew's church in Newgate Street, this Walk includes much of the standing remains of the Town Wall and looks at streets in the w part of the modern city.

115. Walk 5

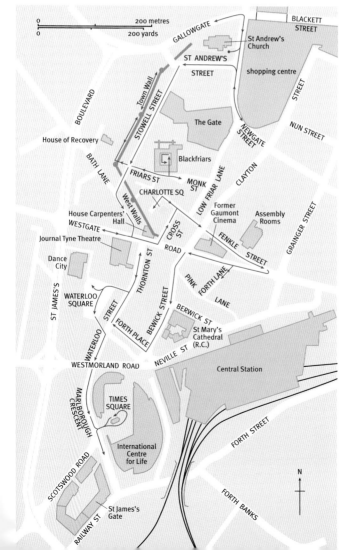

In 1265 Henry III allowed the town to charge murage tax to fund new defences. Work seems to have begun later, its progress proved by problems caused: in 1280 the Dominicans (Black Friars) near St Andrew's church obtained permission for a postern gate through the wall because it crossed their land; in 1290 the Hospital of St Mary the Virgin in Westgate did the same. Building began at the N (along the modern Blackett Street), continuing simultaneously on both sides. At the W it curved in towards the castle, then turned sharply S to the river. At the E it turned to curve round Pandon, granted to Newcastle in 1298. A lane ran inside the wall, and a ditch outside, over which in 1312 the Dominicans were allowed to build a wooden bridge. A modern footbridge has been constructed over this newly excavated section of that earthwork (*see* p. 175). The walls were strengthened in Edward III's reign (1327–77), and in *c.* 1540 Leland could still say that their 'strength and magnificence... far passith all the waulls of the cities of England'. In spite of much C18–C19 destruction,

more wall survives than in any other English town except Chester, Chichester, Southampton and York. It was 7–10 ft (2.1–3 metres) thick and 20–30 ft (6–9 metres) high, including the parapet and merlons protecting the wall-walk. There were six principal gates (clockwise from the river: Close Gate, West Gate, New Gate, Pilgrim Street Gate, Pandon Gate, Sand Gate), and other less important gates and posterns. The seventeen towers were semicircular projections, each with three loopholes; between them, turrets flush with the outside of the wall and corbelled out from the inner face provided extra shelter.

The remains of the lane, sometimes with and sometimes without the wall, begin in St Andrew's churchyard, and with the excavated ditch, run sw behind Stowell Street and se along Bath Lane to Westgate Road and Pink Lane. For the lower western stretches *see* Walk 1, p. 111; for Plummer, Corner and Sallyport towers and the short section at Trinity Gardens *see* Walks 6 and 2, pp. 189 and 130.

116. Town Wall and ditch, late C13 onwards

St Andrew's Church [117] and its churchyard, with tall trees, lie between Gallowgate (N), St Andrew's Street (S) and Newgate Street (E, formerly straddled by the New Gate of the Town Wall). The sturdy W tower, with NW stair-turret and large SW clasping buttress, has C12 lower courses, but is much repaired. It became a gun platform in the Civil War of the 1640s, when the church was probably damaged through being a target in the siege. The upper tower, chancel (its S porch later, and still with a stone-slab roof) and N transept are of *c.* 1300: see the stepped lancet windows under one two-centred arch on the N side of the transept and S side of the chancel. C14 chancel N chapel (1380s endowment by Sir Adam de Athol) and nave S porch, though its Baroque doorway was done in 1726. Perp clerestory. In 1844 the S transept was remodelled in the fashionable Neo-Norman style by *Dobson*. Restoration, and addition of N hall and vestries, 1950s–60s, by *Caröe & Robinson*.

Inside, the earliest part is the late C12 chancel arch, tall and wide, chevron-moulded, of two orders, and additional shafts to the nave with two shaft-rings. The nave arcades may belong to the same building operation: four bays, circular piers with very plainly moulded octagonal capitals and single-stepped round arches. In 1788 the third pier of the N aisle was taken out and a new wide arch made, then in 1866 *Thomas Oliver* restored the N arcade, removed the galleries and renewed the aisle windows. The small blocked clerestory windows on the S side look late C12. In the chancel S wall a double **piscina** of *c.* 1300. The 1866 E window is supposedly a copy of the original. The chancel N chapel, known as the Trinity or Athol Chapel from the image it held and from its C14 benefactor, has semi-octagonal responds and wide double-chamfered arches. In the tower there are springers and wall ribs below the beams of the first floor, suggesting that a C15 vault was removed.

Furnishings. C15 **font cover** of the same type as that in the Cathedral (p. 53), but the upper stage has specially large, eight-light 'windows' with Perp panel tracery. – **Pulpit** and **choir stalls**, 1906–7 by *Ralph Hedley*. – Carved **royal arms** of George IV over the high arch of the SW door. – **Stained glass.** NE chapel, E (Ascension), 1900 by *Kempe*; mid-C19 N window by *Gibson*. Other windows, 1976, clear glazing by *L.C. Evetts*, with varied leading to Monkwearmouth hand-made glass; very attractive, and allowing soft clear light. – **Monuments** include an indent of the brass of Sir Adam de Athol d.1387 and wife, NE chapel. – H. Griffith d.1837, a kneeling allegorical figure above a profile portrait, by *D. Dunbar*.

The **churchyard** has many inscribed stones *in situ*, a wonderful jumble, and late C18 walls, piers and railings. The **Town Wall** runs along its N side (*see* topic box, pp. 168–9), with corbels for a vanished turret.

To the N is **Gallowgate**, originally a medieval suburb. On its S side and to the W, another part of the Town Wall is embedded inside shops and offices of 1898–9 by *Oliver & Leeson* in free Baroque style, overlooking the churchyard with a big roof with tiers of the small steeply roofed dormers associated with the town halls of the Low Countries.

117. St Andrew, C12 and later; south-west doorway, 1726

On the N side of Gallowgate is the former **General Electric Co.** building, 1933–6 by *Cackett, Burns Dick & Mackellar* with *Hetherington & Wilson*, with the same cast-metal figure reliefs of strong diagonal composition representing vigour and work, designed by *Halliday & Agate*, that were used inside Sir Giles Gilbert Scott's Battersea Power Station. Converted *c.* 2002 to student flats called **Magnet Court**, with new top storey and rear wings. Then new blocks by *Lister Associates*: **Time Central**, 2004–7, ashlar-clad, and **Wellbar House**, for completion 2009. This replaces the first high-rise office block in Newcastle, of 1961.

Down **Newgate Street**, s of the church, is the **Newcastle Co-operative Society** [118], rebuilt 1931–2 by *L.G. Ekins*. Ekins worked in Newcastle and Manchester for the Co-operative Wholesale Society before establishing the London CWS architects' department in 1916; his earlier work can be seen in Stowell Street (p. 174). Newcastle's is one of the Co-op's major interwar buildings, a big Art Deco store; two towers with clock (the eleven letters COOPERATIVE mark the hours 7–5) and barometer dials. Vertical motifs, on the German 1920s pattern of Messel and Olbrich (in 1930 Ekins had travelled to study German and Dutch architecture, with the CWS architects W.G. Townsend-Gray from Newcastle and W.A. Johnson from Manchester). Three left bays are a matching addition, 1959. Stairwells, originally marble-lined with corner display cases, with zigzag rails in front of the full-height window strips; solid balustrades with steel handrails on the bent backs of little men, climbing with their load. On the top floor, some beams have the wave motif originally also used in the shop windows' stained-glass frieze. The present unfortunate window frieze is 1990s, when the central entrance was broken through, but a 1930s fragment survives in St Andrew's Street, N, set in a 1902 extension by *E. Shewbrooks* to the 1870s store formerly on the site (future uncertain).

The Gate, s, is a 2½-acre glass-fronted development of 1999–2002 by *Geoffrey Reid Architects*, crossing Low Friar Street by a glazed bridge. The developer claimed that the frontage was the highest glass-walled construction in the UK. Behind are a multiplex cinema, bars, clubs, casino, restaurants, shops and a car park. **Sculpture** in front by *Danny Lane*, 2005; tall, of steel and glass. The brick and stone rear elevations, with service access on Stowell Street, are disappointing. On Low Friar Street's N corner it replaced Newgate House, Newcastle's first modern office block (*c.* 1959), where rock and jazz stars played in the basement Mayfair Club. Across Newgate Street, E, an extension of the Eldon Square shopping centre is under way, replacing part of the complex. The new work is by *Leslie Jones Architects*, and *Haskoll*. Further down on the sw side, as the street curves, the former **Swallow Hotel**, a stereotype slab-and-podium design by *Bernard Engle & Partners*, *c.* 1969, with shops in the podium part. This was Newcastle's first 'modern' hotel. This part of the street has lost all sense of its long history, except for its width from Low Friar Street to St Andrew's, the site of the White Cross where medieval markets were held.

118. Former Co-operative stores, Newgate Street, by L.G. Ekins, 1931–2

Now back to **St Andrew's Street,** formerly called Darn Crook. At its w end, a grand, lively **Chinese arch** [119] by *Yonglai Zhang,* constructed by the *Changshu Classical Gardens Architectural Engineering Co.,* 2004–5, one of several such arches erected by English Chinese communities. Newcastle's Chinatown extends s down **Stowell Street**, with restaurants and shops. The street was begun in 1824; in 1827 Eneas Mackenzie praised the houses as 'well adapted for families of a certain rank, whose convenience is seldom consulted by building speculators'; now mostly redeveloped. Red brick buildings on the w side include the Co-operative Society's **banana-ripening warehouse** of 1907–8 by *L.G. Ekins (see also* p. 172), and its replica s extension. Beyond, Nos. 38–46 are original, simple two-storey, three-bay brick terraced houses.

A lane just past the houses (right) leads to the **Town Wall**, with inner lane and three wall towers. The **Heber Tower**, s, is almost intact, with pointed barrel-vault, and a large upper window inserted by the Company of Armourers, Curriers and Feltmakers in 1770–1. The continuation of the wall s of the Heber Tower is described below, p. 177. To the N, the best-preserved of all the **turrets**, still with the passageway, and external stair to the roof platform, then **Morden Tower** with a

119. Chinese arch, St Andrew's Street, by Yonglai Zhang and the Changshu Classical Gardens Architectural Engineering Co., 2004–5

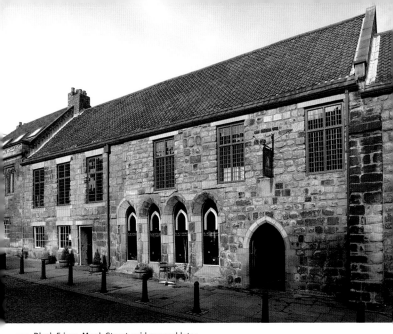

120. Black Friars, Monk Street, mid-c13 and later

picturesque brick upper storey added *c.* 1700 by the Company of Plumbers, Glaziers, Pewterers and Painters. Further N, **Ever Tower** survives up to the beginnings of the deep-splayed arrow slits.

Through the doorway beside Heber Tower to the recently excavated **Town Ditch**. Opposite stands the **House of Recovery**, facing Bath Lane. Built in 1804, on this site outside the town; a fever hospital until 1888. Restrained classical style. Three storeys, five bays, the central three slightly higher and projecting, originally with a stepped parapet. The sash windows had opening top lights for ventilation, copied in the restoration of 1988 for the North of England Museums Service. Diagonally opposite, the domed former **Co-op printing works** (now flats), 1890 by *F. W. Rich*.

Now back across Stowell Street to **Friars Street**, E side, to a building of national importance. We are at the SW corner of **Black Friars** [120]. The Dominicans were established in Newcastle by 1239. In 1250 the prior was criticized by the General Chapter of the order for architectural extravagance: what remains of that and of later building can be seen in the W, S and E cloister ranges, in the usual plan. The church on the N side was demolished in the C16; the friary survived because the property was sold to the mayor and burgesses, who in 1552 leased it to nine of the town's craft companies. Each range was partitioned into three company halls, with ground-floor almshouses and a meeting hall above. After some C18 and C19 rebuilding the companies eventually let their premises, and squalor set in. In the 1930s the many families living on 'Friars' Green' were rehoused, but restoration, and the preceding excavation, did not begin until after 1973, when the city's Planning Committee commissioned a report from *Wales, Wales & Rawson* on how to secure the buildings. Restoration by this firm was completed in 1981. Black Friars now houses craft shops, a restaurant and offices.

The s **range** faces Monk Street. The medieval kitchen, left, became the Cordwainers' almshouse, reconstructed in Tudor style in 1843–4 by *John Wardle*, with an extra floor on the inner face. Next, the refectory with its unmistakable lancet windows. This became the Tanners' and Butchers' almshouses, the upper floor given cross-windows in early C18 refurbishments. Past the refectory and the arched entrance to the slype, or passage to the cloister, the s end of the E range, the friars' warming house, with three lancets. It became the Smiths' hall, and has at the E a big door surround dated 1679 and carved with the Smiths' arms, brought from their property in Low Friar Street by *Thomas Oliver* in 1827–8 for a new staircase extension. The wall above was gabled: a large traceried first-floor window was removed in stages between 1709 (cross-windows inserted) and 1803 (the gable lowered).

Now under the medieval arch to the **slype**. At the right, the big arch supported the day stair to the rooms over the refectory and warming house. A pointed arch opens onto the **cloister**, with buildings on three sides. The restoration used straight-pointed arches to distinguish new openings. Clockwise from here, first the **refectory**, originally with a wall bench. Of all the meeting halls, only those in this s range retain company fittings: a fireplace and painted panels commemorating 1720s restoration in the **Butchers'**; in the **Tanners'** the (altered) oval table and benches with low balustraded backs. Across the stair landing further E, the restored **Smiths' hall** with oval table and benches, and arcaded backs to the wall seats. The w **range** became the Saddlers', Tailors' and Skinners' and Glovers' halls. The tiled floor of the craft shop, in the Saddlers', copies black and yellow tiles found in excavation of the guest hall here. In the cloister, the giant trefoil-shaped recess was the **lavatorium** where the friars washed their hands before entering the refectory; small blocked medieval windows above. The Tailors' hall was completely rebuilt (inscription 1787), with sashes. The Skinners' and Glovers', N, remodelled in 1712, had a building running off w from it.

The plan of the **church** on the N **side** has been revealed by excavations. It was aisled, the cloister walk alongside the nave s aisle wall, the choir extending beyond the E range.

The N end of the E **range** was the sacristy, cleared except for the bases of the round night stairs, w, to the dormitory above, and of the central pier from which sprang the vault ribs. Then a slype, also cleared. Next s, the **chapter house**, its E end blocked off, its elevation with a two-light window with cusped openings N of the arched doorway, a copy to the s. It became the Bakers' and Brewers' hall. Fixed on its s wall, part of a large C15 grave cover from the church site. The **warming room** next,

121. Journal Tyne Theatre, Westgate Road, by W. Parnell, 1867

and **dormitory** above, were bisected for the Fullers and Dyers and the Smiths; the former was largely rebuilt in 1899 by *Matthew Graham*.

The motif of triangular-headed arches from the 1980s restoration is repeated in **Jacobins Court**, houses and flats of 1989–92 by *Jane Darbyshire Associates*, N of the church site and extending also onto Stowell Street, complementing but not copying the medieval fabric. 1990s buildings to the E, replacing C19 warehouses, are less successful.

Back to Stowell Street, and left into Bath Lane along the well-preserved **West Walls**, i.e. the full-height, many-phased stretch turning SE to the old West Gate. The **Durham Tower**, the best-preserved of the circuit, retains its barrel vault. Where the wall meets the N side of **Westgate Road** is a modest ashlar building in Palladian style (with inserted shopfronts), the hall of the **House Carpenters**, whose arms are in the pediment. Built 1811–12 by *William Burnup Jun.*, and perhaps designed by him. It included a toll house. The previous hall was lost with the demolition, as a barrier to traffic, of the West Gate, which straddled the road with its Edward III barbican. Alongside, **sculpture** by *Eilís O'Connell*, called Ever-changing, 2004. Polished stainless steel.

The Italianate pale brick front of the **Journal Tyne Theatre** [121] faces the end of Bath Lane from the s. By *W. Parnell*, opened 1867 as the Tyne Theatre and Opera House, founded by Joseph Cowen.

This mid-C19 theatre survives virtually complete, despite a serious fire in 1985. Three horseshoe tiers of balconies and boxes, a shell-shaped ceiling (good acoustically), a high elliptical proscenium arch. Some embellishments to the balcony plasterwork, box fronts etc., 1901. To the right, a red brick addition by *Oliver & Leeson*, 1892–3, built for Augustus Harris from London's Drury Lane theatre, lessee from 1887. He also bought property behind to make a rehearsal room, and added a second gallery staircase. In 1919 it became the 'Stoll Picture Theatre' (hence the front glass panel). Restored twice by the New Tyne Theatre Trust, 1977–86, the second time after the fire, with reconstruction of the original stage machinery by *W. Day* of Liverpool. w of the theatre, backing onto the new Waterloo Square development, **Blenheim House** by *Cackett & Burns Dick* of 1919–22. Portland stone in Beaux Arts style, with a rear block added: offices, warehouse and factory. ROBERT SINCLAIR TOBACCO COY LTD. prominent on the side wall. At the St James's Boulevard end, facing w, the four-storey Sinclair Building, 1913, for the same firm. Dance City, to the s here, is described on p. 182.

Further e down Westgate Road, across Cross Street, **Imperial Buildings**, 1895 by *J. W. Taylor*, offices (now student flats) above shops. The usual good Newcastle ashlar, in free Baroque style with big attic dormers and corner dome, and large dated and initialled cartouches on second floor. Up Cross Street, and into **Charlotte Square** [12]. Begun 1770 in the Black Friars precinct by the architect and developer *William Newton*, it is Newcastle's only c18 square in the London style: three terraces round a garden, originally with shrubs and trees. Three-storey brick houses with attractive doorcases, the usual floor and sill bands. Newton himself lived in the wide house on the right side; see its two Venetian stair windows from the side lane. The square's character has withstood the addition of extra storeys on some houses. At the NE, an arched passage to Black Friars, introduced when a fire necessitated late c20 rebuilding. No. 6 and the warehousing behind were renovated as offices by *Bill Hopper Design*, 2004, with a tall all-glass atrium inserted in the yard. Levels, boundaries and planting of the garden all changed by late c19 tramlines, a c20 electricity substation and c21 civic landscaping.

Fenkle Street leads SE from the square, passing Low Friar Street (both with modest early c19 brick houses) and crossing Grainger's Clayton Street (*see* p. 158), to the **Assembly Rooms** of 1774–6, also designed by *Newton*, built in the garden of the then St Nicholas Vicarage. The projecting three-bay centre has a pediment on giant unfluted Ionic columns, and an arched central window (compare Newton's later entrance to the Guildhall [13], designed with David Stephenson). Lower one-bay wings. The whole front in high-quality masonry with a rusticated ground floor; the other walls plain brick. Iron lampholders on the drive replace the originals, which guided sedan chairs. In 1882 *Austin, Johnson & Hicks* blocked the central door and inserted double side doors under a canopy. Internal alterations have not

122. Assembly Rooms, Fenkle Street, by William Newton, 1774–6, ceiling detail

greatly changed the principal rooms. The main Assembly Room itself
has coupled pilasters, a clerestory, an apse and a w gallery; delicate
Adamesque plasterwork [122], porcelain plaques, magnificent ball-
room chandeliers. Double-apsed front ante-room with delicate plaster
and carved chimneypieces. Other ceilings also with Neoclassical ornament. The subscribers were very satisfied with this setting for balls and
dinners, as well as with the newsroom, where London papers could be
read; refreshments included tea, coffee, chocolate and negus.

Westgate Road lies ahead. On its N side at No. 56 the former County
Court, 1864–5 by *Charles Reeve*. A five-bay palazzo, quite ornate but not
large. No. 52 was built for the famous Dr Gibb, whose house and
surgery were both here; six bays, giant pilasters above, with an ornamental band at mid height. By *J.E. Watson*, 1861. **Cross House** diagonally opposite, on the wedge-shaped site between Fenkle Street and
Westgate Road, is a *Hennebique* reinforced concrete structure (1911),
with Portland stone cladding, by *Cackett & Burns Dick*. In front, a fine
statue by *Tweed*, 1906, of Joseph Cowen M.P. (1831–1900), newspaper
proprietor, social reformer, friend of Italian freedom and founder of
the Tyne Theatre.

On **Westgate Road** (s side), a good sequence of c18 houses. The early
c18 five-bay No. 53 was 'Lady Clavering's house' on Corbridge's 1723
map. Bright red brick, with (modern) sashes in architrave surrounds

linked vertically by stone aprons. Untapered pilasters at the ends of the three upper floors; moulded bands to each floor below the top cornice. A three-storey ashlar-fronted house, Nos. 55–57, probably includes some C17 fabric. Shopfronts replaced the ground floor; the right part now restored to sashes. Above, bays grouped 2+3+2 by giant Doric pilasters, linked by floor bands and supporting an entablature; sashes all with simple architrave surrounds. Half the roof has original graduated Lakeland slates. Two small segmental-headed C18 dormers. Inside, an open-well stair to a gallery and a long first-floor room. Rococo stucco almost everywhere: a phoenix, portrait medallions, eagles, cornucopia, garlands, putti and clouds. It looks like the work of the York school of *stuccatori*. Behind, a Doric-pilastered Venetian window lights the staircase [123]. Corbridge's map depicts four-storey 'Assembly Rooms' here with gabled eaves dormers, so the front range at least must have been reworked in the mid C18. Nos. 67–75 are now the **Newcastle Arts Centre**. No. 67, C18, was Sir Matthew White Ridley's town house: brick, seven bays, with gauged flat window heads and a modillioned eaves cornice; a round-headed dormer half-hidden by the parapet. Nos. 71–75 have later C18 render, but the gabled rear wing of No. 71 has mid-C18 tumbled-in brickwork. Underneath the bay to its E, **Forth Lane** runs through the buildings to Pink Lane, the old lane inside the Town Wall, named here after the medieval Pink Tower.

Back up Westgate Road, alongside the former **Gaumont Cinema** (1912–13, enlarged and refronted 1927 by *Percy Lindsay Browne & Son*), to **Clayton Street West**. A lively SW corner with the Baroque former Northern Goldsmiths, 1910 by *Cackett & Burns Dick*, with bracket clock (cf. Blackett Street, p. 186). Its domed turret echoes that on the NW corner, on *Armstrong & Knowles*'s **Atlas Chambers**, dated 1894. Both replaced parts of Grainger's developments here, which were probably designed by *John Wardle*. On the SE side Grainger built only one short block between Westgate Road and Pink Lane; on the NW side he built up to Forth Place. His own office was at No. 28, and he lived latterly at No. 36. Like the rest of Clayton Street, these parts were plainer than Grainger's shopping streets, and were entirely domestic when built. His usual ashlar, each house three bays and three storeys, some with steps up to the doors. Nos. 6–24, NW side, are a retained façade to a large housing development of 1979–82 by *Barnett Curry Smith*, replacing the former Crown Hotel. The rear block, brick with long dark oriel windows, faces Waterloo Street (*see also* p. 182). On the SE side, **Clarendon House**, formerly the Clarendon Temperance Hotel. Big, brick-gabled, with an arcaded ground floor and a central oriel. By *Oliver & Leeson, c.* 1896. To its S, **St Mary's R.C. Cathedral** (p. 58) fills the triangle between Bewick Street and Neville Street. Down Bewick Street, E, is **Bewick House**, by *Austin & Johnson* for the Tyne Improvement Commission, 1884, in a Gibbsian-Palladian style; three floors added in 1911 by *W.H. Wood*, with arms of the local authorities involved below the cornice.

123. Nos. 55–57 Westgate Road, stair hall, mid-c18

From the cathedral, sw down Clayton Street West. By the junction with Neville Street, on the right, Forth Place leads to **Waterloo Street**. At the SE is a (relocated) granite **memorial fountain** to Grainger and his wife by the *Elswick Court Marble Works*, 1892. The handsome Art Deco brick building opposite, with jazzy railings, is now **Centralofts** (*see also* below). Built as Co-operative Wholesale Society offices and drapery warehouse, 1935 by *W. G. Townsend Grey*. To its right, Charlton's Bonds, a duty-free warehouse by *Lamb & Armstrong*, dated 1885, with Gothic-derived detail. In **Thornton Street**, just beyond, another C19 terrace (Nos. 56–63).

The area to the N and W between Waterloo Street and St James's Boulevard, the new road from Redheugh Bridge to St James's Park, has been redeveloped as **Waterloo Square**, 2002–6, to a masterplan by *Napper Architects*. From the N end of Centralofts, turn left into the Square. New buildings on the E, W and S sides face interestingly varied spaces and surfaces. Steps between the levels are set off by large stone spheres; paved areas blend with the adjoining lanes. On the E side, the Centralofts building, remodelled by *Napper* with a new glazed and balconied W front. Offices on the ground floor. At the SE, **City Quadrant** apartments and offices by *DLA Architecture*, with varied levels and materials. To the SW a simple rendered hotel. The partly stone-clad, multi-storey **Grainger Town car park** on the W side is by *Napper*. Curved glass pedestrian entrance and stair, S; restaurants on the ground floor. In the NW corner **Dance City**, 2005 by *Malcolm Fraser Architects*; partly blue Staffordshire brick for studios and auditoria, N, partly steel-framed offices, with some timber screens and glazed panels in greens, blues and greys, S. A spirited building. Its entrance and projecting café invite from the square.

Back down Waterloo Street, across Westmorland Road, to **Marlborough Crescent**. On the W side a stone-and-brick warehouse built 1906 for Hunter & Nesbitt, by *Frederick T. Walker*. Four pilastered storeys, pedimented central bay, door framed by long brackets. Opposite, on **Neville Street** and W of the Central Station, the **International Centre for Life** [124] complex, 1996–2000 by *Terry Farrell & Partners*, on part of the old Cattle Market site. Two curved buildings on an ovoid plan, with gaps where Scotswood Road formerly cut across. To the NW, the Bio-Science Centre; to the E, Newcastle University and NHS Institute of Human Genetics; then a lower conference centre abutting the sinuous green roof of the Life Science Centre, which houses exhibitions, lecture theatre, games and interactive displays. Varied uses are reflected in varied materials: render, glass, glass bricks, polished blockwork. In the large central piazza, oddly called **Times Square**, the **Market Keeper's House** of 1840 by *Dobson*. A low Italianate block to accommodate offices and house the market keeper, his assistant, and their families. Wide low eaves, central clock turret, three-arched N and S sides, lower apsed projections E and W. Restored 1998 by *Ainsworth Spark*; now offices with a shiny new stair.

124. Centre for Life, Marlborough Crescent, by Terry Farrell & Partners, 1996–2000

Appropriately, *Charles Jencks*'s steel **sculpture** nearby is a double helix. Further sw, on part of the old cattle market across Railway Street, is a tightly clustered group of tall office and hotel buildings called **St James's Gate** by *DEWJO'C*, completed 2006. Inward-facing to a courtyard, with stair-towers, projecting eaves and varied window types. From here it is a short walk through the Centre for Life to the Central Station (p. 82).

The North-eastern Town Centre

This walk starts at the Monument (*see* Walk 4, p. 153; also for the w part of Blackett Street), then E along Blackett Street, N up John Dobson Street, NE to the University of Northumbria, w to the Civic Centre, and back s down Northumberland Street, resuming the commercial and retail theme.

By the Monument and along the N side of Blackett Street is **Monument Mall**, by *Hugh Martin & Partners*, 1989–92. The w part, stone with simplified classical detail and an uncomfortably proportioned dome to the atrium, respects Grainger's work but is unconvincing because form is at odds with style. Heavy-looking Neo-Art Nouveau ironwork at the entrance, in the dome, etc. The E part, with a dome of glazed lacy metal, picks up some motifs from the

125. **Walk 6**

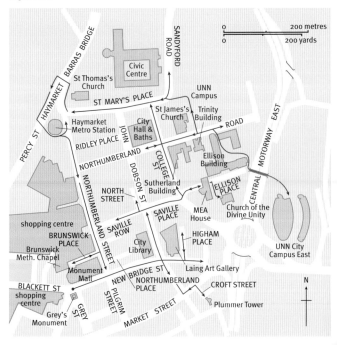

126. Gem House, Blackett Street, by Newcombe & Newcombe, 1904; shopfront by
Benjamin Simpson, 1906

Burton's 1930s white-faience building it replaced. Between them three
tall narrow retained façades: No. 30, 1902 by *Marshall & Tweedy*, Nos. 22
and 18, 1892 and 1895 by *James Cackett*.

On the s side, **Eldon Buildings** (Nos. 29–33), 1893 by *Oliver & Leeson*,
a successful corner to Grey Street. Giant Composite order and some
Venetian windows, parapet with carved panels. Then **Gem House** [126]
(Nos. 23–27), 1904 by *Newcombe & Newcombe*, a hierarchy of orders on
the two broad shallow bows, with serpentine dentil cornice, top
balustrade, and swan-necked pediments on the dormers. Art Nouveau
shopfront of 1906 for Reid & Sons, by *Benjamin Simpson* (cf. Emerson
Chambers to the w, p. 155). The Pilgrim Street corner is rounded by the

tall, showy **Northern Goldsmiths'** building of *c.* 1895 by *James Cackett*, with a red-tiled corner dome on a tall drum. Fine original shopfronts, first-floor windows in blocked surrounds, those on the third floor mostly round-arched under pediments and two-light attic dormers. Bracket **clock**, *c.* 1932 by *Cackett, Burns Dick & Mackellar*, with female figure by *Alfred Glover*. Some excellent original fittings and showcases by *Sopwith*. For Pilgrim Street, *see* Walk 3, p. 141.

New Bridge Street continues E from here, following the line of the Town Wall to the site of Carliol Tower and on towards Byker. It was laid out in 1812 over a new bridge across Pandon Dene, then still a green valley. On the S side, **Watson House**, a 1930 steel-framed office block, then concrete **Dex Garage** of the same period (set back) by *L.J. Couves & Partners*, an early example of ramped access. On the N side, the long bleak 1970s concrete front of the **Pearl building**, then the glass-walled **City Library** of 2007–9 by *Ryder*, replacing that of 1966–8 by *Sir Basil Spence, Glover & Ferguson*, which had its main entrance at upper level, as part of the wider post-war plan for the city (*see* topic box, p. 190).

John Dobson Street runs N, parallel to Northumberland Street; opened in 1970 to designs by *D.T. Bradshaw*, City Engineer. The consequent demolition of the former library of 1880–4 exposed the blank brick W wall of the **Laing Art Gallery** [127], 1901–4 by *Cackett & Burns Dick*, the wine merchant Alexander Laing's gift to the City to celebrate fifty years in business. Like other citizens, he was anxious at Newcastle's failure to follow the example of other major cities and encourage the arts.

The site was bought despite objections that its front was only to Higham Place, a minor street. The resultant unsatisfactory approach from the town centre, exacerbated by John Dobson Street, was partly remedied in 2001 by pedestrianizing part of New Bridge Street. The Laing was given a glass-bowed S-facing entrance by *City Design*, and on the street in front, *Thomas Heatherwick*'s **Blue Carpet** [32] was commissioned. Resin tiles (rather faded except when wet, or dramatically lit at night) incorporating blue glass from sherry bottles, are laid carpet-style, corners turned up against tree and building; strips torn up suggest a fibre-optic-lit underworld and provide benches. It fills the space – ambitiously called a 'square' – and tries to unify its disparate elements. At the E end, against the hotel, Heatherwick's **spiral stair** of laminated timber, crafted by *McNulty Boats*, links to a pedestrian bridge over the Central Motorway East, which cut mercilessly through C19 terraces here in the late 1960s. The whole, although difficult to maintain, has transformed a dull street.

127. Laing Art Gallery, Higham Place, by Cackett & Burns Dick, 1901–4

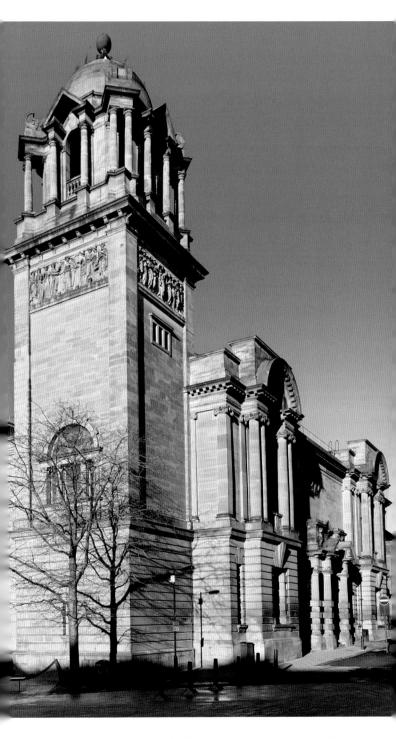

128. Former Lying-in Hospital, New Bridge Street, by John Dobson, 1825–6

The gallery itself, neo-Baroque with Art Nouveau elements, has a corner tower with high-relief frieze, open octagonal lantern, and stone dome. The ornate original entrance in Higham Place, w, has wrought-iron gates. Inside, a splendid marble stair, with much Frosterley marble and (reinstated with changing tastes) stained glass by *J. Edgar Mitchell*. In the galleries, murals depicting scenes from the history of Newcastle fill the lunettes; artists *Byron Eric Dawson, Louisa Hodgson, R.J.S. Bertram, A.K. Lawrence, Thomas W. Pattison, James Walker Tucker, J.H. Willis* and *Ralph Bullock.*

Outside are three early C19 buildings. Diagonally opposite the original entrance in **Higham Place**, three brick houses (stone dressings, Tuscan doorcases) are remnants of the terrace that *Richard Grainger*, right at the start of his distinguished career, built for William Batson in 1819–20. At the s end of the street and to the E, *John Dobson*'s own restrained house (altered), 1823, painted stone, with a honeysuckle frieze, and bracketed window cornices on the main floor. Some internal stucco decoration by *Ralph Dodds*. On the s side of New Bridge Street, diagonally opposite, *Dobson*'s small Tudor-style **Lying-in Hospital** [128] of 1825–6, in pale ashlar. Perp oriel over the doorway, flanked by cusped windows and cusped niches over canopies. It was the BBC's North East headquarters until 1987; now subsumed in offices of 1992 for **Newcastle Building Society** by the *David Ash Partnership* (studio additions of 1932 by *Wells Coates* demolished).

s of the former Lying-in Hospital in Market Street, **Plummer House**, 1911 by *Newcombe & Newcombe*, eleven bays, in the Dobson-Grainger style. To the E in **Croft Street**, the Town Wall, with the **Plummer Tower** [129]. The medieval tower has a D-shaped plan with flat inner front. The Palladian front was added *c.* 1743 by the Company of Masons for their hall, a showpiece for their skills. The rusticated ground floor has keyed moulded surrounds. Above is the sharp contrast of plain stone, setting off a grand Venetian window, with rusticated arch and full Doric order, framed by pilasters set in from the angles and supporting a deeply modelled cornice. The sashes still have their original broad glazing bars, one of the few early C18 examples in Newcastle. Low part-conical roof. Attached to the left, the Masons' small C18 brick addition.

Back past the Laing Gallery to **John Dobson Street**. On a deck above the street, **Bewick Court**, 1969–71 by *T.K. Powell & Partners*, a twenty-one-storey tower block; first-floor entrance from Princess Square, W. Refurbished with new cladding by *Red Box Design, c.* 2000. Beyond and to the W, three-storey late C18 brick terraces, recognizably Georgian despite insensitive shopfronts: a fragment of **North Street** (N–S), and **Saville Row** (E–W), 1770s, described as a 'retired and elegant street' in 1827. Some moulded window keystones. S side rebuilt, 1970s. Off the E side of John Dobson Street, alongside Durant Road (the 1960s link to

129. Plummer Tower, Croft Street, medieval with front range of *c.* 1743

The Post-war Plan for the City Centre

The principles behind Newcastle's *Development Plan* of 1963 included the vertical separation of pedestrians from vehicles, and the removal of through traffic to the E and W Central Motorways, of which only the E one was built (the present St James' Boulevard is the reincarnation of the W route). A raised road was planned along the line of Percy Street. External faces of the Eldon Square shopping centre on this street were therefore blank brick panels.

The entire central area was to have had the main floors of buildings opening onto platforms linked by elevated walkways. At the 1960s Central Library, the entrance faced W onto a platform called Princess Square, with vehicle access from John Dobson Street to the E. Walkways from Princess Square across to M.E.A. House and beyond, and from the E end of New Bridge Street across the motorway, both survive in 2008.

130. Proposed Development Plan, Northumberland Street and Percy Street, 1963

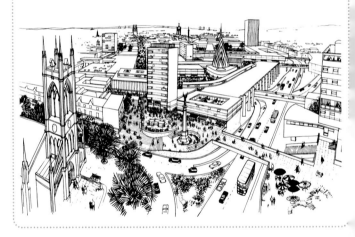

the motorway), is the remnant of the E block of **Saville Place**, a brick terrace with full-height end bay window, *c.* 1820.

Then the terraces of **Ellison Place** (1810s), where, in a back garden, *W.B. Wilkinson* built a pioneering patent reinforced-concrete cottage, 1854 (dem. 1954). At right angles is **M.E.A. House** [131] by *Ryder & Yates*, completed 1974: the first British building to be purpose-built to house many voluntary services. The main block mirror-glass-clad, with three internal service towers. The structure, with floors hanging from the nine steel yokes which form the roof, allowed the road-way to go under, and pedestrian ramps to link with, the first floor.

131. **M.E.A. House, Ellison Place, by Ryder & Yates, completed 1974**

132. Church of the Divine Unity, Ellison Place, by Cackett, Burns Dick & Mackellar, 1938–40

The pedestrian deck is part of the upper-level walkway system. At the w, an elegant curved brick auditorium. Heights were kept to those of the adjacent terraces, attractively reflected in the glass wall on good days. On the s side of Ellison Place beyond, the **Church of the Divine Unity**, 1938–40 by *Cackett, Burns Dick & Mackellar*. A Unitarian church with meeting room (Durant Hall), its origins a c17 congregation in The Close. Concrete and steel frame clad in light brick. A tall tripartite portal screen of reconstituted stone to a small forecourt; straight-headed windows, square E tower with a taller window, all in the rectilinear style of Hilversum town hall. The fine interior [132] has cantilevered aisles, so no arcades; clerestory, raked w gallery, coffered ceilings; the whole in wonderful condition. Excellent wood **furnishings**: pews and stalls with patterned ends, inlaid wave pattern on pulpit, altar with patterned reredos. *Dobson*'s church of St Peter (Gothic, 1843; *see* p. 236 for reused fabric) was formerly on the site.

E of M.E.A. House, the **University of Northumbria at Newcastle (UNN)** stretches N to Sandyford Road. Formerly the Polytechnic, founded in 1969, which incorporated the Rutherford College of Technology. It has also adapted some older buildings, and the area includes other buildings not in university ownership. We approach N up College Street, w of M.E.A. House. At the SE corner with

Northumberland Road, the **Sutherland Building** [133] was the **University of Durham Medical School** of 1887 by *Dunn, Hansom & Dunn*: Late Gothic, dark red brick and red terracotta with ashlar dressings. Entrance tower like a gatehouse, with barrel vault, stone benches, niches, oriel. The main block has mullion-and-transom windows, gargoyles and battlemented parapets. s extension 1906. NE of the crossing are the former **Dame Allan's Schools**, now College House, UNN offices; 1882–3 by *R.J. Johnson*, in Norman Shaw's Queen Anne style. A charming building: fat Tuscan columns flank the entrance under an 'Ipswich' oriel; ogee-domed towers, thick-framed sash windows; fine entrance piers, repeated on the Northumberland Road wing, and railings. At the NW, the **City Hall and Baths**, one structure, 1928 by *Nicholas & Dixon-Spain*. Neo-Georgian, brown brick, with Doric porticoes. The Hall (E) has an arcaded, marble-lined foyer and galleried auditorium; the Baths have groin-vaulted corridors, coffered ceilings; the Turkish Bath has Doric pilasters, and retains mahogany-panelled changing rooms, glazed domes and marble slabs in the steam room.

Facing City Hall (Northumberland Road, s side), the former **Riding School** of the Northumberland Yeomanry, 1847, by *Dobson*. Brick, with stone-dressed tall-arched recesses under a pediment. The hall had bare brick walls; its complex roof trusses are now barely discernible. Restored 1991 by *Ainsworth Spark* for the (then) Polytechnic college. Next to it, at

133. Former University of Durham Medical School, Northumberland Road and College Street, by Dunn, Hansom & Dunn, 1887, now UNN Sutherland Building

134. University of Northumbria at Newcastle, City Campus East, by Atkins, 2007

the corner, **Burt Hall**, 1895 by *John W. Dyson* for the Northumberland Miners' Association, commemorating Thomas Burt M.P. Brick and terracotta, ashlar dressings, Lakeland slate roof. On the gable a statue of a miner, by *Canavan*, modelled on Ralph Hedley's painting 'Going Home'. Now also part of UNN.

Now E along Northumberland Road. E of the Sutherland Building, **Trinity Building**, originally Trinity Presbyterian church, 1895 by *Marshall & Dick*. A fine group, with school and caretaker's house. A free treatment of Perp forms, with a tower. Another church on the N side: **St James (United Reformed)**, formerly Congregational; 1882–4, by *T. Lewis Banks*. A big raised central tower (reconstructed in the C20) dominates this group of cruciform church, Sunday School, church hall and caretaker's house. Free C13 style. Much C19 **stained glass**, some by *Atkinson Bros* and *G.J. Baguley & Son*. The Queen Anne building next door is the former office and warehouse of Brady and Martin, chemical manufacturers, 1890–7. By *W.L. Newcombe*. More Ipswich oriels, below giant pilasters of C17 English type.

To the S is the **Ellison Building**, built for Rutherford College in 1949–65 to designs by *George Kenyon*, City Architect. A quadrangle of plain elevations of varying heights, faced in Portland stone, slate or brown brick. Like the later grouping N of Ellison Place, intended to be linked to the central shopping area and Civic Centre by overhead walkways. Entry from the NW by a broad open passage between pilotis. On the diagonal path across the quadrangle, **sculpture** by *Nico Widerberg*, 2007; five herm-like figures.

The path leads to where the University of Northumbria at Newcastle spread E of the motorway in 2007, via a cable-stay **footbridge**, to **City Campus East** [134]. New buildings and footbridge by *Atkins*, the buildings glass- and steel-clad with mesh solar screen panels, and making maximum use of natural light. Landscaping by *Insite Environments*. The site held a multi-screen cinema, and before that the massive New Bridge Street Goods Station, built on landfill in Pandon Dene in the early 1900s.

Paths N of Northumberland Road lead through to an irregular courtyard within later UNN buildings, also by the City Architect. Much use of dark brick here, including the **Library**, W side. On the N side the former **Sandyford Building**, 1960s, remodelled in 2007 by *Red Box Design Group* for **Newcastle College** with dark glazing or zinc cladding and solar screens of steel. Many more buildings further N. S of the Library the **University Gallery**, **Baring Wing** of 2004 by *Carey Jones*. In front, another sculpture by *Nico Widerberg*, Pillar Man, a tall bronze (2004). Also a polished aluminium abstract sculpture by *Austin Wright*, 1981, against the blank wall of the Library complex. The sculptures face the Rates Hall at the back of the Civic Centre (*see* Major Buildings, p. 76).

135. St Thomas, Barras Bridge, by John Dobson, 1827–30

From here, w along **St Mary's Place**, with an ashlar-fronted terrace by *Dobson, c.* 1829–30. In Tudor style to complement his **St Thomas's Church** [135] of 1827–30 opposite. This stands in tree-fringed open grounds off Barras Bridge. The church is a 'peculiar', without a parish, because it combined the charities of the medieval Bridge Chapel (p. 108) and the medieval hospital of St Mary Magdalene, which was near here. Gothic, in a personal interpretation of E.E. w tower with very high, slender bell-openings, an openwork effect; clasping aisles of the same height as the nave. The buttresses have tall pinnacles; flying buttresses over the pierced sloping w parapets support the tower. Tall lancet windows, paired in the five-bay nave, triple with shafts in the E front. Dobson's w doors and gates have been replaced with full-height plate glass and iron. Large, light interior, with slim clustered piers from which plaster vaults with stone ribs spring over nave and aisles. Trefoil-panelled galleries, part of Dobson's design, were built in 1837 and provided the seating needed for the spreading suburbs (stone stairs integral with the organ loft). No deep chancel, only a slight projection to hold the altar. (Master of the Hospital at the time of rebuilding was Robert Wastney, a noted Evangelical.) Reordered *c.* 1970 with a large projecting platform. – **Organ case** of 1837, inserted in the w gallery 1960. – **Stained glass**. E window by *Baguley*, 1881, with other windows. Malta memorial window by *Helen Whittaker*, 2000. – **Monuments**. Tablet to Robert Wastney, d.1836, by *C. Tate*; standing woman beside altar with profile portrait. – Wall plaques (N aisle, w) to the Hawkes family, whose Gateshead ironworks produced iron for the High Level Bridge.

In the grounds, two **war memorials**. To the sw, a beautiful composition to the 6th (Territorial) Battalion of Northumberland Fusiliers, by *John Reid*, unveiled 1924. Portland stone and granite, with curved benches flanking a statue of St George. Facing Barras Bridge, The Response [136], a powerful group by *Sir W. Goscombe John*, 1923, to the Commercial Battalions of the Northumberland Fusiliers. The front shows the 5th Northumberland Fusiliers, who marched down the Great North Road to the Central Station, their families alongside them, in April 1915: an emotional bronze group against a high block of grey Shap granite with an angel above. On the back the Newcastle militia of 1674 are honoured.

136. Northumberland Fusiliers war memorial, by Sir W. Goscombe John, 1923, detail

Barras Bridge crossed the Pandon Burn here (the stone arch now beneath the road), connecting the town to the **Great North Road**, the main route to Edinburgh in days before the Tyne Tunnel to the E and the Blaydon route to the W. Opposite, a first glimpse of the University (*see* Walk 7). To its S, the former **Grand Hotel** (now **Blackwells**), 1889, a long flat Free Renaissance front, and the Crow's Nest Hotel, 1902, more ornate, in red sandstone and red granite. These face the **Haymarket** (not a medieval market, but established here in 1828 on the militia's parade ground of 1808). Further S, on **Percy Street**, the former **Newcastle Brewery offices**, 1896-1900 by *Joseph Oswald*. Red sandstone and brick, with quirky Flemish gables and a corner turret. Some interiors faience-lined. Ahead, the **Eldon Garden** development of 1987–9, an extension of Eldon Square shopping centre, crosses the road by a covered bridge.

Return to where **Northumberland Street** – the route of the old Great North Road – meets the Haymarket. The **South African War Memorial,** signed 1907 by *T. Eyre Macklin*, dominates the skyline in the angle. A heroic-sized winged Victory on a tapered hexagonal column, a figure with unfurled flag clasping its base; the effect heightened by steps and big low-relief panels and garlands. The adjacent **Metro station** was suitably simple, a spacious low brown drum. In 2008–9 it was being replaced with a huge glazed dome, with parabolic-arched sides; the interior filled with shops. Design by *Reid Jubb Brown*.

Northumberland Street, pedestrianized in 1998, leads S to Pilgrim Street. In the C18 it was a suburb of the medieval town, with three-storey brick houses.* At the N end, their proportions may be discerned above garish modern fronts. More is preserved in **Ridley Place**, E, of *c.* 1810. Further S, the C20 takes over. Large shops were developed here in the early 1930s; when the national economic depression was accompanied by increased spending power for those in employment. **British Home Stores**, E, 1967, replaces most of a 1931 Art Deco block for C&A (mass-market clothing). On the Northumberland Road side large coloured reliefs by *H. & J. Collins*, 1974, depicting scenes from Newcastle's history. Across Northumberland Street, the 1970s **Marks & Spencer**, its concrete encrusted with grey chippings (popularly thought to be intended to blend with the then grey and grimy stone all around). Next, the ramp to **Eldon Square shopping centre** (*see also* Walk 4, p. 154). Its side wall is blank save for **sculpture** salvaged from 1970s demolitions: the old Central Library in New Bridge Street (1881), the YMCA in Blackett Street (1889), and the 'Old' Town Hall of 1858–63 between Cloth and Groat markets. The adjacent canopied entrance bears the words **Eldon Square** (replacing the original more subtle 'E's), where a

---

*Old deeds mention the number of riggs (ploughed strips) each plot contained – a reminder of town fields here, outside the Town Wall; the town's pasture (Town Moor) was beyond.

sloping mall leads into the shopping centre itself. The interior detailing has also changed character, from playful to explicit: clusters of huge pencils for seats have been replaced with round benches on steel cones, and much more top lighting introduced. On the w side of Northumberland Street, a former Boots (chemists) shop at No. 45, designed by the firm's architect *M.V. Trevelyan* in 1912. Four arched niches hold statues of famous Newcastle men: Thomas Bewick, Sir John Marley, Roger Thornton and Harry Hotspur (stretching a point – he belonged to Alnwick!).

Further s, **Fenwick's** department store. J.J. Fenwick, from Richmond, Yorkshire, opened a shop in two houses here in 1882. It was enlarged, then elaborately rebuilt by *Marshall & Tweedy* in 1913 with the shop specialist *Cyril Lyon*, in cream faience with a giant Ionic order, and extended N and behind (for the sw extension of 1937 on Blackett Street *see* p. 155).

To the s of Fenwick's is **Brunswick Place**, made in 1820. Little evidence of its origins except for the **Methodist Chapel** of 1820–1 at the end, the successor to Wesley's Orphan House in Northumberland Street. E. Mackenzie wrote in 1827 that it was 'built after the plan of Waltham Street chapel at Hull, constructed by Mr [*W.*] *Sherwood*, architect, who liberally sent all the necessary drawings and specifications'. The outside is handsome, brick with ashlar dressings, arched openings, three-bay pedimented centre with Doric porch. In 1983 a floor was inserted at gallery level, and the ground floor converted for various pastoral needs. Above, Corinthian pilasters frame the apse, with a wide, panelled pulpit; the ceiling retains its delicate stucco, and ventilation grilles.

Back on Northumberland Street, on the E corner with Queen Street is a small early C19 house-turned-shop, with jolly pargetting introduced in 1953 to commemorate Elizabeth's coronation. To the s is Blackett Street once more, its edge defined by *Ray Smith*'s **sculpture,** Heralds, 1997–9, tall black-painted figures of slender iron strips. The crossing of the streets was the site of Pilgrim Street Gate, so we have returned to the medieval walled town.

Walk 7.

Newcastle University, and some Inner Suburbs

137. Walk 7

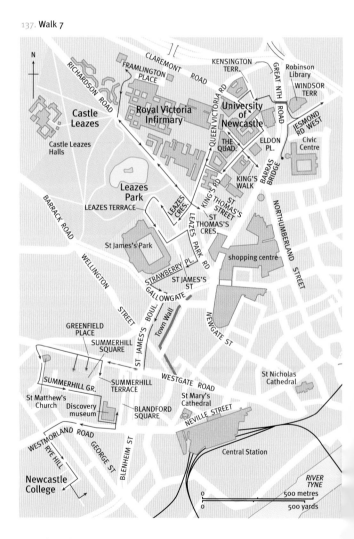

This Walk goes through C19 development and C20 redevelopment outside the Town Wall, skirting medieval Newcastle between the old Great North Road (NNE) and Westgate Road (SW). The area is now dominated to the N by the University and the Royal Victoria Infirmary, and to the SW by Newcastle United F.C., mostly on the Town Moor. The land belongs to the Corporation, but the herbage to the freemen, whose cattle grazed on the meadows or leas – hence 'Leazes'. The C19 houses around the edges of the Moor are mostly modest and of brick, for professional and commercial families, but the striking houses in Leazes Terrace are ashlar-fronted. SW of the football stadium we see fine early C19 terraces at Summerhill.

Newcastle University

Like many later C19 provincial universities, Newcastle's has its origins in science and medicine. A School of Medicine and Surgery, founded in 1832, was incorporated into Durham University in 1870, and moved to Northumberland Road in 1887. The College of Physical Science, founded in 1871 behind the Mining Institute, followed in 1874, and moved to the Barras Bridge site in 1888. Lord Armstrong, the industrialist, public benefactor and builder of Cragside in Northumberland, laid the foundation stone, and in 1904 the science college was renamed Armstrong College in his memory.

Early C20 expansion made the roughly four-sided group now known as the Quadrangle, followed by new buildings to the W on Queen Victoria Road. The College of Medicine moved here in 1938, having merged with Armstrong College in 1935 to form King's College, part of the then federal University of Durham. The 1,105 students and 135 full-time staff of 1936 had become 2,975 and 273 respectively by 1947, and a masterplan for the expanding site was drawn up by *W.B. Edwards*, the Professor of Architecture, and *Sir Howard Robertson*, only to be abandoned by the late 1950s.

In 1963 King's became the University of Newcastle upon Tyne, expanding to 5,905 students and 840 full-time staff by 1970. The medical school moved to a new site, other campus buildings were enlarged or replaced, and halls of residence and flats were built further W on the edges of Castle Leazes. The campus now covers 45 acres. The University is in 2009 working to a masterplan by *Terry Farrell & Partners* which will give it a new southern aspect, facing and welcoming the town, with selective demolition to reveal the Armstrong Building's Jubilee Tower. On Barras Bridge, *Bond Bryan*'s Student and Administration Services (SAS) building will be the 'front door' for the University.

138. Carlton Terrace, Jesmond Road West, by John Dobson *c.* 1838

The University and Surroundings

The start is at **Barras Bridge**, beside the Civic Centre (*see* Major
Buildings, p. 76). Near the Council Chamber moat, a Town Moor
boundary stone, with the town's heraldic three castles. Across the road
on the corner, a **monument** to the 1st Lord Armstrong, 1905–6, with
statue by *Hamo Thornycroft*. The University (*see* topic box, p. 201) lies
to the w, spreading behind the street frontages. Demolitions have left its
tall post-war buildings more visible, but still looking away from the city
centre. Present proposals will change that orientation, and an imposing
gateway building by *Bond Bryan* is under way in 2009.

139. Newcastle University, Robinson Library, by Faulkner-Brown Hendy Watkinson Stonor, 1980–2

To N the **Great North Road** passes into a 1960s cutting with ribbed concrete retaining walls. The C19 terraces begin with Nos. 14–20, E, three-storey brick, *c.* 1830. The University now occupies many of the houses further N and to the W.

Jesmond Road West turns off right. It was a country lane until the opening of the General Cemetery of 1834–6 (p. 242) necessitated a carriage road. Development here was spasmodic, shown by detailed changes in the terraces. First the W end of the S side, then another S block further on. Brick – by then fashionable again – for the fronts, homely sandstone rubble for the rear. The gap was filled in the mid C19. On the N side *Dobson*'s symmetrical and well-proportioned **Carlton Terrace** block [138], *c.* 1838.* End pavilions with tripartite windows and plain antae. Next to the left return, facing the Great North Road, is the University's **Robinson Library** [139], 1980–2 by *Faulkner-Brown Hendy Watkinson Stonor*, extended 1996 by *FaulknerBrowns.* Red-brown brick, with long slit windows set diagonally to filter the light. Much glass in the newer part, its proportions reflecting those of Carlton Terrace. To the N is **Windsor Terrace**, substantial 1870s, its N side rebuilt in dull imitation as students' flats.

*For a few years that name also applied to the plain terrace facing, but no evidence of Dobson's involvement in designing these s terraces is known.

A covered footbridge leads w over the cutting. To the s, the former Hancock Museum; *see* below. Ahead, the University's rather flashy **Devonshire Building**, 2002–4 by *DEWJO'C*. It houses the Institute for Research on Environment and Sustainability, its High Tech exterior and curving roof demonstrating its purpose; but it lacks a clear entrance and seems to ignore its neighbours. **Devonshire**, **Kensington** and **Park terraces**, N, are large late C19 houses in white brick, now University offices. The **Drummond Building** on Devonshire Terrace, 1975 by *Sheppard, Robson & Partners*, is plain darkish brick, unrelieved except by recessed windows with deep shade-emphasizing downward-sloping sills.

Wedged between Kensington Terrace and the NE side of Claremont Road, the University's first major post-war buildings face each other across a footpath. To NW is the wide **Stephenson Building**, 1952 by *Edwards & Manby*. Classical proportions, four storeys, chiefly grey brick, with recessed central entrance framed by dark columns. Smaller and SE of it, the **Cassie Building**, 1955. Walk between these two to see the core of the University, facing **Claremont Road**. Post-war development reaches here from the NE side of the original quadrangle. Beyond wide lawns, set well back, an elegant apse-like extension of 1959 by *Easton & Robertson, Cusdin, Preston & Smith* to the rear of the **Old Library**, with mosaic decoration; now the **Research Beehive** (restaurant, meeting and seminar rooms). NW of it, **Merz Court** (1959–63), to the SE, the twelve-storey **Claremont Tower** and the **Daysh Building** (completed 1968), all by *Sheppard, Robson & Partners*. Sharp-edged in brown brick with window bands [140], enlivened by recessed external galleries and occasional breaks in the rhythm occasioned by the higher windows of taller laboratories; Merz Court with a well-proportioned SE front, ground-floor piers flanking the wide courtyard entrance. These blocks were conceived after the abandonment of Edwards's post-war masterplan; the architects sought instead 'an atmosphere of massive calm amongst the warring elements'. The slab bridging Claremont Road was needed after the City rejected a twenty-storey tower because it would compete visually with the Civic Centre.

On the left side, the former **Hancock Museum**, 1878 by *John Wardle Jun.* for the Newcastle Natural History Society (now Natural History Society of Northumbria), 1880–4. It is astonishingly Dobsonian for that date, with Dobson's beautiful ashlar, his Doric pilasters and heavy attic, and the name cut into the frieze in the sans-serif letters of the pre-Victorian C19. Enormous sandstone slabs from quarries at Fourstones in Northumberland form the entrance steps. Aisle-like side ranges were added; the E by *Wardle*, the w by *F. W. Rich*, 1889. Restored 2006–9 and given a new rear extension by *Terry Farrell & Partners*, as the **Great North Museum: Hancock**. Its holdings include the collections of the

140. Newcastle University, Claremont Tower and Daysh Building, by Sheppard, Robson & Partners, completed 1968

Natural History Society, the University's Greek or Shefton Museum, and the Society of Antiquaries of Newcastle (from the former Museum of Antiquities).

Now SE down Claremont Road under the slab. Right into King's Road, then left to a pair of modest brick houses: a sad fragment of a terrace of *c.* 1811, **Eldon Place**. Next a white-faience car saleroom of *c.* 1930 (perhaps to be replaced by *Bond Bryan*'s Northern Writers' Centre), then a wedge-plan corner filled by **Claremont Buildings**, 1894 by *William Hope*, extended 1905. A speculative development of shops and showrooms with houses above. Red and yellow ashlar with tall copper-clad corner dome; now including the University Chaplaincy.

King's Road leads SW into the heart of the University area. On the NW side are additions by *Sheppard, Robson & Partners* to the **Schools of Art and Architecture**, part of the same scheme as their brick-walled blocks but with smooth concrete finishes, and kept low to respect the rear of the older Quadrangle buildings. On the SE side, *William Whitfield*'s former **University Theatre and Gulbenkian Studio**, 1969–70, reworked by *RHWL Arts Team* and *Arup Acoustics* in 2006 and now called **Northern Stage**. Much of Whitfield's brick structure is visible: his curved stair-towers remain, now with cast-glass lift towers set back beside them, and the wide brick piers supporting the stage in the former foyer. The clever entrance extension (W) with bar and eating space is simply brick, with a glazed wall for the shorter, upper restaurant. Varied fenestration in both side walls. *Cath Campbell*'s roof-top **installation**, Escapology: a palisade disintegrates into a tumbled mass of planks, falling into an open space over the recessed NW entrance, and concealing services. The remodelled auditoria are slightly smaller, but can become one large space; the acoustic has been improved by lining side walls with dark timber. Sadly, Whitfield's distinctive roof form is now overpowered by the extensions; but the theatre is now partly hidden by *Bond Bryan*'s new gateway SAS building to the SE (*see* topic box, p. 201).

The older University buildings start to appear beyond. SW, across **King's Walk**, the Neo-Jacobean **Students' Union** of 1923–5, by *Cackett, Burns Dick & Mackellar*, in red brick and Portland stone. Behind, facing King's Road, extensions with refectory and other rooms (**King's Road Centre**), 1960–4 by *W. Whitfield* (the debating chamber straddling King's Road dem. 2004). Strong shapes in exposed aggregate, granite and bronze mesh, assertively interesting among their historicist neighbours. On King's Walk, SE of the Union, the former University Physical Education centre, now **Culture Lab**, built by *Lamb & Armstrong* in 1889 as the **Grand Assembly Rooms** with a jolly, over-decorated façade. Behind, the **International Centre for Music Studies**, by the *Howarth Litchfield Partnership*, under construction 2009.

At the head of King's Walk **the Arches** lead to the Quadrangle. The fine Tudor **gate tower** [141], red brick with twin arches, is part of the King Edward VII School of Art (now **School of Fine Art**), already seen on King's Road. Designed in 1911 by *W.H. Knowles*. J.B. Simpson of

141. Newcastle University, the Arches, King's Walk, by W.H. Knowles, designed 1911

Bradley Hall (near Ryton, Co. Durham) gave £10,000 to build it, so that wood, metal and craft design could be taught. Latin motto on frieze below a statue of Edward VII in a niche surrounded by blind tracery, and large mullioned-and-transomed windows beneath the battlemented and pinnacled parapet. Attached to its w wall, a simple two-storey building of 1949 by *W.B. Edwards & Partners* for the Department of Physical Chemistry, later the Department of Archaeology and Museum of Antiquities (demolition planned).

Through the Arches to the **Quadrangle**, of several periods. On the right, a wide flight of steps to the School of Fine Art: imposing entrance of paired Ionic columns and large open segmental pediment with the Royal Arms. Left of the steps, the low **Hatton Gallery** in front of the teaching block, again Tudor and red brick. To the left of that, the former **School of Agriculture** of 1913 by *Knowles*; later the Department of Architecture (now School of Architecture, Landscape and Planning), with mullions and transoms, and oriel windows in buttressed end bays. Now part of the same department is the adjacent **School of Bacteriology**, 1922 by *Knowles, Oliver & Leeson*, with large stair-hall window. The ground level rises to the last of this range, the handsome **Old Library Building** of 1923–6 by *A. Dunbar Smith*, with diaper-patterned brick, high canted bay windows, and large hipped roof of plain tiles – a strong simple building which continues the vernacular revival of the early C20. (Behind, steps down to a plain extension of 1949 with the present entrance, and then the 1959 extension facing Claremont Road, p. 204.) The NW end of the Quadrangle is closed by the long brick **Percy Building** of 1958–9 by *W.B. Edwards & Partners*, built for the Schools of English and Classics, with an airy glass-domed entrance hall. It was also part of the post-war masterplan.

The whole of the Quadrangle's sw side is the buttressed **Armstrong Building**, with four ranges round a service yard. Facing, the first build of 1887–8 by *R.J. Johnson*, who described the style, large stone-mullioned windows and carved detail, as 'early Jacobean English'. The left return range has the **Jubilee Tower,** with an arched, wide-vaulted gateway to the courtyard, in an exuberant block of 1890–4, also designed by *Johnson* but executed by *F.W. Rich*. The tower (using money remaining from the 1887 Town Moor Exhibition, which celebrated Queen Victoria's Jubilee) has a four-storey oriel, and octagonal corner turrets. The Farrell masterplan proposes to reveal it by demolishing the building in front (*see* above). Beside it, the lively banded chimney of the boiler house (*c.* 1925 by *Cackett & Burns Dick*). The NW range, facing Queen Victoria Road, is the formal entrance, added 1904–6 by *W.H. Knowles*, revising *Johnson*'s design and including the **Armstrong Tower**. The Edwardian details owe more to Knowles than to Johnson. Among its delights are a marble-lined main entrance and stair, **King's Hall**, with hammerbeam roof and minstrels' gallery, and several memorial plaques, some in fine Art Nouveau metalwork. Statues on the tower by *W. Birnie Rhind*.

The Quadrangle's pleasantly low-key layout, with planting, gentle steps, and low, wide-topped walls of stone and soft-coloured brick, is a **war memorial**, 1947–9, by *J.S. Allen*, Professor of Town and Country Planning.

Back through the Arches and sw along **King's Road**. All on the right is brick. sw of the boiler house, the near-rectangular **Bedson Building**, built for the School of Chemistry by *W.B. Edwards & Partners*, 1949 and 1959: a simple modern design of four storeys with a canopy roof, its entrance round the left corner. On the other side of King's Road, after the Union extensions, the impressive **Herschel Building**, by *Sir Basil Spence & Partners*, 1957–62 for the then Physics Department. Up to eight storeys, the clean lines of the long elevations set off by the recessed ground floor with dark piers and second floor with gleaming white piers. Facing of brick, grey mosaic and dark slate. Behind the parapet is a penthouse. At the Haymarket end, s E, green slate on the cantilevered Curtis Auditorium. On the forecourt of granite setts, a tall metal **sculpture** (Spiral or Swirling Nebula) by *Geoffrey Clarke*, 1962. A new block for international students, by *FaulknerBrowns* is proposed on the Haymarket. Lastly on the left, the eight-storey **Agriculture Building** of 1964, by *W.B. Edwards & Partners*, with cantilevered auditorium towards the NW and formerly with a spider-like greenhouse on the roof.

A lane leads NW from King's Road to Queen Victoria Road, the Bedson Building on the right, the red brick **King George VI Building** on the left. Three long blocks with corridors and stairs between. Built for the Medical School 1938–9 by *P. Clive Newcombe,* heightened in the 1950s; now part of the School of Agriculture. It faces the hospital gates. Large forecourt and classical doorway. The entrance hall ceiling is like that added in 1931 to No. 41 Sandhill (*see* p. 107), in a mid-C17 strap-work style.

Queen Victoria Road was also laid out using money from the 1887 Exhibition. On the right, NE, the former **School of Mining,** 1929 by *A. Dunbar Smith*, Tudor with a tiled roof with dormers, is at the N angle of the Bedson Building. Then the NW range of the Armstrong Building, for which *see* above.

The Royal Victoria Infirmary and Castle Leazes

Across Queen Victoria Road from the former Medical School, the **lodge** to the **Royal Victoria Infirmary** (RVI), 1900–6 by *W.L. Newcombe & Percy Adams* (demolitions, alterations and new buildings in progress, 2008). The most important building is the **Administration Block** facing sw [142], containing the Peacock Hall, former boardroom, and library (the Nightingale wards, good examples of the pavilion plan, may be demolished within a few years), approached from the lodge by a sweeping drive, as if it were a large house. The Baroque architecture, bright red brick, ashlar dressings, soft grey-green Borrowdale slates, and the internal decoration, sustain that illusion as far as is reasonably possible. Seventeen bays, with a porch in the three-bay centre and

142. Royal Victoria Infirmary, Richardson Road, 1900–6, by W.L. Newcombe & Percy Adams, with Queen Victoria Monument, by George Frampton, 1906

three-bay end pavilions; pediments over the middle bays of the end and centre sections. The high roof, hipped over the end bays, has a dormer storey and a central lantern. Groined inner porch; hall, staircase and gallery have inlaid woodwork, a plaster frieze of briar roses and a ceiling also with lavish floral plasterwork. The **chapel** is a Greek cross in plan with central dome, rich mosaics and fine stained glass. In the children's wards sixty-one charming *Doulton* tile pictures, mostly nursery rhymes, with landscapes in a side room. Signed by the artists *J.H. McLennan, William Rowe* and *Margaret E. Thompson,* and paid for by the Lady Mayoress and her friends. (Due to be demolished, with the ceramic pictures relocated.) The white marble **statue** of the young Queen Victoria [142], a wonderfully slim and graceful figure in the centre of the garden, is of 1906 by *George Frampton.* Superb (resited) gates on Richardson Road, sw. Most of the boundary has excellent wrought-iron **railings**, principals formed by tapering groups of four uprights supporting a dome.

To w and visible from Richardson Road, the **Leazes Wing**, a simple red brick ward block by *RMJM,* 1988–92. To N and NW, teaching and research blocks including the **William Leech** and **Catherine Cookson buildings**, also by *RMJM*: buff brick, each enclosing large central gardens/yards, seen from a service road, and (at the N) the **Medical School,** 1981–5, and **Dental Hospital and School of Dentistry,** again by *RMJM,* built 1974–8. The glass-enclosed N extension of the Medical School is the **Henry Wellcome Building**, by *FaulknerBrowns,* for the School of Psychology. Between it and the Dental School is the **David Shaw Lecture Theatre**, 2003 by the same, jutting out and upwards on two clusters of tubular steel stays. On the w side of the service road and path, **Richardson Road Flats,** 1959 by *Kendrick Lynn,* spreading low-rise blocks with an interesting plan-form, in pleasant brick.

To the NE of this group, **Framlington Place**, part of the mid-C19 suburb which spread alongside the Town Moor. Mostly terraces, in the cream-coloured brick fashionable then; at the NW end two pairs (Nos. 18–21) quite unlike any local types, where the central four bays project under a pediment from which the roof ridge runs back. Entrances in recessed outer bays. At the E end a pleasant villa, **Framlington House**. Beyond to NW the beautiful **Paul O'Gorman Building** for cancer research, 2003 by *FaulknerBrowns.* A square site. Outer elevations of pale unglazed terracotta panels or light brown brick; glazing with brises-soleil to the paved forecourt; careful proportions.

Return s to Castle Leazes and Richardson Road. w, across the grass, the big **Castle Leazes Halls**, by *Douglass Wise & Partners,* project architect *Alan Moody.* Work began 1966; official opening 1969. Originally planned as a collegiate system, so the three distinct halls each has its own dining room. Variation in size and mass, and careful grouping around greens, produce a community with its back to the surrounding moor.

Returning SE down Richardson Road towards the city centre, on the right is **Leazes Park,** taken out of the Castle Leazes to form a public park in 1873, designed by *John Laing*; restored 2001–4 with lodges, lake and bandstand. At the end of Richardson Road, ahead, the start of **St Thomas's Crescent** (with **St Thomas's Square** and **St Thomas's Street**, NE). Small houses in dark brick with ashlar dressings, uniform despite their range of dates, *c.* 1840–60; restored 1980s. Doorways with the sturdy Doric pilasters and heavy architraves characteristic of the first half of the C19 in Newcastle. Brick was used only for front elevations; rubble sandstone for the rear. Behind No. 14 St Thomas's Crescent is the brick **outhouse** used as a studio by William Bell Scott (resident 1859–64), which Rossetti visited; so optimistically called 'the Rossetti studio'.

w of St Thomas's Crescent is the ambitiously named **Leazes Crescent** [143], begun 1829, by *Thomas Oliver* for Richard Grainger, gentle curve, now facing Leazes Park, NW. Charming terraced cottages, two storeys and stuccoed. Quite Regency in style, with pale-coloured render; rinceau frieze in the end bays of each block (some surviving) and pretty serif-lettered street-name panels. A delightful preliminary to the much grander **Leazes Terrace** [144], 1829–34, also designed by *Oliver* for Grainger. The terrace is really a rectangle with canted narrow end at NW. It is probably the grandest terrace on Tyneside, and as a single development has no equal of that period in the north-eastern counties. With open moor on three sides, it was a startling addition to the town. Eighty-six bays to NE, twenty-one to SE. Houses each of three bays.

143. Leazes Crescent, by Thomas Oliver, from 1829

144. Leazes Terrace, by Thomas Oliver, 1829–34

Three storeys over a basement, Corinthian pilasters accentuating angles and centres, pedimented centre to the narrow NW elevation. Honey-coloured ashlar fronts, with moulded artificial stone for the rinceau frieze (where present) and capitals. Brick rear; back yards cleared away for car parking. Much good interior detail survives to the NW, and possibly elsewhere. King's College Education Department was the first to colonize it (1940s–50s), and since the 1980s the whole block has been restored, mostly for University residences (part as private flats). Some steps were removed in the conversion.

Walk anti-clockwise round Leazes Terrace, admire its details, see its relationship with Leazes Park – and then Newcastle United F.C.'s concrete E stand at **St James's Park** confronts the Terrace. The lowest and oldest part is of 1970–3 by *Williamson, Faulkner-Brown & Partners*, of its time, with massive concrete struts. Subsequent additions (1993, 1995, 1999–2000, latterly by *Taylor, Tulip & Hunter* with *WSP*, structural engineers) have created the W (Milburn) and N (Sir John Hall) stands with four huge mast-hung tiers each, the S (Newcastle Brown) stand with three tiers; the E remaining comparatively low out of respect for Leazes Terrace. The stadium dominates not only the terrace (and the brick-built **St James's Terrace** and **St James's Street** to the SE, also *c.* 1830), but also the city's skyline. Astonishingly, this is the club's 1892 ground, originally a pitch enclosed by earth banks; suggestions of moving to a site nearer main roads have been resisted. The result is a certain excitement in town on match days; just SE, **St James Metro Station** and an underground spur line cope with the crowds.

145. Greenfield Place, Summerhill Square, *c.* 1823

From the sw corner of Leazes Terrace, e along Terrace Place to **Leazes Park Road**. Originally Albion Place, *c.* 1811, probably designed by *David Stephenson*. One block of mostly three-storey houses with some original doorcases. Then, in the s block, a former **synagogue**, 1879–80 by *John Johnstone*, now flats (after a fire, 1990). An imposing gabled front of ashlar with pink granite shafts. Lombard frieze on the central part of the gable. Upper windows paired under round arches with the Star of David carved in the tympana.

Strawberry Place runs w from Leazes Park Road, past the steps to the football ground. On the left here *Ryder HKS*'s big office drum, called Strawberry Place, is expected. Then left down the steps to **Gallowgate** (*see* Walk 5, p. 171, for Magnet Court etc. and for the Town Wall and Stowell Street to the e). On the w side, the research development **Science City** will cover the site of former Scottish & Newcastle Brewery outside the historic centre. The tall curved offices of 1965, by the brewery's architect *C.P. Wakefield-Brand*, may be replaced or refurbished. Beyond is **St James' Boulevard**, a wide 1990s road from Redheugh Bridge to St James's Park. On the left side, **Citygate** by *Ryder*, 2002–4: tall thin buildings, squeezed onto the site. Fine concrete panels to the road, glass to the rear, towards the Town Wall and its ditch.

Further down, **Westgate Road** runs off to the right, with 1820s–30s three-storey terraces on the n side, c20 shops filling many front gardens; two-storey on the s, almost all now shops, with narrow lanes between. **Summerhill Terrace** leads to **Summerhill Square** [145], built 1820s–*c.* 1840 on former nursery gardens. Fine brick houses around a grassed square. The n side terraces (**Greenfield Place**, **Ravensworth Terrace** and **Swinburne Place**) three-storeyed with Georgian doors and sashes; on the s, **Summerhill Grove**, *c.* 1840, linked semis. At the sw **St Anne's Convent**, built 1828 by *Ignatius Bonomi* as The Priory for Cuthbert Rippon M.P. Good ashlar, mixed Perp and Early English styles. The chapel (w), second floor and other alterations of 1878 by *Dunn & Hansom* for the Convent; presumably also the high boundary wall and gate. Second gate, e, inserted *c.* 1990. **Winchester Terrace**, w, *c.* 1860, has plate-glass sashes proving the skill of local glass-makers. On Houston Street, sw of the square, the former **Barber Surgeons' Hall**, 1851. A late work by *Dobson* in Italian Renaissance style; later part of a school.

Further w is **St Matthew's Church** at the top of Summerhill Street, an important landmark. 1878–80 by *R.J. Johnson*, tower 1894–5 and outer aisles 1900–5 by *Hicks & Charlewood*. The tall w tower can be seen from far away: big windows, pinnacles, wind-vanes. Clasping double aisles balance this weight. Dec tracery in the tower, Perp elsewhere. Splendid interior [23]: high five-shafted tower arch with delicately carved flower capitals; nave piers of four shafts and four hollows with carved capitals, the e pair repeating the tower capitals. Outer arcades echoing the local medieval style, with octagonal piers and double-chamfered arches springing without capitals. Inlaid marble chancel floor; sedilia; E wall of stone panelling. Magnificent six-light E window. Much glass by *Kempe* and *Kempe & Co.*, 1892–9.

From the SE corner of Summerhill Square, a path leads E then s to **Westmorland Road**. To the E is the **Discovery** science museum (also Tyne and Wear Museums offices and Tyne and Wear Archives), established in 1978 in **Blandford House** [20]. Built as the warehouse and offices of the Co-operative Wholesale Society, 1897–9, by *Oliver, Leeson & Wood*: a striking manifestation of commercial success. U-plan, the main front facing E onto Blandford Square. Fifteen bays, four storeys, with shaped central gables rising two further storeys. Red brick with sandstone and terracotta, with ogee copper domes on the corner turrets and rooftop cupolas. 1930s alteration to entrance hall and directors' suite (now the Archives department) in Art Deco style, with marble stairs, a stained-glass wheatsheaf in the landing window, walnut panelling, and glass-and-chrome light fittings. The gentlemen's toilets are the most amazing in the city, with blue tiles glowing like lapis lazuli. Refurbishment by *City Design*, with a new glazed entrance, was completed in 2004. The *Turbinia*, Sir Charles Parsons's pioneering steam-turbine yacht of 1894, is displayed in the long central yard, now glassed over.

To the w, Westmorland Road leads to **Newcastle College**. Founded in 1956, in 1964 split into the College of Further Education and Charles Trevelyan Technical College, merged in 1972 to form the College of Arts and Technology, renamed Newcastle College. The campus has a long, steep N–S site along **Rye Hill**. On the E side first the only remnant of the 1840s houses, a stone villa of 1+4+1 bays, **Rye Hill House**. Enlarged as the college's administrative centre by *RMJM*, 2006, with partly glass-walled extensions. On the w side, within railings and not part of the college, the **almshouses** of **St Mary the Virgin Hospital**, 1858, with C13 Gothic details. Extended N at each end and remodelled, 1916. Halfway down Rye Hill is a stepped piazza cut by diagonal routes from a central circle. To the w, N and E of here are big first-phase blocks with bands of render and glass (**Trevelyan**, *c.* 1966 by *W.B. Edwards & Partners*, **Rutherford** and **Parsons**, 1973). At the NE, the **Mandela Building (School of Art and Design)**, High Tech of 1987 by *George Oldham*, City Architect. Long and low, with blue and grey glazing and tubular framing. Big eaves, the upper edge of the roof canted back. Long balconied atrium, under a pitched, part-glazed roof. Stained glass in its gable-end by *Susan Bradbury*: diagonals of graduated colour. To the sw the **Performance Academy** [34] (2004), further SE the **Lifestyle Academy** [146] (2008), both again by *RMJM*. Bold blocks with cladding of dark or light-coloured metal panels, lit by small slit windows or all-glass walls according to the functions inside.*

---

*At the NE of the site, facing streets of C19 houses, a Sixth-form Academy by *RMJM* is planned for 2009.

146. Newcastle College, Lifestyle Academy, by RMJM, 2008

Gateshead Town Centre

History

After Roman occupation of the North ended, Gateshead seems to have become a monastic site. Bede's *History of the English Church and People* mentions the priest Utta as abbot here in 653. In 1080 there was certainly a church, in which Bishop Walcher and his knights took refuge, and died when the 'men of Gateshead', enraged at the Normans' violence, burnt it down. That building was probably somewhere near the medieval parish church of St Mary. In 1164 Bishop le Puiset of Durham granted borough rights, and so the town grew, near the church and the bridge. By 1264 markets were held, and by 1576 the town had 400 house-holders. The value of coalfields in Gateshead became apparent (*see* p. 10); deep mining, with improved underground drainage, began in the early C18. Iron foundries and glassworks developed, taking advantage of the availability of coal and of water transport, and continued into the C19. Chemical manufacturing, rope-making, and heavy engineering followed. The population was 8,597 in 1801, 19,843 in 1841, 65,845 in 1881, 109,888 in 1901, and peaked at 125,142 in 1921. In 1971 the figure was 94,457; in 1981, 74,644, despite boundary changes which enlarged the borough.

Between Speed's early C17 plan and Thomas Oliver's of 1830, Gateshead changed little. Its streets made a T-plan, with High Street, carrying the Great North Road across Tyne Bridge, meeting two short-er riverside streets. The modern town plan began by *c.* 1830, when the back lane to High Street was formalized as West Street, with mostly open fields on its w and a mixture of gardens, quarries and new terraces on its E. The North Eastern Railway's Greenesfield works was established NW of High Street in 1854, and the settlement also expanded to the E of St Mary's church. The 1890s map shows many terraced houses, often 'Tyneside flats' (*see* topic box, p. 33), but also streets of superior houses, including villas.

Built evidence of the original riverside settlement is now scarce. Extensive clearance began with the construction of the High Level Bridge and its railway approaches of 1845–9 and the catastrophic Quayside fire of 1854 (p. 122), then increased before the 1914 war, and again before construction of the New Tyne Bridge in 1925–8. In the mid C20, blocks of multi-storey flats began to replace the houses along the

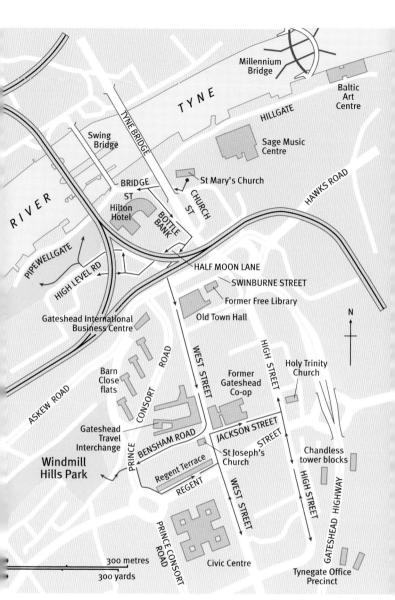

147. Walk 8

roads from the centre and just beyond: tenemented since the 1880s, slums by the 1930s. With the construction of the Felling by-pass (1960), Gateshead Highway (1961) and Western by-pass (1971), little remained of the old town centre. As industries closed down, the riverside also changed completely. Since then, imaginative schemes have refurbished old buildings and set new buildings on old sites, reinforced by a vigorous programme of public art.

148. St Mary's church (now heritage centre), Church Street, mostly C14 and C15, tower by George Cansfield, 1739–40

The East Riverside

Tyne Bridge (*see* p. 97) allows unsurpassable views along the river, with Newcastle's Byker Estate (p. 232) on the horizon, its Quayside below left, and to the right, Gateshead's Quayside, with Baltic, Sage and St Mary's church. Dominating both, for the time being at least, the unsophisticated and unsympathetic bulk of **Tyne Bridge House**, a concrete and glass 1960s block beside the bridge.

The first landmark downstream from the old river crossing, at Swing Bridge, is **St Mary's church** (since 2008 a heritage centre). The general impression is of a pinnacled Perp church with C18 W tower [148]. A small C12 window in a roll-moulded surround, on the chancel N inner wall, is the earliest fabric *in situ*. Some nutmeg moulding on the hood-mould of the round arched S doorway. Later nave arcades [6], of the local C14 type with high, pointed arches flowing from octagonal piers without capitals. They continue across the transepts. The fabric has been altered many times: the nave roof was rebuilt in the C15, but the church was seriously damaged by fires in 1854, 1979 and 1983. The tower was rebuilt in 1739–40 by *George Cansfield* with classical arched windows; *Thomas Oliver* changed the galleried interior in 1838–40. The full restoration needed after 1854 was done by *John Dobson*, who may have added the pinnacles. In 1874 *Austin, Johnson & Hicks* removed the organ from the W gallery to an organ chamber on the N, heightened the tower arch and made a larger, Gothic W window, thus completely changing the relationship of tower to church. Further restoration and a new s porch, 1908–22 by *W.H. Wood* of *Oliver, Leeson & Wood*. After the late c20 fires the former anchorage attached to the N wall of the chancel, c14 in origin but much rebuilt, was not saved, and the 1874 organ chamber next to it was demolished, its arch now holding a new glazed entrance. A mezzanine chancel floor inserted for an auction-house conversion (1991) has been removed. Early medieval grave slabs displayed in the s porch are further evidence of the earlier church.

Much of the **churchyard** was lost when Tyne Bridge was begun in the 1920s. A brick-walled **mausoleum** to the SE was built by the Trollope family, of whom Robert (d.1686) was the architect of Newcastle's Guildhall (p. 70). Later the burial place of the Harris and then of the Greene families, it was rebuilt in 1850, reusing some original masonry. Trollope's flourishes – scrolled finial, frieze with mottoes – have been diluted, repeating the c17 open-crown finial but without much of the carving.

Downstream, across St Mary's Square, the Sage (p. 91), then across Baltic Square the Baltic (p. 88) and the Gateshead Millennium Bridge (p. 95), or upstream.

The West Riverside

From St Mary's, **Bridge Street** leads down under Tyne Bridge. Up **Bottle Bank**, left, past the large, plain **Hilton Hotel**, 2004 by *Red Box*. The road continues as High Street. Then right into **Half Moon Lane**. A flavour of Victorian Gateshead here, with c19 pubs, notably **The Central**, 1854 by *Matthew Thompson*. Further w, under the railway line of 1849, the walk crosses the High Level Bridge approach. Just before another railway viaduct is reached, a large bright red brick building is a further sign of the railways' eminence in Gateshead, for this was the **Railway Workers' Club**, begun in 1887, probably designed by *William Bell*. To the w, remains of Gateshead's second railway station, of the later 1840s: ramps to the viaduct (*see* topic box, p. 228). Continue w beyond this second viaduct to the site of the North Eastern Railway's **Locomotive Works**. Much of the workshops have been replaced with a housing development (**Ochre Yards**), begun in 2002 by *PHS Architects*. The masterplan, developed with *EDAW*, incorporates parts of the engine sheds and the workshops. What remains is a large L-shaped block to the N, in origin a tinners' shop of 1884 (heightened 1894), now converted to housing, and partly derelict buildings to the s, including (sw) some of the shell of the machine shop of 1851–2 (extended 1868), with big rusticated-arched windows. Formerly adjoining it to the E was a very early station hotel of 1844 by *G. T. Andrews*, a two-storey Classical building, dismantled in 2003. Part of the York, Newcastle & Berwick Railway's first station for Tyneside, it lost its importance when the High Level Bridge and Newcastle's Central Station (p. 82) were built shortly after. The new street names commemorate NER locomotive engineers: Worsdell, Fletcher, etc. Varied blocks, with some 600 apartments, are informally arranged, using a palette of pale and dark bricks and coloured render, with steel and glass balconies. Reinforced concrete podiums, incorporating ground-floor car parking, support timber frames – an interesting structural method.

A path alongside the nearer viaduct leads s to High Level Road. This runs w, following the stone boundary wall of the railway works. N of the road, wooded river banks are now a **sculpture park**, begun by the Borough Council in the 1980s, perhaps the first project of their very successful public art programme. The first installation was **Bottle Bank**, a sequence of stone piers with steel ribs, graduating from complete arcs to mere abutments (by *Richard Harris*, 1982–6). *Colin Rose*'s **Rolling Moon** of 1990 is a rainbow arch with the moon set upon it. Other work installed before the Gateshead Garden Festival of 1990 includes *Andy Goldsworthy*'s **Cone** (1990), of layers of soldered steel. More pieces have been added, all by the side of paths meandering along the steep hillside and down to Pipewellgate, the old riverside road.

The Town Centre

Back now to Half Moon Lane, and s beneath another railway bridge to **West Street** for a group of later C19 civic buildings. The former **Town Hall** [149] on the E side looks over a cleared area. Built 1868–70 by *John Johnstone*, the architect of Newcastle's now demolished Town Hall of 1858–63 in St Nicholas Square. An earlier scheme was abandoned because old mine workings were encountered during construction. Free Venetian Renaissance, with rock-faced basement. Two storeys of paired arched windows, the upper more elaborate, light the stair hall and public spaces. Bays are defined by superimposed pilasters, floors by cornices, that at the eaves bigger and with widely spaced dentils; hipped roof. The projecting, taller entrance block has a balustraded parapet with Queen Victoria presiding over a central (depleted) group of statuary. Rectangular in plan, the public spaces forming a U. The entrance has a colonnaded stair hall, with double-flight stone staircase. Corridors to right and left originally led to the public hall and the Magistrates' Court respectively; the space between held fire engine, cells, drill ground and prisoners' airing ground, ancillary rooms, cloakrooms and refreshment rooms. There is some excellent stained glass.

In front, an elaborate cast-iron **clock tower** of 1892 by *Gillett & Johnson* of Croydon, restored 2001, each side with a tiny figure of Old Father Time. Also a sculpture of patinated and stainless steel, **Acceleration**, 2005 by *John Creed*. The large, gleaming building further w is the **Gateshead International Business Centre** of 2004, designed by *Gateshead Council*.

The Italianate former **Post Office** round the left corner in **Swinburne Street** followed the Town Hall *c.* 1873; then *John Johnstone* again with the former **Free Library**, 1882–5, its style a more fanciful Baroque, appropriate for its purpose: a mixture of education and entertainment (the first floor originally included an art gallery). The street

149. Former Town Hall, West Street, by John Johnstone, 1868–70; clock tower by Gillett & Johnson, 1892

150. Villa, later dispensary, West Street, 1830s

continues with the former **Gateshead Institute Permanent Building Society** (plain classical, *c.* 1880), and the former **National Provincial Bank** (a palazzo of *c.* 1873 by that bank's usual architect, *Gibson*), all used as offices for the expanding Borough Council until the 1980s Civic Centre (p. 227) was built.

s of the old Town Hall in **West Street**, a plain red brick villa of the 1830s: four by three bays, giant pilasters defining them, and big eaves on paired brackets [150]. In 1855 it became the town dispensary and is still used for council offices. s of that is a fine **Lloyds Bank**, 1914 by *George Reavell* of Alnwick: Baroque style with rusticated ground floor and pilasters. Between end bays projecting under broken pediments the recessed first floor has attached giant Ionic columns, and the first-floor windows have tall segmental pediments with long keystones. The last of this interesting C19 group is squashed up against the bank: the former **Post Office**, 1897 by the *Office of Works*. A cheerful building in Free Tudor style of bright red brick with stone dressings and steep slate roof. A big gable over the two right bays, its peak carved with foliage and a high-relief crown, under a ball finial. At the left, a doorway with mullioned trefoil-headed overlight. A little hip-roofed dormer set back above. A plaque records the site of the house of Thomas Bewick, the celebrated engraver and illustrator, who died there in 1828.

The clearance which isolated the old Town Hall and its neighbours was part of Gateshead's post-war scheme to demolish slums. In 1954 the Borough decided to replace the old terraces with high-rise housing, to designs by the *Architect's Department*. Some can be seen to the w of here: the **Barn Close** [151] flats of 1955–6, four nine-storey blocks with flat roofs designed as communal spaces. After Bensham Court, 1964, and Redheugh Court of 1965, the Borough adopted a new strategy, building villages rather than massive blocks. New development was made more difficult by the multitude of old mine workings.

151. Barn Close flats, by the Gateshead Borough Architect's Department, 1955–6

s of the Old Town Hall group, the post-war reconstruction of the commercial centre. The major presence, on the E side, was being demolished in 2008–9: **Trinity Square**, a reinforced-concrete shopping centre and multi-storey **car park** of 1964–9, by the *Owen Luder Partnership* for E. Alec Coleman Investments Ltd. Like the same team's Tricorn Centre in Portsmouth, also now demolished, it was a good example of 'Brutalist' sculptural massing of concrete, with interesting shapes and relationships: tightly packed shops and market on two levels below [31], car-park decks and a top-floor enclosure intended to be a restaurant above, famous for their appearance in the 1971 film *Get Carter*.

To the w is the **Gateshead Interchange**, a late 1970s structure remodelled in 2002–3 by *Jefferson Sheard*. The bus station (sw) now incorporates a steel and glass **screen** by *Danny Lane* called Open Line, with images of the region's heritage. Below ground, the **Metro station** opened in 1982 has **mosaics**, Nocturnal Landscape, Night, and Day, by *Keith Grant*. On West Street there is also a gargantuan **sculpture**, *Mike Winstone*'s concrete-covered polystyrene Sports Day of 1986, painted black in 1991.

To the s is **St Joseph's Church (R.C.)**, on the corner with Bensham Road. Of 1858–9 by *A.M. Dunn*. An imposing group of church and presbytery, dark sandstone and steep slate roofs, its varied masses full of interest. The church Dec style. Nave, aisles and gabled SE chapel, big traceried windows, prominent buttresses; an octagonal steep-roofed baptistery, NW; chancel roof stepping down from the nave. Interesting **stained glass** by *Barnett*. **Presbytery**, s, in modified Gothic style with segmental window heads under hoodmoulds. High-gabled s wing with a tall bay window.

By the church, two mid-C19 terraces isolated by the late C20 road system, **Walker Terrace**, w (1842–3) and the parallel **Regent Terrace** (1852–4), represent many that have gone. Brick with local sandstone dressings, plain Late Classical style, with moulded surrounds to the ground-floor openings. Both were built for the professional classes, but Walker Terrace is the grander: five-bay houses with big corniced chimneystacks. The front gardens with gatepiers of Walker Terrace probably survive because they are raised above the street. Some windows on Regent Terrace still have their margined sashes.

w of Walker Terrace and across Prince Consort Road, the former **Windmill Hills Industrial School**, built 1879–80 to designs by *Oliver & Leeson*, a landmark on the crest of the hill. Bright red brick, varied masses and roofs with many shaped gables. The boys' and girls' entrance porches on the w front have paired round arches. Now in community use. **Windmill Hills Park**, w of the school, became Gateshead's first public park in 1861. The site of one windmill is marked out. At the N edge a platform allows wonderful views; no wonder the Scottish cannon were set up here to bombard Newcastle in 1644. Beside the park's gatepiers is a marble **statue** by *Joseph & Robert Craggs* of **George Hawks** (d.1863), first mayor of Gateshead; paid for by his

152. Civic Centre, Regent Street, Council Chamber, by D.W. Robson, 1978–87

friends and the workmen of his ironworks. First set up outside the Town Hall. To the N, **Windvane,** a tall steel sculpture, 2001 by *Richard Woods*, working with local schoolchildren.

Regent Terrace looks s across Regent Street to the **Civic Centre**, 1978–87 by the Borough Director of Architecture, *D.W. Robson*. Almost vernacular: warm red brick, low and spreading; red-tiled hipped roofs. It has a central block housing the Council Chamber [152] (with stained glass by the architect), and a quadrangular block projecting from each corner, housing council departments. The U-shaped block of flats to the W is **Regent Court**, 1958.

Back N, to where **Jackson Street** runs w opposite St Joseph's church. Here was the headquarters of **Gateshead Co-op**. Buildings of three stages. First a block of 1964. Then an impressive Baroque building of 1925. Giant attached columns to the three central bays, recessed under an entablature with a strong stone balustrade. Bronze panels, now painted, between lower and upper windows. Wide end bays, with tall stepped voussoirs on the tall, round-arched windows. Then six lower bays, the entablature inscribed GATESHEAD INDUSTRIAL CO-OPERATIVE SOCIETY LIMITED 1881 (it opened in 1884). Big arched first-floor

Early Railways*

Tyneside's first railways were horse-drawn wagonways, carrying coal from pithead to river. Steam locomotives were developed to work some of these lines from the 1810s. Improved versions of these early engines helped to make possible the first passenger-carrying public railways, notably the Liverpool & Manchester (1830, engineers George and Robert Stephenson).

Railways of this kind appeared on Tyneside in 1837, when the Newcastle & Carlisle Railway opened a temporary terminus at Redheugh, Gateshead. This was followed in 1839 by the Brandling Junction Railway. It was carried through Gateshead on a half-mile-long viaduct (the arches were intended as warehouses, and are still in commercial use), reaching the Redheugh terminus by a steep incline and a cutting. The eastern terminus was at South Shields, so that the North Sea and Irish Sea were effectively linked by railway, via Gateshead.

The next railway development of significance had considerably more impact on the town. The Great North of England Railway, opened between York and Darlington in 1841, was unable to complete its line to Tyneside because of financial difficulties. It therefore relinquished its powers to George Hudson's Newcastle & Darlington Junction Railway (later York, Newcastle & Berwick Railway). This opened to Gateshead in 1844, by a circuitous route including the BJR and other lines, none of which had been promoted as part of a N–S main line. In order to achieve through running to Newcastle and the North, a short section of line (with a new Gateshead station) was built up to *Robert Stephenson*'s High Level Bridge of 1845–9, which crossed to the new Central Station. Thus, for all that Tyneside is called the Cradle of the Railways, its most conspicuous monuments of the new technology date from the 'Railway Mania' of the later 1840s rather than the pioneering years.

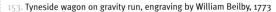

153. Tyneside wagon on gravity run, engraving by William Beilby, 1773

* By Stafford Linsley.

154. Metropole pub, High Street, by William Hope, 1896

windows, attached Corinthian columns under the two-bay end gables; in the centre, a square pilaster. The Co-op movement beehive in the left gable, the arms of Gateshead in the right. Set back to the E, a high rubble wall hints at the earlier character of this area. Old maps show a ropery.

Jackson Street meets **High Street**, along the E side of the Trinity Square site. At the SW corner the gabled **Metropole** pub [154], 1896 by *William Hope*, built with a theatre (now demolished). On its E side, Trinity Community Centre is the former **Holy Trinity Church**. Its S aisle is **St Edmund's Chapel**, one of the town's two surviving medieval buildings. Part of the hospital (almshouse) of the Holy Trinity after 1248, it became a private house after the 1530s; a later C16 doorway from that house, with fluted Doric pilasters and entablature, has been set in the S wall of the forecourt. In the fine C13 W front, the doorway with three orders of columns is flanked by two tiers of blank pointed trefoil arches (one lower arch with nailhead decoration) below a stepped arcade of seven lancets, three with windows, all with nailhead. The hoodmoulds end in little volutes. On the S and E sides lancet windows, with nook-shafts. *Dobson* restored the chapel for worship in 1836–7;

Stephen Piper made a second parish church for the swiftly growing town in 1894–6 by adding a new nave, the chapel becoming its s aisle. The new w front imitates the medieval, with the addition of a large porch and an octagonal vestry at the NW corner. In 1980 it was converted to a community centre by *Hayton, Lee & Braddock*.

High Street further s has mostly C19 houses, shops and pubs, with some C20–C21 rebuilding. On the corner of Charles Street, w, a pair of three-storey three-bay houses (Nos. 270–274), late C18 or *c.* 1800; two shops built in the front garden, left, and the corner house extended as a pub. The proportions, stone floor band and big lintels all suggest they were good houses once. Opposite, further s, No. 297 has a whole faience façade with green touches on the cream. The three pale sixteen-storey blocks behind belong to the **Chandless** redevelopment of 1960–3, which includes maisonette blocks and old people's bungalows. **Sculpture**. A bright object at the s end of the street demands attention: a tall mirror-faced door frame (Threshold, 2003 by *Lulu Quinn*) on the path into the grassed area below the elevated Gateshead Highway. Walk through it the better to appreciate it.

Beyond the Gateshead Highway here, on an island site by Sunderland Road, the **Tynegate Office Precinct** by *Hubbard Ford & Partners*, 1967–70; of eight blocks planned, only three were built.

The civic buildings at Shipcote, s, are described on pp. 262–3.

Outer Areas

The Byker Estate

By Elain Harwood

Byker was developed in the 1890s with lines of Tyneside flats (*see* topic box, p. 33) ignoring the contours. It was rebuilt in 1970–81 to the designs of *Ralph Erskine* (*see* topic box), with 2,001 houses and flats divided almost equally between low-rise housing of no more than three storeys, and a spine 'Wall' to the N, a mile long and mostly of three to eight storeys skimming the contours. Designed as a shield to an intended motorway to the coast, it now serves as protection from the by-pass cut through *c.* 1988–90 and the Metro to the N, as well as from north winds. Car access is restricted, with parking around the perimeter, and the planting by Erskine's in-house specialists is as imaginative as the building work. Erskine had developed this plan form in the Swedish Arctic, but Byker is its greatest realization, and also of his intricate, personable detail of contrasting brick colours and stained timber.

Ralph Erskine

Ralph Erskine (1914–2005) was born in Mill Hill, London, but was working in Sweden at the start of the Second World War and, as a conscientious objector, decided to stay there. Erskine's work not only embraced Swedish conditions and materials but also the humane ideal that attracted British architects towards Scandinavian Modernism in the late 1930s. His first commissions were for tiny individual houses, followed by rural housing schemes and New Town developments. The concept for Byker can be traced back to a theoretical scheme of 1959 for an Arctic town, based around a wall of housing that created a microclimate for lower buildings in its lee. A fragment of this plan was realized at Svappavaara, Sweden, in 1963, and at Resolute Bay, Canada, in 1973. Erskine's dense, largely pedestrian schemes are related to those of Team 10, the international planning forum of which he was a fringe member, but are more attuned to people and place. In the 1960s Sweden embraced system-building in a political campaign for 'a million new homes', and Erskine sought work in England, designing Clare Hall, Cambridge, and private developments including the housing at Killingworth which led to the Byker commission.

155. The Byker Wall, by Ralph Erskine, 1971–8

First proposals for rebuilding accompanied demolition *c.* 1960, which separated southern Byker from the Shields Road shops. Many people moved away, leaving a predominantly elderly population. In 1964 the City Corporation agreed a comprehensive redevelopment, supported by a residents' poll in 1968. A report in 1967 proposed a 'solid line' of system-built slabs (like those in nearby Howard Street) as a barrier to motorway noise. Control then passed to a Conservative administration determined to bring in private architects; ironically their principal appointment went to an architect noted for humanitarian, left-wing views, but the Leader, Arthur Gray, valued Erskine's experience with community groups in Sweden. He was appointed in early 1969.

Erskine leased an undertaker's shop in Byker as his British office and residents' 'drop-in' centre. The Skeffington Report on public participation in planning (1969) recommended more dialogue with residents, and Byker tenants knew from an early stage what was happening. Their comments on the first low-rise phases influenced the bright colours, introduction of semi-private courtyards and children's play areas in later neighbourhoods. They had no say in internal planning, and none in the design of the perimeter block. The estate was designed here and in Drottningholm, with Erskine scuttling between them. *Vernon Gracie* ran the Newcastle office, with *Pär Gustafsson* and *Gerry Kemp* responsible for the landscaping.

In February 1970 Erskine's 'Plan of Intent' recommended low-rise housing behind a protective perimeter block at a density of 100 persons per acre, retaining schools, churches, pubs and the Shipley Street Baths. To preserve the community, the first areas developed were the fringes, leaving the central core until last. About 40 per cent of the new Byker was occupied by former residents, nationally a high percentage. It was redeveloped in a rolling programme of some 250 units at a time, creating neighbourhoods each with a shop and community facilities. Erskine envisaged that other architects would build schools and industrial units. Byker was abandoned in 1981 with the last (SE) phase, Harbottle, unbuilt, when the Thatcher government cut support for public housing. It is nevertheless the most ambitious and imaginative of Erkine's housing schemes anywhere, owing much to the ebullient timberwork and planting; given the vulnerability of such details, the estate's condition is remarkable.

Erskine exploited the contours of the s-facing site – a bowl with views across the city – developing pedestrian routes and giving individuality to each neighbourhood. The pilot scheme was Janet Square, in the SE corner, with dark brick and a limited colour palette. The first phase of the 'Wall' followed, its form determined by noise abatement. Patterned brick, cheery ventilators and tiny bathroom and kitchen windows face N, but to the s a riot of balconies and walkways exploit the benign microclimate [155]; a gap (thus avoiding cold bridging) between the walkways and main structure is concealed by timber

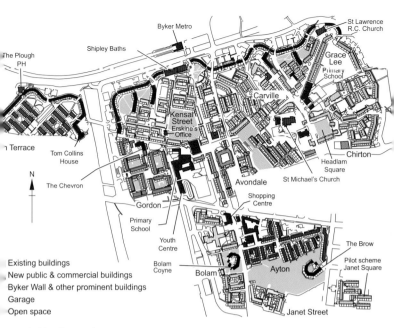

156. Byker Estate, plan

benches and planters, brightly coloured with Swedish impregnated stains and preservatives. The snaking blue metal roofs of the Wall dominate views of E Newcastle. The early low-rise housing has similar roofs and timberwork, while the district heating system's thick pipes span terraces at first-floor level, forming timber bridges or pergolas topped with large bird boxes. Similar boxes terminate the over-scaled downpipes, derived from Erskine's Arctic work. Lower link ranges and isolated blocks of flats, and the later Carville and Avondale areas on the high central ground, use concrete blocks and brick (of an over-size 'metric' dimension).

A chronological walk is impossible. Instead, head s from the Byker Metro through **Raby Gate** into the scheme's heart. The contrast is immediate between the N side of the 'Wall' (1971–8), with its few windows, and the exuberant s side. The ground floor has maisonettes for families, with small flats set above. The **Shipley Street Baths** of c. 1900, integrated into the Wall, served the district heating until a boiler house was built. Turn right through Norfolk Square and down Brinkburn Street to **Erskine's Shop**, which survives (extended) as a housing office. This early phase, **Kendal Street** (1972–5), established the pattern of short terraces found in the low-rise areas, with semi-private courtyards elaborated by kerbs and salvaged sculptural details from the old Town Hall, YMCA and Royal Arcade then being demolished (*see* topic box, p. 146). Across the old railway to the w, **Dunn Terrace** of 1975–8 has bolder brick patterning to its outside wall – pick out 'BYKER' –

book-ended by **Tom Collins House**, sheltered housing of 1976–8, a thirteen-storey wedge immortalizing a hostile Labour councillor. In contrast are low-rise patio houses, each L-shaped unit shielding the garden of the next.

Back across the tracks, **Gordon Road** (1974–6) has large greenswards, and **The Chevron** provides a landmark of three-storey flats. More incident was introduced s of Commercial Road, historically the most socially disadvantaged part of Byker, which in 1975 Erskine tried unsuccessfully to alleviate with a shopping centre, park and an irregular outcrop of the Wall, **Bolam Coyne**, and with stronger colours. Tighter budgets simplified **Ayton Street** (1978) to the E, while **Janet Croft** to the s was abandoned by inexperienced contractors in 1980.

To the E across Ayton Park is **The Brow**, flats from 1978, and then **Janet Square**, the pilot project of 1970 – a large square with service streets to the rear. The assessment made by the first volunteer families here initiated the pattern of more private space and brighter colours in later phases. They also recommended grouping families and elderly people rather than trying to mix them, and encouraged more hobby rooms. These lessons are seen in the NE quadrant, at **Chirton** – where the planting and bird boxes are most imaginative – and **Grace Lee** (1974–6) [27], linked by **Headlam Square** (1976–8), sheltered housing around a bowling green.

The spine of Grace Lee is **Spire Lane**, an axis between the Victorian **churches** retained by Erskine. At the E end, attached to the Wall, is **St Lawrence (R.C.)**, almost a stone-by-stone rebuilding of 1897 by *W.L. Newcombe* (transepts and one spirelet) of *Dobson*'s Trinity Presbyterian Church, New Bridge Street (1846–7). Lancet Gothic, with a NE spirelet. Inside, galleries, and a splendidly Gothic roof structure. To the sw, **St Michael**, 1862–3 by *W.L. Moffatt*. Dec style, with a N aisle and vestry added in 1936 using materials from *Dobson*'s St Peter, Oxford Street (1840–3). Restoration and reordering 2008 by *Xsite Architecture*.

Cut through Michaelgate and sw down the steps of **Carville**, the steepest part of Byker, where in 1977 Erskine adopted an earthier brick palette and tiled roofs in short terraces set across the contours. On **Raby Street**, the heart of Byker and the last fully completed phase, the two styles are juxtaposed and you have come full circle.

Jesmond

The C19 suburbs of Jesmond and Heaton lie respectively w and e of the Ouseburn, as did the two medieval villages. The Ouse Burn and the deep valley of Jesmond Dene form Jesmond's eastern, and the Town Moor its western, boundary. It is good fortune for such a large town as Newcastle to have both a dene, with its burn and now densely wooded banks, and the grassy pasture of the Moor, crossed by footpaths, so close

157. Jesmond

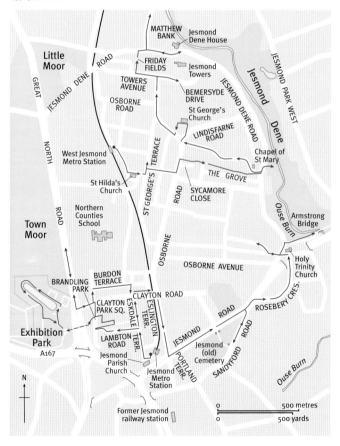

to its centre. Until 1835 Jesmond was a township in its own right, outside Newcastle. It remained no more than a village up to the mid C19, when it became the suburb for Newcastle's wealthiest inhabitants (population 2,100 in 1851, 6,100 in 1881, 21,400 in 1911). By 1900 most of Jesmond had been built up with terraces and large villas. There are none of the Gothic doorcases, shafted windows and turreted roofs then fashionable elsewhere in England; just good bricks and slates and good craftsmanship with, perhaps, some bands of coloured brick, and pierced bargeboards. The area also has back lanes, the earliest being in Brandling Village. Sufficiently isolated from the town to support a full range of shops and services, yet close enough for a brisk walk to the universities, Jesmond still prospers and is still largely residential.

South Jesmond

This walk explores south Jesmond between the Central Motorway East and Jesmond Dene (for which *see* p. 244). As seen in Walk 7, Newcastle's expansion along the Great North Road began by 1830. It continued with Brandling Village, then NW along what is now Jesmond Road, with *Dobson*'s cemetery, opened in 1836.

The start is at **Jesmond Parish Church**, Jesmond Road, just N of the motorway (reached from the centre via Jesmond Road West, *see* Walk 7, p. 203, or via Metro to Jesmond station). 1857–61 by *John Dobson*; N vestry 1874 by *R.J. Johnson*. The church was paid for by public subscription to commemorate Richard Clayton, a leading Evangelical minister. Late E.E. style, it has a big pinnacled tower, planned to receive a spire which was never built, and cross-gabled aisles. Six buttressed bays, a two-bay chancel; inside, octagonal piers; no clerestory. Much rich carving, with gargoyles and varied tracery. The interior expresses Evangelical principles, and has no separate chancel (the communion table originally stood on a timber floor, with rails on three sides) and N and S galleries. The galleries were given new fronts in 1907, and the W gallery removed so that a baptistery could be made. An enamel roundel of great beauty set on the N gallery (now moved to N aisle wall). Other interior changes have been made to suit the parish style of worship. Fine **stained glass** by *Atkinson Bros* of Newcastle, in S baptistery and N aisle; E window of N aisle, 1886 by *J.B. Capronnier*, Brussels. Tall five-light E window of 1956 by *Lawrence Lee*. Johnson's **vestry** is cosily domestic, with wide stone fireplace and hammerbeam roof.

Jesmond Metro Station [158] lies to the E. 1978–80 by *Faulkner-Brown Hendy Watkinson Stonor* and *L.J. Couves & Partners*, part of the first phase of the Tyneside Rapid Transit System (*see* topic box, p. 38), and like many of the stations, embellished with public art. The blank dark-glazed N walls are the backdrop for a lawn and *Raf Fulcher*'s playful **sculpture** Garden Front, 1978, a fanciful composition of obelisks and a mock-C18 arch with stalactite rustication. Below ground, the stairwells have *Simon Butler*'s vivid enamelled 1983 **murals**, geometrical compositions in the modular wall panels.

158. Jesmond Metro Station, by Faulkner-Brown Hendy Watkinson Stonor and L.J. Couves & Partners, 1978–80; sculpture by Raf Fulcher, 1978

Eskdale Terrace leads N from the parish church. On its W side is the **Royal Grammar School**, the original blocks of 1905–7 by *Sir Edwin Cooper*. Low brick and stone ranges in friendly Neo-Early Georgian, connected by colonnaded galleries; clock turret above the half-round porch. Just behind the railings are two medieval stone **piers** salvaged from the Hospital of Mary the Virgin at the foot of Westgate Road, the C18 home of the Free Grammar School founded under Queen Elizabeth. Much extended and added to, e.g. the science block, S, 1997 by *FaulknerBrowns*.

N of the school, Lambton Road runs W to the early C19 suburb of **Brandling Village**. At its W end and to the N, the *c.* 1820–30 houses of **Brandling Park** face the Moor. The northernmost block was raised by a storey towards the end of the C19. **Brandling Place South** runs back E from the W end of Lambton Road. It is a terrace but not uniform, stone or brick, with a few roofs in the London style with stone-coped party walls running back behind front parapets. Most are two storeys high and two windows wide. Many alterations, but still with a mid-block alley running underneath to the back lane. Through the alley, a lane leads W and then another lane runs N; from it a path cuts between the houses of Brandling Park. Beyond this second lane and to the N is the rear of **Clayton Park Square** on the S side of the Clayton Road, both part of the 1870s spread over Jesmond's fields. Two-storey terraces of white brick, rising straight from pavements.

159. Exhibition Park, bandstand, 1887

Before looking at later Jesmond, a w diversion may be made to
Exhibition Park at the SE corner of the Town Moor, via an underpass
beneath the Great North Road w of Brandling Park. Like Leazes Park
(*see* p. 212), this was established by the 1870 Town Moor Improvement
Act; it opened in 1878. The highly successful Royal Jubilee Exhibition
was held there in 1887, when the **bandstand** [159] was built and the **lake**
formed. In 1929 the North East Coast Exhibition provided a showcase
for local arts and industries (perhaps inspired by the success of the 1924
British Empire Exhibition at Wembley); more than 4 million people
visited over twenty-four weeks. Most of the pavilions, kiosks and layout
were designed by *W. & T.R. Milburn* of Sunderland. These were
temporary, save for the **Palace of Arts** [160] with portico and dome, of
artificial stone cladding on block walls. Later it became a science
museum then the Military Vehicle Museum.

The fields to the N of Brandling Village, the property of the Mary
Magdalene Charity, were developed with a fine group of public buildings originally facing open moor (now playing fields). The institutions
have private drives from Tankerville Terrace (w), and Burdon Terrace
(s), but all can be seen from the Great North Road to the w. First, the
former **Fleming Memorial Hospital for Sick Children**, 1887–8 by *John
Quilter* and *George Wheelhouse*. Fine Flemish bond brick and ashlar
dressings, in a free Jacobean style, with good lodges to SW and NE. Now
the **Fleming Business Centre** and **Fleming Nuffield Unit**. Next a site
shared by two former orphanages: the Jacobean-style **Northern
Counties Orphan Asylum**, 1869 by *R.J. Johnson*, w, and to its E, with
round-arched windows and dark-and-light voussoirs, rather Italian,
the **Phillipson Memorial Orphanage**, 1873–6 by *G.T. Redmayne*;
both in vivid red brick and sandstone, gabled, the latter with central

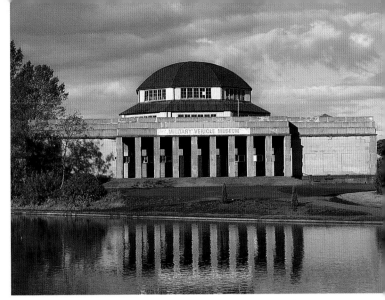

160. Exhibition Park, former Palace of Arts, by W. & T.R. Milburn, completed 1929

projecting chapel, and tall saddleback tower at the s end. In 1939 they became the **Princess Mary Maternity Hospital**, and now form **Princess Mary Court**, flats with newly built houses behind by *Stringer & Jones*. To its n the **Northern Counties Deaf and Dumb Institution** (later School for the Deaf, now the **Northern Counties School** of the Percy Hedley foundation), the only one of these institutions still used for its original purpose. 1860–1 by *Johnson Hogg* with *T.W. Goodman*. Gothic, with interesting use of varied materials – sandstone, granite, whinstone – and Ruskin-inspired carved details. Success brought expansion: plans of 1892–3 by *W.L. Newcombe* were only partly executed; large additions in 1904–5 by *Stephen Piper* were followed by further additions and adaptations. Further n, a **cemetery** for St Andrew's church, Newgate Street (*see* p. 170), 1855–7. Designed by *J.P. Pritchett & John Middleton Jun.* of Darlington. Lodge and chapels as usual, but somewhat altered.

Burdon Terrace leads e from just s of the Fleming Hospital. On its n side, **Jesmond United Reformed Church** (formerly Presbyterian), 1887–8 by *W.L. Newcombe*. Sandstone and Lakeland slate, free Gothic style. Windows fill the liturgical w wall (actually s), above paired doorways with pink granite shafts and stiff-leaf capitals; tall sw tower. Consistently well designed and decorated inside, with more pink granite columns and a kingpost roof. Behind the chancel arch the space is filled by the organ, a familiar Presbyterian arrangement. Excellent **stained glass**: by *Kempe & Co.*, ritual e, 1904, and transept, 1913; 1921 by *H. Dearle* of *Morris & Co.*, w, above the doors; s clerestory and n and s aisle windows by *H. Hendrie*, 1933 and 1938. Beautiful high-relief **war memorial**, *c.* 1920 by *Walter Gilbert*, with St George and an angel flanking the Crucifixion.

מה טבו אהליך יעקב משכנתיך ישראל

161. Former Jesmond Synagogue, Eskdale Terrace, by M.K. Glass, 1914–15, porch

Burdon Terrace then turns s to **Clayton Road**. A little to the E is the N end of Eskdale Terrace, with on its E side the former **Jesmond Synagogue**, now the art department of the Central High School for Girls. 1914–15 by *M.K. Glass*. A striking building. Red brick with stone bands. The high, round-gabled entrance front has a large round-arched window, with Star of David. Below it, the triple-arched porch [161], with alternating dark-and-light voussoirs under a mosaic Hebrew frieze, links projecting corner stair-towers. The next N–S road is **Eslington Terrace**, alongside the railway cutting: to the s, three-storey houses in the white brick seen elsewhere in 1870s Jesmond, to the N two Arts and Crafts-influenced blocks in red brick with attractive details. With other terraces behind, these are by *J. Newton Fatkin*, 1909 onwards.

Just E of the railway, **Osborne Road** runs s to Jesmond Road, past **Blythswood** (E side), private flats by *Barnett Winskell* with *Keith Banyard*, 1976. Hard red brick, with rounded corners to the stair-towers. At its s end, Osborne Terrace allows a view w to the former **Jesmond railway station** of 1864 (Blyth & Tyne Railway), now a pub and restaurant. Red brick and stone dressings in Tudor style, with mullioned windows and octagonal chimneystacks. Probably by *J.F. Tone*. The railway made it possible for businessmen to travel to lunch in their suburban homes. To its sw, dull 1970s concrete office blocks (**Archbold Terrace**, named after the Victorian street they replaced).

NE along **Jesmond Road** are tall brick terraces of the 1870s, now flats, offices and hotels. On the right side is a large 1930s **bus depot**, facing Portland Terrace, s, with sturdy Doric columns and triglyph frieze. Then along the main road a high stone wall with the entrance to **Jesmond Cemetery**, 1834–6 by *John Dobson* for the Newcastle General

Cemetery Co. Beautiful ashlar **chapels** face the road. Sombre pedimented fronts with paired Greek Doric pilasters [162]. Between, a
square recess with a high arch joining tall square twin towers with
lattice-grille bell-openings. Tall iron gates, with spearheads and
acanthus principals. The long walls have sash windows facing the drive.
J.C. Loudon wrote in 1843 that it was 'the most appropriate cemetery
lodge' that he knew, because it 'can never be mistaken for an entrance
to a public park or to a country residence'. The chapels were converted
to offices in 1978. The single s **lodge** and its wide **gatepiers** on
Sandyford Road are more modest, but still severely Greek, with antefixae and acroteria. The **graveyard** was laid out by *Dobson* with two
long mounds, straight drives along the N side and down the centre, and
winding picturesque paths at the s and w. Many professional and commercial people are buried here: architects and artists, shopkeepers and
writers, engineers and doctors, in Tyneside's equivalent of Père
Lachaise cemetery in Paris, with a wonderful variety of styles.
Perhaps the oddest **monument** is the huge granite log of the building

162. Jesmond Cemetery, Jesmond Road, chapels, by John Dobson, 1834–6

contractor Richard Cail (d.1893). The architect *Thomas Oliver* has a fluted column at the NE. In the SW part, *Dobson*'s own grave (d.1865) is commemorated by a disappointing marble headstone of 1905 and an earlier slab inscribed J.D.. Contrast the tall Gothic tower of 1843 to Archibald Reed (NW section), signed by *Dobson*. By the W side of the central path, a touching monument with a baby on a couch under a Tudor canopy commemorates the Keenleyside children, d.1841–2 in cholera epidemics, aged one, twelve and ten.

Further E, on the left, is **All Saints' Cemetery**, 1855–6 by *John Green*. High-gabled Gothic arch with elaborate iron gates; original railings: the sobriety of Dobson's 1830s design gone, all now lively and elaborately carved. The **chapels** are set well back from the road, not sombre and powerful but rather cheerful, with nook-shafts and dripmoulds, buttresses and belfries.

A little way NE, then SW down **Sandyford Road**, where *Dobson*'s early domestic work can be glimpsed. Set back from the road is the Villa Real, a modest 1817 design for Capt. Dutton, with a Greek Doric porch. Now **Chapman House**, part of Central High School. Further NE, **The Minories** in Rosebery Crescent is a sheltered housing scheme of 1986 by *George Oldham*, City of Newcastle Architect. Pleasantly informal; low buildings of soft-coloured brick with wood balconies and pitched roofs, set in attractive gardens.

Rosebery Crescent curves N across the dual-carriageway underpass to **Holy Trinity**, Churchill Gardens. The chancel by *Hicks & Charlewood*, 1905, followed by the nave, aisles, tall W tower and spire, built as a war memorial by *Hoare & Wheeler*, 1920–2, the gift of the Dalgliesh and Hoare families. Conventional Gothic style with Dec tracery and stepped buttresses. Excellent ashlar; fine windows, with military insignia in contemporary **stained glass** by *Nicholson Studios*. The fall of the land emphasizes the tall, pinnacled spire, commanding Jesmond Dene beyond.

A short detour W to see a fine 1960s development. From Holy Trinity W into Shortridge Terrace, then right into **Buston Terrace**. Among dark brick C19 terraces, a light cream brick wall on the right shields **Fenwick Close**, a short terrace of very attractive low, one- and two-storey brick houses, 1962–5 by *Brian Robson*, built on the large garden of the adjacent terrace-end house. Beautiful in their simplicity, with E clerestories in westward-sloping boat-shaped roofs; a few alterations have not marred the whole composition.

Back to the junction of the old roads at Jesmond Road and Benton Bank, beside Holy Trinity church (the new road is carried seamlessly over the Ouseburn). From here, **Jesmond Dene** opens out before you. In the mid C19 the industrialist and engineer W.G. Armstrong, later 1st Lord Armstrong, bought the C18 Jesmond Manor House (dem. 1929) and the land of the dene. He transformed the valley, where old water wheels powered ironworks and mills, into pleasure grounds, incorporating part of the grounds of Heaton Hall on the E bank (dem. 1933).

In 1883 he gave this wonderfully romantic park to the city. With his gift of land in 1880 to the s, it forms a string of public parks, Jesmond Dene, Armstrong Park and Heaton Park, extending to the industrial Ouseburn valley (p. 136). Many houses now cover the site of his house and its grounds, which will be seen in the northern Jesmond walk (*see* below).

The first evidence of Armstrong's reworking is the **Armstrong Road Bridge,** now only for pedestrians, by *W.G. Armstrong & Co.*: a unique structure, designed and constructed in 1876–8. Eight wrought-iron lattice girder spans, the overall length between the stone abutments being 552 ft (168 metres), are supported by seven pairs of square wrought-iron box-section columns, cross-braced with wrought-iron ties and resting on rock-faced sandstone piers. What makes it special are the rocker bearings at foot and head of each column, the sliding bearings at the central columns, and the fact that each girder is separately supported, all to provide articulation to compensate for mine subsidence and thermal variation (clearly a wise precaution, for in the 1970s a trial boring between the E columns was unhappily directly on a mineshaft!). Pedestrianized in 1960, the bridge has become the setting for a Sunday arts and crafts market. Threatened with demolition in the 1970s, it was rescued in 1982 thanks to a late-discovered underspend by Central Government. Columns have been replaced with steel replicas, cast-iron pilasters replaced in fibreglass, and some decorative brackets have been omitted in the restoration.

A well-proportioned tower block, **Vale House**, Lansdowne Gardens, can be seen to the s: 1966–8 by *Douglass Wise & Partners* with the *City Housing Architect (D. Cunningham)* [27]. Uncluttered white surfaces with a contrasting black central recessed strip at the centre of the two shorter sides. Poured profiled concrete panels here were formed using shuttering designed by *Derwent Wise*, brother of Douglass.

163. Jesmond Branch Library, St George's Terrace, by Williamson, Faulkner-Brown & Partners, 1962–3

North Jesmond

This Walk starts at **West Jesmond Metro Station** on the former Blyth & Tyne line, opened 1900 by the North Eastern Railway. Much altered 1978–80 for the Metro (*see* topic box, p. 38). Then s along West Jesmond Avenue, to **St Hilda's Church** on Thornleigh Road. 1900–5 by *Hicks & Charlewood*, with attached school, dated 1900. Perp style; copper-covered flèche. Good glass, good snecked sandstone and graduated Lakeland slate roof. A daughter church of St George's, Osborne Road (p. 248). Next E, then N up St George's Terrace to **Jesmond Methodist Church**, 1900–2 by *W.H. Knowles*, with hall and school. Big, of stone, with a copper-domed tower. Alterations and the attractive wide w door by *Christopher Downs*, 1995. On the site of an intended larger chapel to the N, **Jesmond Branch Library** [163], 1962–3 by *Williamson, Faulkner-Brown & Partners*. The narrow frontage is used to advantage by setting a circular reading room in a bed of whinstone and granite setts. The perimeter wall is zigzag in plan, each glass-fronted fin enclosing a bookcase against a lower panel of red granite chips in its longer side. These full-height glass fins lead the eye by stages round the corner.

Across St George's Terrace, s of the supermarket, Acorn Road runs E into **Osborne Road**. On the E side a little to the N is **Sycamore Close**, a small group of pleasant 1990s brick houses. Then right, into a narrow lane, and past the rear of some 1890s villas (possibly by T. R. Spence). After a bend this becomes a wide (unmarked) lane called **The Grove**. On the s side is **Grosvenor House,** formerly Jesmond Cottage (until recently **Akhurst School**). Built for Matthew Anderson (rainwater head 'MA 1831') and bearing all the trademarks of *Dobson* design: Tudor style in excellent ashlar, big gabled roofs of Westmorland slate, and interior details such as are found in his Tudor houses elsewhere. The main entrance was on the s side in Grosvenor Avenue; W.G. Armstrong's Jesmond Manor House (*see* p. 244) was beyond. A short way E along the Grove, a sign indicates that one garden on the left has **St Mary's Well**, restored after excavation in 1982; possibly of medieval origin, certainly a well by the C17, then an C18 bathing place for the large house called The Grove that was nearby.

The lane then enters **Jesmond Dene Road**. Opposite, the early C19 **Dene Terrace** juts into the Dene. N of The Grove off **Reid Park Road**, trees surround the ruined **Chapel of St Mary** [164], with chancel, sacristy and fragment of the nave, all in coarse sandstone. C12 chancel arch on fat, semicircular responds; the s capital with simplified volutes, the shafts with cushion capitals; voussoirs with roll and chevron mouldings. In the s wall of the chancel, a two-light window with cusped tracery. The N chapel (or sacristy) is curiously long and seems to be mid-C14 work. In its N wall, two cusped ogee-headed lights in a square-headed opening. Piscinae in the chancel s wall and sacristy E wall.

164. Chapel of St Mary, Jesmond Dene Road, C12 and C14, ruins

A short way N, on the E side of Jesmond Dene Road opposite Glastonbury Grove, Armstrong's **gatehouse** of 1869–70 for his banqueting hall happily survives intact. Rock-faced masonry in late Gothic/Tudor style, with a pointed-arched doorway, mullioned-and-transomed windows and steep roof. Carved over the door, panels with WGA, left, and 1870, right. By *R. Norman Shaw*. (Shaw was at that time also greatly enlarging Cragside (Rothbury), Armstrong's country house in Northumberland.) Behind it is the **Banqueting Hall** by *John Dobson*, built 1860–2, now a roofless shell best seen from the valley. It is large, rather dull Italianate with many niches that once held statuary by *Lough*. Diners had wonderful views over the dene.

The valley footpath, accessible from several points along Jesmond Dene Road including the N side of the Gatehouse, allows views of the park landscape that Armstrong made – with waterfalls and meadows, quarries and trees, footbridges and a ruined **water mill** (for grinding corn, and later, flints for the local pottery industry).

From St Mary's chapel, **Reid Park Road** leads w through early C20 houses to Osborne Road. Across Lindisfarne Road here (N) the **Church of St George** is in full view, its tall campanile dominating the suburb, a landmark for miles around. Of 1886–90 by *T.R. Spence*, an ambitious church following the precepts of the Arts and Crafts Movement, integrating decoration with structure; all expensive and well executed, and progressive in style for its date. It was built and furnished at the expense (over £30,000) of Lord Armstrong's partner Charles Mitchell. Mitchell's son *Charles W. Mitchell* was a painter and contributed to the decoration; Spence had already enlarged Mitchell's house, Jesmond Towers (p. 250).

The church is a strong E.E.-style composition of good sandstone ashlar, with a steep roof of graduated Lakeland slate. The high clerestory has five large windows rising above wide aisles with paired lancets, the gable of the sw porch rising over the eaves at one end, and the campanile with its pyramidal top standing forward at the other. The E wall has three high lancets; at the w, a long two-light window rises above a wide gentle baptistery. Here, over a row of lancets, is a band of low relief carved with natural forms in the firmly controlled flowing manner found in all the other external decoration.

The interior is high and dramatic, with something of the glittering atmosphere of the churches in Ravenna [165]: an inspiring setting for ritual, and now a unique witness to Spence's importance as a designer of such schemes (e.g. his decoration, now overpainted, of the former All Saints, Ennismore Gardens, London; was the campanile there the inspiration for this one?). The s porch prepares one for the quality beyond for it has fine swirling wrought-iron **gates** made to Spence's designs by *Alfred Shirley* (who did all the metalwork) and delicate stained glass. High, simple arcades with round piers are the foil for the richness to E and w. The w wall is panelled with tracery in Caen stone above the three baptistery arches, and has a central canopied niche containing a

165. St George, Jesmond, by T.R. Spence, 1886–90, interior

bronze **statue** of St George designed by *Spence*. The superb **stained glass** above, by *John W. Brown*, is filled with angels at the Last Judgment. All the windows were made by the *Gateshead Stained Glass Co.*, except for the two w aisle windows, by *O'Neill Bros. Brown* also designed the figures in the E window, a rich, glowing Nativity. It is matched in splendour by the surrounding **mosaic** in the chancel, with figures designed by *C.W. Mitchell*, the benefactor's son, and executed by *Rust & Co.* Below the mosaic, glazed tile with roundels of the Evangelists by *G.W. Rhead*, set in a surround of natural and abstract curving, interlacing leafy shapes. The focus of all this is the richly carved **altar and reredos** of Pavonazza marble, by *Emley & Sons* of Newcastle, who also made the matching **font**. – Richly carved wood **pulpit** by *Ralph Hedley*, and **screens** by him and *Messrs Robson & Co.* – **Roofs** stencilled and painted by *C.S. Wardropper* of Gosforth to designs by *Spence*. – Superb **memorials** by *Frampton*, in the N wall to Charles Mitchell (1898) and in the S wall to Charles W. Mitchell (1903), in bronze, carved stone, and enamel. Fine brass and alabaster war memorial (1920) by *Hicks & Charlewood*.

s of the church is a green, with on the E side the attractive block of **church hall and verger's house**, with sunflower-finialled gables, dated 1887. Replacing the original vicarage w of the church is **St George's Close**, with at the right a new vicarage and at left a terrace of five interesting houses, long garden extensions to this side, plain front and hipped roof to the street; 1968–9 by *Cyril Winskell*.

Osborne Road runs NW from here. Where it swings to the left, North Jesmond Avenue continues N. On the E side the former **South Lodge** to Jesmond Towers, signed and dated 'CM 1883' (Charles Mitchell) in the pargeting of the coved eaves; on the w the Georgian-influenced **Church of the Holy Name (R.C.)**, by *Dunn, Hansom & Fenwick* (1939). An attractive mixture of semis and detached houses in Mitchell Avenue, w, with good coloured glass in hall and stair windows. Then a T-junction with **Towers Avenue**, lined with magnificent trees, once the drive to the big house.

The right arm of the junction is Bemersyde Avenue (with some *Crittall* 'Sunshine' windows). From here the drive leads to the former **La Sagesse** school and convent (closed 2008). The school occupied **Jesmond Towers**. The first part was built as West Jesmond House in the early C19, and added to in 1817 and 1823–7 by *Dobson* for Sir Thomas Burdon. It was enlarged by *Thomas Oliver Jun.* in 1869, and twice by *T.R. Spence* for Charles Mitchell, 1884 and 1895 (*see also* St George's Church, above). As might be expected from its slow evolution, it does not have a clear plan. An overall Gothic atmosphere prevails, especially on the front elevation to the S, which is mostly *Dobson*'s. There are traceried windows, blind traceried buttresses with big polygonal pinnacles, pierced parapets and battlemented gables. The additions by *Spence* respect Dobson's design and high-quality mason-work. Internal detail of this period includes much fine carving by *Ralph Hedley*. The entrance is through a vestibule with a tiled floor incorporating many medieval motifs. To the right is a stone-arched **entrance hall** (now partitioned). The main stair of Dobson's building, at the rear opposite the entrance, has gone, but at the right of the entrance and hall is a Gothic **stair** probably designed by him, with a slender traceried timber balustrade. At first-floor level, a triple arch with pendants, and the soffits of the doors off the stair have blind tracery. The stair is lit by an oriel window. Off this stair hall to the E on the ground floor is a **morning** or **drawing room**, with an Arts and Crafts dado painted with flowing leafy

166. Jesmond Towers, by John Dobson, Thomas Oliver Jun. and T.R. Spence, early c19–1895; detail of Picture Gallery by Spence, carving by Hedley, 1884

stems bearing many-petalled flowers; similar flowers appear in the lights of the stone tracery of the square bay window at the s end. This window and the dado seem to have been added between 1885 and 1910; Mitchell's son, the artist *Charles W. Mitchell*, may have been involved. It was to provide him with a studio that the central tower was raised between 1869 and 1884. To the left of the entrance, the former **billiard room** (now library), lit by an oriel window and with a traceried stone arcade. The door surrounds were elaborately carved by *Hedley*, and the richly coloured stained-glass window to the corridor is by *Sowerby* and *Barnett* (information from Neil Moat). It belongs to the 1884 work, as do the delicate grisaille windows with inset panels of flowers in the top-lit former **Picture Gallery**, which was added to the w end of the house by *Spence* to display Mitchell's collection. It also has an elaborately carved triple-panelled door surround [166], and an ornate stucco frieze and cornice to the panelled ceiling.

Back w to Towers Avenue, and n along Friday Fields, an unmarked lane to Jesmond Dene Road, then e to see **Jesmond Dene House**, now a hotel, sitting within the dene. The house built in 1822 by *Dobson* for T.E. Headlam and altered by the architect in 1851 was subsequently enlarged for Sir Andrew Noble, a partner in Armstrong's business. First the rear wing (1870–1), then rooms towards the front (1875), and a billiard room (1885), all by *Norman Shaw*. All this was extended or replaced in 1896–7 by *F.W. Rich*. He continued Shaw's Tudor style in a more cheerful vein, with some half-timbering, some render, an oriel window, and a corbel table with Arts and Crafts carving. Inside is a Great Hall with gallery, Jacobean-style panelling, a large fireplace, rich use of stone (Frosterley marble fender) and tiles, and a roof with moulded beams, corbelled arch trusses, and bosses. The staircase is not grand, only a small affair tucked in the thickness of the fireplace wall. Tiles by *de Morgan* in the sitting room fireplace. The hotel has added an entrance porch, stair and conservatory (by *Darbyshire & Kendall*). The former **stables** to the w are simple but well built; two ranges with a gabled lodge attached, and some original stalls. On **Matthew Bank,** further n, is the house's wonderful **real tennis court**, built *c.* 1900 by *F.W. Rich* and still used by a private club. Bright red brick (Flemish garden-wall bond), and the plain tiles which are almost Rich's trademark. He made a large block lively by the application of buttresses, tall octagonal corner turrets, and big round windows high in the s wall. Pent entrance at one end and a single-bay two-storey apartment for the professional player at the other.

Matthew Bank is a bus route. Alternatively, Jesmond Dene Road runs w to Ilford Road, with a Metro station to the n.

Gosforth

Before 1974 Gosforth was in Northumberland, but local government reorganization made it part of the new City of Newcastle District. It retains its distinct identity, principally because the Town Moor separates it from the former City. Gosforth has grown around the Great North Road, its present line being that of the c18 turnpike crossing the Moor. Before quarries and coal mines brought workers to the area, there is little evidence for anything other than two medieval churches: St Nicholas, at the long-vanished colliery village of South Gosforth, and a chapel in North Gosforth, now ruined.

167. Gosforth

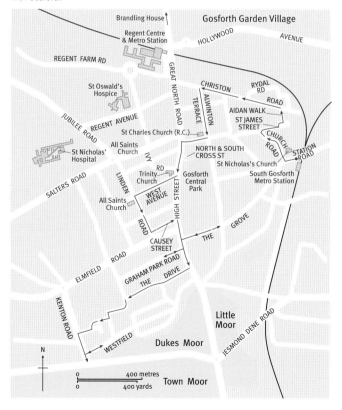

168. St Nicholas, Church Avenue, by John Dodds, 1799, galleried aisle and south porch by John Dobson, 1820 and 1833, extended by Hicks & Charlewood, 1913

Modern Gosforth began near **South Gosforth Metro Station**, Station Road. The Metro line (*see* topic box, p. 38) was originally part of the Blyth & Tyne Railway (1865); a sturdy cast-iron **footbridge** of *c.* 1891 survives. The Tudor-style station was demolished for the **Control Centre** of 1980 by *Ainsworth Spark Associates* in the cutting, a smoked-glass box, the upper floor projecting over the w platform. A curved corrugated canopy shelters the other platform.

Across the road, **St Nicholas's Church** [168] (Gosforth Parish Church) of 1799 by *John Dodds*, a classical church on a medieval site, on high ground w of the Ouseburn. 1799 saw a simple box: nave, apsed chancel, w gallery, and w tower with sturdy octagonal stone spire. *John Dobson* in 1818–20 added galleried aisles with Tuscan columns and wide elliptical arches, with a new doorway between the two w windows in the s aisle; tower s porch 1833. Restoration, and N porch, by *R. J. Johnson*, 1884. In 1913 *Hicks & Charlewood* extended the building E, lengthening the nave by one bay, blocking Dobson's s door, building a wide chancel, a Lady Chapel, and a second N aisle, and removing the galleries. To this much-altered building a clergy vestry was added in 1959. Local sandstone was always used, hammer-dressed blocks with tooled dressings, cleaned in the early 2000s and now varying shades of grey. The N tower porch has two re-set fragments of medieval dripmould. Plain tower arch; recessed round-headed windows throughout. The 1913 alterations, including the Venetian window with keyed surround, curved to fit the apse, are in keeping, but have Ionic columns at the chancel and apse arches. The *œil de bœuf* windows originally lit the galleries. – **Reredos** and chancel wood-panelled, **altar** in the same restrained classical style, all by *Hicks & Charlewood*. – **Stained glass**. E windows, 1917, and w tower window, 1893, by *Kempe* or *Kempe & Co.* s aisle w window by *Wailes*, c. 1840, resited from the apse. Strong blue and red in Gothic style, with the Evangelists and their symbols. Several windows to young men who died in the Great War, e.g. that signed by *Swaine Bourne*, N aisle. Above the vestry door, Flight into Egypt, c. 1952, by *L. C. Evetts*. Two more by him in the chancel, 1985. – **Monuments**. Plain early C19 tablets, some by *G. Green* and one by *Davies*; and one to William Vincent von Hompesch Count of the Holy Roman Empire, d.1839 (N aisle). The **churchyard** has many headstones still fortunately *in situ*, and to the NE of the church the large severely Greek **vault** of the Brandling family, probably early C19.

Beside the NW path a fallen **stone** inscribed Main Dike marks the main or 90-fathom dike, a geological fault running across SE Northumberland below this point and displacing the coal seams. In 1829 Gosforth Colliery broke through it to coal on the other side, and celebrated by holding a ball a 1,000 ft below ground.

N of St Nicholas, in a group of streets named after Northumbrian saints, lies a cluster of pebbledashed *Tarran* bungalows [169], i.e. **prefabricated houses** provided by the government under the Housing (Temporary Accommodation) Act of 1944. They are reached from the church NW along Church Road, then E along St James Street. At the E end of **Aidan Walk**, to the N, is another **Main Dike stone**, a round-topped slab dated 1828 set in the grass verge. Further N, beyond the flats along Christon Road, **Rydal Road** has the 'Howard' type of prefab, designed by *Frederick Gibberd*: two storeys, now brick-clad with porches.

169. Aidan Walk, Tarran prefabricated bungalows, *c.* 1946

w along Christon Road, and s down Alwinton Terrace to **St Charles (R.C.)**, 1911. By *C.J. Menart*, born in Belgium and trained in Great Britain, whose work was mainly in the Glasgow diocese. Darkened rock-faced sandstone, with vaguely Perp windows and ashlar w towers; a large glass 1970s w porch. Large parish centre by *Darbyshire Architects*, 2005, to the N. Porch and reordering by Bill Stonor of *Faulkner-Brown Hendy Watkinson Stonor*, 1985–6. Striking **stained glass** of 1946 by *Harry Clarke Studios*, two very large windows in the transepts, and one in the s clerestory.

Then w along Church Road, and s into the C19 **High Street**, passing on the w side a small Romanesque former Wesleyan Methodist church. On the E side **North Cross Street** and **South Cross Street**, of early C19 origin: cobbled lanes, low stone cottages now in commercial use. To the s, in the gable of the building N of the Brandling Arms pub, a re-set stone records the name used locally until *c.* 1950 for High Street and its houses: Bulman Village. Opposite, a block of small shops, built in the early C20 as the stone frontage of a tram shed. Next, on the angle between Ivy Road (with its castellated chimney pots) and West Avenue, **Trinity Church.** This former Methodist church of 1877 by *Septimus Oswald & Son* unites three Nonconformist congregations; adapted and enlarged by *Stephen Crichton Architects*, 2007–8. The adjacent ex-United Reformed church, Gothic with the customary paired pointed arches to the lobby, is now a restaurant. On the E side is **Gosforth shopping centre**, a two-storey 1980s block: modest in scale, and for its time comparatively respectful of its setting.

Up West Avenue to Linden Road, and **All Saints**, a good prosperous suburban church of 1885–7 by *R.J. Johnson*; prominent w tower of 1896 (executed by *W.S. Hicks*), a memorial to Lyulf Cochrane. Battlemented, with high buttresses. Big seven-light Dec E window, triple w lancets and straight-headed Perp aisle and clerestory windows; Tudor-flowered corbel tables. Inside, the five-bay nave and two-bay chancel have tall octagonal piers; tall chancel arch. Much **wood carving** by *Ralph Hedley*, including a lacy chancel screen, choir stalls with poppyheads, and the reredos and screen (designed by *Johnson*). Excellent **font** and cover, 1906 by *Crawford Hick*. High-quality **stained glass**: N aisle, one with Northumbrian saints by *Bayne* (to F.W. Bindley, Rector, d.1892); another to the architect W.S. Hicks, 1904 by *Bryans*. The striking E window of 1887 is by *Heaton, Butler & Bayne*.

From All Saints, s down Linden Road, and into the narrow Causey Street, second left; note the C19 terrace of stone **cottages**, supposedly built for the corve-makers of Coxlodge Colliery (corves were baskets in which coals were brought up the mineshaft). Back on the **High Street**, a stone villa of *c.* 1840 and two terraces of *c.* 1860 on the E side, followed by **The Grove**, another terrace of *c.* 1860, running E. On its N side still much original detail, although the coachhouses behind would not now be recognized by their first owners. The mid-C19 character of this area is defined by trees and leafy gardens, (restored) iron railings, and

170. Graham Court, High Street, by Clifford Wyld, built 1951–2

especially the high stone walls of the crossing with Moor Road. The s
side of The Grove has Gothic semis, and pleasant houses of *c.* 1900 in
bright red brick.

Now back s down the **High Street** to **Graham Park Road** on the w
side, and **Graham Court** [170]: three groups of six council flats and
their garages, designed 1948–9 by the District Surveyor *Clifford Wyld*,
and built 1951–2. Pale brick, metal windows with projecting concrete
surrounds, balconies, big sloping canopies over three entrances.
Ingeniously planned interiors, with glazed bricks to light letter boxes,
glazed screens between living and dining rooms, and chutes for
rubbish. Two turnings further s is **The Drive**, with No. 2, perhaps
c. 1900, formerly the lodge to Coxlodge Hall (rebuilt after a fire,
1877, dem. *c.* 1936). Oddly French-looking amidst Northern sobriety:
keyed stone surrounds to elliptical-headed windows. Further along

The Drive, the former **stables** of Coxlodge Hall (now offices), built *c.* 1796 for Job Bulman. A symmetrical sandstone building with a clock tower over a pedimented centre, and a keyed oculus in the pediment. The incongruous Corinthian porch is an addition of *c.* 1950. Between here and the Town Moor the **Graham Park Estate** was developed from 1905 by *William Hope* and *Joseph Maxwell*: semis, villas and Queen Anne terraces.

A diversion to the w: opposite the Moor at the corner of Grandstand Road (so called because Newcastle racecourse was at one time on the Moor) and Kenton Road, stands **Kenton Lodge** (now a residential school). A Queen Anne house of *c.* 1908 by *Newcombe & Newcombe* for Max Holzapfel (i.e. crab apple; hence the central bunches of iron apples on the wrought-iron gates, s). Good lettering in low relief on the later Newcastle Education Committee panel above. To the E on Westfield, **Moor Court**, private flats by *C. Solomon*, 1938, in the streamlined style.

Other Buildings, to North, East and West

The description runs chiefly from sw to N, for those wishing to walk.

St Nicholas's Hospital, Jubilee Road. 1869 by *W. L. Moffatt* as the borough lunatic asylum; additions 1886–8 by *A. B. Plummer,* 1892–6 by *J. W. Dyson*, and later; some parts sensitively converted to flats by *Darbyshire & Kendall*, 1990s. An assortment of buildings punctuated by two square towers. The recreation hall has large round-headed windows with two sub-arches and a roundel in each, not very different in style from the buildings around, but there is one astonishing feature: a *Doulton*-tiled proscenium arch by *W. J. Neatby* in Art Nouveau style, dated 1896: the only one of its kind in any hospital. Female figures in flowing robes float beside richly coloured trees with sinuous branches and roots, while tall flowers rise from ground carpeted by simple daisies.

St Oswald's Hospice, Regent Avenue. 1984–7 and later by *J. & D. Darbyshire* (project architect *Jane Darbyshire*); landscape architects *Kendrick Associates Landscape*. Warm brick, timber verandas, low-pitched roofs, and an interesting garden with roofed walks give this small group of buildings a reassuringly domestic air. Bedrooms look onto the garden, and the whole group is sheltered from the street by a high-walled car park.

Regent Centre, Great North Road. A 1960s office complex, a swimming pool of 1967–8 to the s by *Waring & Netts*, with the adjacent library (storey added in 2007), and a **Metro station** and **bus interchange** of 1981 to the w. Exposed aggregate piers, vitreous enamel panels for the station and the rooftop car park, with an open-deck roof over the porte cochère for buses. The original **office blocks**, now mostly refurbished, had plain lines and much glass. The most interesting was Northern Rock House, 1967–8 by *Richard Turley Associates*, a tall slender tower demolished in 2006. Its replacement of 2007–8 belongs with extensive work here by *Red Box Architecture*. D-plan, brick to the s, glass-clad to the N.

171. Brandling House (formerly Gosforth House), by James Paine, 1755–64; now racecourse grandstand

To the SE, **Gosforth Civic Hall**, concert hall not town hall, 1974 by *Mauchlen, Weightman & Elphick*. On a more domestic scale, with warm red bricks and a polygonal theme carried through from entrance hall to raised flowerbeds and tiled forecourt.

Opposite Regent Centre Metro, E of the Great North Road along Hollywood Avenue, the **Gosforth Garden Village**. Streets of neat red brick houses built by the North Eastern Railway to designs by *Stephen Wilkinson* for purchase by workers at the nearby railway sheds. All have gardens; many still with 'sunburst' iron gates. The Gosforth Garden Village Trust, 1921–59, managed the estate.

Gosforth Park (Newcastle Racecourse), North Gosforth, 1¾m. NNE of the Regent Centre. Gosforth House, now called **Brandling House** [171]. By *James Paine*, 1755–64 for Charles Brandling, coal-owner and M.P. Deep within the park, it backs onto the drive, facing s over the landscape towards Newcastle, largely undeveloped until the C19. The original interior was destroyed by fire in 1914; the s front suffered the addition of the grandstand of the racecourse established there in 1881 by the High Gosforth Park Co. The **entrance front**, N, has lower wings breaking forward. The large main block – almost 90 ft (28 metres) square – has three storeys and seven bays, the projecting centre with a dentilled open pediment. Rusticated half-basement. Those windows at the centre and ends of the *piano nobile* have *Paine*'s blind balustrades to the aprons, jambs with long slender outswept curves, and segmental pediments, the central one on brackets. Over the corresponding window of the attic storey is a floating cornice, carrying the eye to Paine's typical open pediment. Similar discipline controls the plainer wings flanking the yard, which have E and W sides developed as minor façades, also with projecting middle bays and pediments. On the s front, seven bays, but only the rusticated basement with end niches, and the first-floor windows with architrave surrounds, are visible: the whole composition can be imagined only with difficulty. It had a slightly projecting three-bay centre stressed by coupled pilasters at the angles and single pilasters between. The principal windows are pedimented, the central first-floor window arched; a three-bay pediment. The **grandstand** which obscures so much is itself interesting: late C19 quasi-Ionic cast-iron columns support the glass roof.

Park House, across the drive to the NE, was the estate steward's house, and may be of 1760 by *Paine*. Sandstone, with two-storey, three-bay centre and lower two-bay wings. The main block has a central open pediment, but alterations have destroyed its original symmetry, which had a central door below a round-headed window. Deeply cut voussoirs to the other windows, and rusticated quoins. The entrance to Gosforth Park and the racecourse from the w is thoroughly impressive: two large **gatepiers** of 1830, by *Dobson*, incorporating the Brandling arms carved in high relief. The **lodge** is simple, with a classical doorcase.

For other buildings in outer Gosforth *see The Buildings of England: Northumberland*.

Shipcote and Gateshead Fell

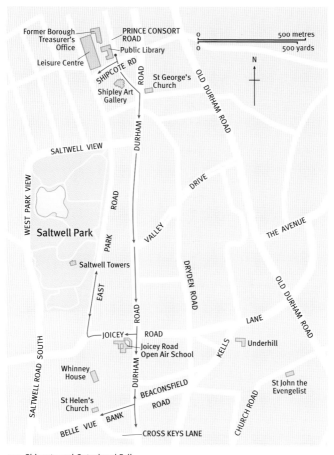

Former Borough
Treasurer's
Office

PRINCE CONSORT
ROAD

Public Library

Leisure Centre

SHIPCOTE RD

ROAD

St George's
Church

Shipley Art
Gallery

OLD DURHAM ROAD

DURHAM

SALTWELL VIEW

WEST PARK VIEW

ROAD

DRIVE

Saltwell Park

PARK

VALLEY

THE AVENUE

Saltwell Towers

EAST

DRYDEN ROAD

OLD DURHAM ROAD

ROAD

LANE

JOICEY

ROAD

Joicey Road
Open Air School

KELLS

Underhill

SALTWELL ROAD SOUTH

Whinney
House

DURHAM

St Helen's
Church

BEACONSFIELD

ROAD

St John the
Evengelist

BELLE VUE

BANK

CHURCH ROAD

CROSS KEYS LANE

0   500 metres
0   500 yards

N

172. Shipcote and Gateshead Fell

In 1800 Gateshead was still essentially three main streets forming a **T** at the s end of Tyne Bridge. The upright, the old North Road from London, ran s over Gateshead Fell towards Chester-le-Street and Durham. The early development of the area was summarized by Mackenzie in 1827: 'Thirty years ago, the Fell was studded with

173. Gateshead Borough Treasurer's Department, Prince Consort Road, by A. Leslie Berry, 1954, Ratings Hall ceiling

miserable mud cottages, inhabited by tinkers, cloggers, travelling potters, besom-makers... A sod cottage is now a rarity even on Gateshead Fell; and this year the gentry of the place had a concert ... for the benefit of Mr G. Bagnall, organist of St John's on the Fell [*see* p. 268] ... most fashionably attended.' Also in 1827, the windswept road on High Fell was by-passed by a new route lower down to the w, the New Durham Road (later Durham Road). This passes through Low Fell, which was distinguished by its denes, partly wooded, cut by streams running w to the River Team. These drew wealthy C19 businessmen to build their villas on the hillside looking across the Team Valley towards Ravensworth Castle.*

This walk starts just w of the 'new' Durham Road at the group of civic buildings in Shipcote, reached from central Gateshead by bus or on foot along Prince Consort Road, through pre-1878 terraces. Then from High Fell down to C19 Low Fell, in 1879 'a pretty village ... [with] several handsome residences of merchants and manufacturers of Gateshead and Newcastle' (Kelly's *Directory*) and back N via Saltwell Park.

The start is the group of C20 civic buildings in Shipcote, by the corner of Prince Consort Road and Shipcote Lane, just w of the 'new' Durham Road, at **Gateshead Public Library**, 1925–6. This was designed in 1918 by *Arthur Stockwell* of Newcastle, who then died. His plans were adapted by *David Ditchburn* to meet reduced funding. It is in a subdued

---

***Ravensworth Castle**, 2m. sw, is now a romantic ruin in dense woods. Of C14 origin, it was transformed for the Liddell family with works of 1724 and before 1759 (by *James Paine*). These were demolished in 1808 for a new house for Sir Thomas Liddell by *John Nash*, who incorporated two of the C14 towers. The Nash work was completed after *c.* 1822 by *Thomas Henry Liddell*, the owner's amateur architect son. The house was demolished in 1950–3 because of subsidence caused, ironically, by coal mines, the source of the family's wealth. The medieval towers remain, with an early C19 stable block, and the fine E lodge alongside the A1 road.

Baroque style with the doorway recessed between shallow-domed pavilions, linked by a big cornice and balustrade. Quoins, pedimented eared window surrounds. One-storey wings set back slightly behind. Entry is via the right return and a glazed stair hall of 1975–6 to the red brick extension of 1973 by *Leslie Berry*, Borough Architect (restoration of the original entrance is expected). Inside, a striking ceramic **mural**, Across the Waters, from exchanges with Gateshead's twin town Komatsu, 1996. By *Christine Constant, Jane Hufton, Junko Tokuda* and *Shuhei Koshita*, collaborating with local people. Set back N of the library, the former **Borough Treasurer's Department**, 1954, red brick, meant as the first stage of a new Civic Centre. The s part contains a circular Ratings Hall [173]. N part successfully enlarged (by *Berry*, 1972–4) by an added storey of tinted glass and anodized aluminium. Immediately to the w is the wide-spreading, uncluttered, red brick **Leisure Centre** by the *Borough Architect* for Gateshead, 1982. Here another mural of 1996, Bridges of Friendship.

s of the library, the **Shipley Art Gallery** [174], 1914–17. Also by *Arthur Stockwell*, larger than his library, and again Baroque. Wide portico with four Corinthian columns between rusticated end towers. On the towers, seated figures of Art (left) and Industry and Learning (right) by *W. Birnie Rhind*. Inside, original galleries, parquet floors, excellent fittings. J.A.D. Shipley, d.1909, had left his large art collection and a bequest of £30,000 to Newcastle to provide a gallery and Mansion House. Despite suggestions that Newcastle's Public Library Committee might provide a site next to the Laing Art Gallery (p. 186), built in 1903–4 without a permanent collection, this was eventually rejected. His executors turned instead to his home town, and were accepted.

174. Shipley Art Gallery, Prince Consort Road, by Arthur Stockwell, 1914–17

Just s of the entrance, a remarkable **memorial** by *George Burn* to James Renforth, one of the rowing heroes of Tyneside, who died in 1871 during an Anglo-American race at New Brunswick (huge levels of betting caused suspicion of foul play, but he had suffered a heart attack). Renforth is supported by his fellow rower; the plinth has carved ripples, and the inscription IN THE MIDST OF LIFE, WE ARE IN DEATH. Moved from Gateshead East Cemetery in 1992.

Across the way, the town's superb **war memorial** [175] faces down Durham Road. 1922, signed *J. W. Spink*, architect. Projecting centre, high rusticated base with a bronze door, with relief coat of arms and inscription. Well-cut inscription above, MORS JANUA VITAE ('Death the gate to life'). An Ionic aedicule frames a large high-relief bronze by *Richard Goulden*, a powerful figure, caped and wearing a helmet, with sword at rest, standing in front of a broad-armed cross. The chamber formerly held a Book of Remembrance. E of the busy junction, the church of **St George**, 1894–7 by *Stephen Piper*. A strong presence among the C19 and C20 suburban terraces N and s of it. Tall, gabled sw tower, and a high w window over three low gables; E.E. style; all in rock-faced stone.

One turning further s on the w side of Durham Road is **Gateshead Technical College** of 1949–55 etc. Due for demolition in 2008–9; housing by *Feilden Clegg Bradley* may take its place. On this stretch of road, professionals and industrialists built villas after 1850, picturesquely set on the lower fellside. (The College replaced three of these: Enfield House, possibly by *Septimus Oswald*, Neoclassical with an Italianate tower by *Newcombe & Knowles*; Park View; and Bloomfield, originally Walker Villa.) Next to the s (inaccessible from the road), **North Dene House**, *c.* 1860, ashlar with a pilastered porch flanked by tripartite windows, big eaves and prominent quoins. C20 houses surround **Heathfield House**, a simple two-storey villa, canted bays flanking the door, big eaves on paired brackets. 1856 by *John Wardle*; alterations *c.* 1900. Its imposing **gateway** on Durham Road has Doric entablatures supporting lions carved by *Anthony Kell* and *John Lamb Burnie*. The grounds are enclosed by high stone walls. Across Durham Road to the E, **Musgrave House**, 1854–5. Recently a school, but empty at the time of writing. Tudor/C17-style ashlar. Three bays with raised quoins, and mullioned-and-transomed windows; bargeboarded gables on the end bays, fish-scale roof slates.

Back on the w side, at the s corner with Joicey Road, the former **Joicey Road Open Air School,** 1936–7. A fine example of a once-common type. The *Borough Engineer*'s plans were based upon those of 1904 for a school at Charlottenburg near Berlin, copied in London by 1907. Brick, with Neo-Georgian arched windows to the main buildings, and fully opening windows on one side of the square classroom pavilions behind. The school was built in part of the wooded grounds of **Whinney House**, now **Gateshead Academy for Torah Studies**, built *c.* 1865 by Edward Joicey, a partner in the colliery-owning firm of Joicey & Co. Large, Italianate, with a pyramid-roofed tower to allow views.

175. Gateshead,
War Memorial,
Durham Road, by
J.W. Spink, 1922

Doric pilasters frame the windows. The elevations have moulded corners and projecting centres; deep eaves with paired, moulded brackets.
The architect is not yet known. The grounds (not accessible) were
equally ambitious, the existing dene landscaped by *Albany Hancock*,
brother of John, the Newcastle naturalist (*see* footnote below).
The conservatory, gazebo and greenhouses have gone, but a fountain
remains. C20 office block, E, presumably on the site of stables. The
grounds are enclosed on Durham Road by slender iron railings.*

At the S of the garden a timber footbridge across Whinney House
Dene gave private access to **St Helen's Church** on Belle Vue Bank.
Edward Joicey gave the land and paid £13,000 for this lovely E.E. church
by *John Wardle Jun.*, 1873–6. Of rock-faced stone, the porch-tower with
broach spire. The foundation stone was laid by Joicey's children –
Edward, Ellen and Mary Kate. Fine late *Morris & Co.* stained glass in the

---

*The *Gateshead Observer* noted (26 August 1876) that Mr Mawson, the Newcastle chemist
who built the modest **Ashfield House**, now a nursery, off East Park Road and S of Heathfield
House, with gardens by the Newcastle naturalist, *John Hancock*, had 'placed a light railing on
the side of his grounds . . . so that every passer-by might partake of the enjoyment afforded
by gazing upon the beauties of nature'.

lancets: nave s side E, 1900, and N side, 1901 (E) and 1920, all to *Burne-Jones* designs; nave N, 1920 (Simeon) by *H. Dearle*; two-light window of 1923 with designs by *Dearle* (Good Shepherd, left), and *Burne-Jones* (Humility). Also one in the s transept signed *G.J. Baguley*, Newcastle, and apse windows by *Wailes*.

Durham Road at the junction with Belle Vue Bank becomes the high street of **Low Fell** except in name, still with the character of a village, although no building is earlier than the 1820s turnpike. The use of the grainy local sandstone, often turned black from decades of coal smoke, has mellowed it, and there is little sign of Victorian exuberance: a barge-board here, a porch there. It is very pleasant to wander among the lanes and streets and genteel houses of the C19, whether villas or terraces. On the w side of Durham Road, N of Cross Keys Lane, No. 516, a stone building with a domestic air. It was a **reading room** and school for workers and their children, built by subscription at the instigation of Thomas Wilson in 1841 to designs by *Thomas Oliver*. In front of the shops, w, a **South African War memorial** of 1903, signed *Morrison*: a soldier, with rifle.

The return N, via Joicey Road and East Park Road, takes in **Saltwell Park** and the most remarkable of the villas, **Saltwell Towers** [176]. It was built from 1862 for *William Wailes*, a renowned Newcastle stained-glass designer and manufacturer, in an eccentric castle style with lively turreted roofscape. Probably designed by him, using engineering bricks of dark red, with black bands and light buff details. He developed the extensive grounds in 1853–70 with features including castellated belvederes, before financial difficulties made him sell it all to Gateshead Corporation in 1876. He remained as tenant. The house was a hospital 1914–18, in 1933–69 the town museum. Empty, it suffered fire damage and lost most of its interior. The restoration of house and park since 1999, assisted by the Heritage Lottery Fund, has been one of Gateshead's recent triumphs.

The **park** was designed by *Edward Kemp* in 1876, the town's second public park after Windmill Hills (p. 226), with modifications and additions by the Borough Surveyor *James Bowyer*. It was extended s in 1920. The park incorporates Saltwell Dene, and has winding paths, a boating lake and bowling greens, a maze, a promenade on the E side with rustic shelters, a drinking fountain which Wailes moved here in 1872, 1880s stable block and aviaries, and E and w lodges, the former of 1882. s of the house, **memorial** to seventy-seven local men who died in the South African War. A bronze figure of winged Peace by *F.W. Doyle Jones*, on a tall, tapered square column, its frieze with cartouches on each side. Unveiled 1905.

Outlying Buildings

Underhill (**No. 99 Kells Lane**), reached from Durham Road up Beaconsfield Road E of the crossing with Belle Vue Bank, became the first private house anywhere lit by electricity, *c.* 1878. It is triple-gabled,

176. Saltwell Towers, Saltwell Park, probably by William Wailes, from 1862

of roughly dressed snecked sandstone with bright red and white dressings. Here Joseph (later Sir Joseph) Swan conducted pioneering experiments in photographic processing and in electricity, fitting his house with the circuits and incandescent light bulbs that he had invented.

177. St John the Evangelist, Church Road, by John Ions and Ignatius Bonomi, 1824–5

St John the Evangelist [177], Gateshead Fell, a short way down Church Road, E of Durham Road. A new church, authorized by the 1809 Enclosure Act and built 1824–5. Designed by the mason *John Ions*, subject to improvements by the architect *Ignatius Bonomi*. A modest ashlar building, without aisles, its four-bay nave and lower single-bay chancel with Y-traceried windows. The w tower has similar tracery in its battlemented topmost stage. Raine's biography of the Rev. John Hodgson of Heworth (1857) claimed that Hodgson suggested the tall, slender spire, a landmark for miles around. In the extensive church-yard, E, a tall **obelisk** commemorates a quarryman (i.e. owner) killed in an 1840 railway accident. S of the nave, the Leathart family **tomb** has two large plain slabs bridged by a parallel richly carved red slab.

Excursions

St Paul, Jarrow

Church Bank, East Jarrow. 6m. E of central Newcastle and
Gateshead; 0.3m. NW of Bede Metro Station

When the Durham historian William Hutchinson visited Jarrow in 1782
he noted only 'two or three mean cottages' near the church. The town
grew in the C19 as chemical, coal-mining and shipbuilding industries
developed, but in the 1930s became the victim of economic problems.
The 1936 'Jarrow March', when 200 men petitioned Whitehall for
employment, is famous. But so too is a man who lived there 1,300 years
earlier: Bede, the great historian of the English church. Now the town
celebrates the scholar monk with a museum and a re-created Anglo-
Saxon village at Bede's World on Church Bank.

The monastery was founded by Benedict Biscop, a Northumbrian
noble, in 681–2, on land given by King Ecgfrith. It was a sister-house to
his earlier foundation (674) at Wearmouth – modern Monkwearmouth
(Sunderland). Biscop became a monk, admired Roman culture and
frequently visited Rome, returning with books and pictures for his two
monasteries. He placed those monasteries directly under Papal jurisdiction.

The Tyne at Jarrow then had a nearly square tidal inlet, Jarrow Slake
or Slack. The monastery was near the water's edge, and salt marshes
bordered the River Don as it crossed the mudflats. Ballast-dumping
changed the shoreline, until mid-C19 river improvements deepened and
narrowed the Tyne's channel. The Slake became timber ponds, then a
car-shipping depot was built on it, and now the sinuous Don that Bede
knew is channelled along the Slake's western edge.

The Church

St Paul's church [178] was begun in 684. Re-set in the E wall of the nave,
above the tower arch, the oldest surviving church **dedication stone** in
the country gives the date, 23 April 685. The present chancel is the survivor of two Saxon churches here, the other, w, larger, probably that
referred to in the inscription. Both seem to have had square E ends.
Linking walls were built between the two, and upon them was raised the
C11–C12 tower.

178. St Paul, Jarrow, 684–5, with C11–C12 tower, and nave by Sir G.G. Scott, 1866, left

179. St Paul, fragments of reset Anglo-Saxon glass

The visitor sees first the twin-roofed **nave and** N **aisle** by *Sir G.G. Scott* of 1866, which replaced an C18 nave. This itself replaced the large Saxon basilica/church described in 1782 as being 'in a very ruinous State & Condition . . . so dangerous & unsafe to assemble therein that for some time past divine service has been regularly performed in the chancel'. A glass floor panel reveals cobble foundations of the Saxon N wall; the s wall was under the present wall. In the N aisle are displayed impressive early sculptured stones found during alterations to the church. The tower has a plain ribbed quadripartite vault, and round-headed E and w arches.

Entering the **chancel**, the change of scale and fabric is immediately felt; a tall, narrow space; tiny, deeply splayed windows; large quoins. The simplicity is deceptive: in Bede's time there would have been religious paintings, richly carved and painted sculpture, and other furnishings. High in the s wall, three round-headed original windows, two still with thin stone slabs (transennae) that held the precious coloured glass, one without that slab; two are filled with pieces of Anglo-Saxon **glass** [179] found in C20 excavations. To the right of the altar, a round-headed aumbry. In the N wall a round-headed doorway, now blocked, with narrow monolith jambs. C14 three-light windows: E, with intersecting tracery; w end of s wall, with cusped tracery. In the N wall, w, a slightly later straight-headed window with elliptical rere-arch to three trefoils above lancet tracery.

The Monastery

Of the first stone **monastery**, s of the church, no original buildings survive, and of the later ones none stand to full height. Professor Rosemary Cramp's excavations between 1963 and 1978 have revealed their plan. Anglo-Saxon walls are now indicated by lines of plain flat stones, later medieval walls by cobbles. The first monastery had rows of buildings and fruit and vegetable gardens filling the slope down to the river. Beside the church was the monks' burial ground; then a row with refectory with kitchen added to the s, and upper dormitory. Separated from it by a narrow passage, there was a hall, an oratory, and another dormitory above. There were *opus signinum* floors (concrete and crushed red tile); walls were plastered, the roofs covered in tiles and lead; windows had coloured glass. To the s, beside the Don, was a richly decorated building, probably a guesthouse, which later became workshops.

That Saxon monastery was eventually abandoned in 874–5 after Viking raids. In 1072 Aldwin, Prior of Winchcombe, brought two monks from Evesham to establish the restored Benedictine rule at Jarrow. Bishop Walcher of Durham gave financial help, and eventually both Jarrow and Wearmouth became cells of Durham. The Benedictine monastery, built by 1083, followed the by then usual plan, with the church along the N side of the cloisters, three ranges along the other sides, and at the SE a reredorter (latrine) attached to the upper dormitories and draining into the Don. The highest standing wall, at the w, has two original doors, one with a triangular head, and one blocked door at the s. So much has survived of this wall because it was incorporated into a C17 house, since cleared away.

At **Bede's World** on Church Bank, N, excavation finds are displayed, and the story of the monastery told, in the 1995 **gallery** designed by *Evans & Shalev*. On the high ground next to it is **Jarrow Hall**, red brick Late Georgian. Built *c.* 1785 for Simon Temple, who acquired wealth from coal mines, glass manufacturing and shipbuilding, it was for a time the site museum.

Tynemouth Priory and Castle

Pier Road, Tynemouth. 8m. ENE of central Newcastle and Gateshead; 0.3m. E of Tynemouth Metro Station.

Northumberland is famous for its castles; the early medieval kingdom of Northumbria, between the Humber and Forth rivers, is renowned for its early Christian sites. This headland had both, until in 1539 Henry VIII closed the monastery; the monks left, the buildings decayed. The fortress remained to defend the Tyne. For a fuller account *see The Buildings of England: Northumberland.*

History

This is a densely layered site, occupied from prehistoric times to the C20. High cliffs on three sides made seaborne attack difficult, and the peninsula's neck controlled landward access. There were round Iron Age houses, timber-walled, probably behind a western bank and ditch. Then the first monastery had rectangular timber buildings, one with a round end perhaps the church. The body of St Oswine was brought here in 651 and King Osred of Northumbria buried here in 792. Those relics brought fame and pilgrims to the headland. Less welcome visitors were Danish raiders, looting Lindisfarne (793) and other East Coast monasteries. At Tynemouth in 794 the monks drove them back to their ships, but Matthew Paris records that the monastery was finally destroyed in 875. By 1066 there was a new monastic settlement here, with a church for the town. The monastery was a daughter house first of Durham (where the successors to St Cuthbert's Lindisfarne community settled in 995) and then of St Alban's Abbey in Hertfordshire, by gift of the Norman Earl of Northumberland, Robert de Mowbray, who had quarrelled with the Bishop of Durham.

William II besieged Tynemouth in 1095, so there were stone defences by then. The monks built a stone church, and on 20 August 1110 St Oswine's remains were transferred to a richly decorated shrine in this Norman church. Before 1200 the church was given a magnificent E end to hold that shrine. A gatehouse was probably built in 1296, but became derelict, and was rebuilt in the 1390s to ward off increasing Scottish raids. In the church, the shrine was moved, perhaps to prevent disruption of services, probably to the new Lady Chapel at the NE corner of the Presbytery. A small, richly decorated E chapel was added in the C15.

180. Tynemouth Priory, east end and south transept west arch, C12 and C13

Henry VIII knew the value of the Castle in protecting Newcastle, an important port if attacks were threatened from Scotland, and the source of vital coal supplies to London. Advised by the Italian *Gian Tommaso Scala* and the English engineer *Sir Richard Lee*, he improved its defences; the present altered earthworks still reflect the style of that period with big, pointed bastions at N and S. The Royalist garrison was captured and retaken more than once in the 1640s. Although the church nave became the parish church, destruction of the monastery increased after the Civil War. Parliament repaired the Castle and in 1658 began a parish church in North Shields, built from 1663 by *Robert Trollope* (rebuilt 1792). In the 1660s the Castle Governor Col. Edward Villiers employed Trollope to build new barracks, a lighthouse and a Governor's house (where the disused Coastguard Station now stands), and, in the upper level of the church, a magazine, using stone from the Priory.

During the C18 and C19 the Board of Ordnance built gun batteries, magazines and nearby barracks for 1,000 men, damaging monastic buildings and the Gatehouse. From 1905 the site was managed by the Ministry of Works (later English Heritage) and gradually restored, while gun batteries remained in use until the 1940s.

The Castle

From Front Street, the medieval castle dominates, with massive ramparts flanking the high stone gatehouse and its barbican. C19 quarrying of stone for Tynemouth's North Pier has changed the medieval ditch, but the **barbican** still controls the entrance. Attackers, once within it between the first gate and the barred inner gate, were at the mercy of soldiers on the walls above. The **Gatehouse** was perhaps improved in the C15 (it reputedly bore the coat of arms of a C15 prior). It had battlemented walls with machicolations and corner turrets, lost when in 1780 a barrack block was built on its upper part (removed in 1936). The Constable of the Castle lived here, with a richly furnished hall on the first floor over the vaulted gateway passage, and a private chamber above it now represented only by a fireplace and joist holes. The kitchen's lower room is now the ticket office and shop. Its E window has become the door to the site, a ramp outside leading to the upper floors, where a solid floor replaces a drawbridge. The first-floor kitchen, S, has an oven and wide fireplace. The doorway high in the N wall of the gatehouse opened onto the castle wall-walk.

The castle **walls** have been much repaired and rebuilt since the C13, and along the S edge of the promontory have been removed by erosion and by the C19 North Pier approaches. Medieval work can be seen at **Whitley Tower**, on the cliff N of the gatehouse, and on the S flank of the castle down the steep slope to Pier Road. Flanking the gate, the sloping walls have bold C17 roll mouldings outside, and raised gun platforms inside.

181. Tynemouth Priory, west front, c13

The Priory

The Priory had the usual monastic **plan**: church along the N side of the cloister, chapter house off the S transept in the cloister E range, refectory on the S side.

The w **elevation** of the church has a richly decorated C13 doorway and trefoil-headed niches for statues; above the door and left, remains of later windows. Outside are foundations of a small square-plan building: the base of a tower which may have been a belfry, later used as a prison. Inside, at the NW, the outlines of the original vaulting, with signs of disturbance; possibly *Trollope* built his magazine here (*see* above). The column bases of the **nave** arcades show that the w bay is an extension of the Norman church: two C13 pairs made up of several shafts; E of these, round bases of Norman columns. The NE Norman pier survives intact, preserved when that E bay of the N aisle was used as part of the post-1539 arrangement. Most of the vaults have gone. The high stone **rood screen** closes the E end of the nave, with arches at each end; heightened to mark off the parish church. **Transepts** and **crossing** are behind the screen; four substantial piers would have supported the crossing tower.

E of the crossing the triple-apsed E end of the small first stone church is marked out. There are foundations of C13 walls to N and S, and bases of the choir arcades. The **Presbytery** at the E end, where the monks sat, is still a fine composition of tall tiered lancets, and on the outside, blank arcading, filling the C13 E gable. At unknown date the E wall was made higher, plain stone walls being inserted between the pointed gable and the corner pinnacles; perhaps a platform was inserted in C16 for a light to warn ships of the treacherous rocks nearby.* A richly moulded C15

*In 1581 the Privy Council reminded the Mayor of Newcastle that a light had been kept 'in the Castle Church', and the papers of Newcastle's Trinity House also mention it.

182. Tynemouth Priory, from the pier, engraving, 1895

door low in the E wall opens to a C15 **chantry chapel**, with superb ribbed vaulting. Sometimes mistakenly called the Lady Chapel; now called the Percy Chantry, because the Percy arms decorate the armorial vaulting bosses. This lovely space, strengthened and its windows blocked, became one of the magazines of the castle during the Napoleonic wars, but *Dobson* restored it in 1850 with new altar and windows, putting a rose window at the E.

Monastic Buildings

The **plan** has been revealed by C19 and C20 excavations and interpreted on the basis of a late C16 survey. At the SE the more substantial remains of the **reredorter** (latrine), and s of that the probable **Prior's Lodging**. This has a vaulted ground-floor room, at present containing interesting architectural fragments from the site.

Other Remains, and Coastal Landmarks

After the new church was consecrated the parish still used the monastic graveyard, holding funeral services in the Percy Chapel. The **graveyard** is fascinating, the inscriptions referring to sailors and merchants, and to John Wright who built many streets in North Shields.

The most significant monument is the C9 **Monk Stone**, brought here in the 1930s; sadly eroded, but old engravings show it richly carved with interlace and animals.

To the E, C19 gun batteries remained in use until the mid C20; ammunition stored below was hoisted to the guns, three facing the sea, two the river. Near the batteries, the sculptural former **Coastguard Station** of *c.* 1968.

Further s, remains of the **Spanish Battery**, mid-c16 outworks. The harbour **piers** and **lighthouses** are of 1854–95 (the N pier rebuilt 1909). Facing s, the **Collingwood Monument** of 1845 by *Dobson*, statue by *Lough*. Nearby, the **Watch Club House**, 1886–7, of the first Life Brigade in the country. At the sw, **Clifford's Fort**, c17, and the **High** and **Low Lights** of 1811 for Newcastle's Trinity House (*see* topic box, p. 125), originating in 1536. 1m. to the N, at **Cullercoats** the arc of the bay ends with the fine spire of **St George**, Beverley Gardens. 1882–4 by *J.L. Pearson* for the 6th Duke of Northumberland; sombre and elegant.

The Angel of the North

Between the A1 and Durham Road (A157), 4 m. SSE of central Gateshead

As the last Northumberland and Durham colliery closes, and ship-building yards make oil rigs, it seems fitting that this pithead (colliery) baths site now holds another piece of North-East engineering made for sculpture- and leisure-loving late C20 society.

Gateshead's National Garden Festival of 1990 left a legacy of sculpture on former industrial land. The Metropolitan Borough Council then decided that this mound at the approach to Gateshead, overlooking the Team valley, A1 road, and East Coast railway line, should carry a monumental piece. In 1993, after consultation with arts bodies, selected sculptors were approached; in January 1994 *Anthony Gormley* was appointed.

The site was difficult, with old mine workings threaded through the strata. The engineers *Ove Arup & Partners* designed a vast concrete sub-structure to reach rock 65 ft (20 metres) below, stabilizing the figure against high winds. The gigantic body, defined by deep vertical ribs, is modelled on the sculptor's, and arm extensions recall an aeroplane's wings. Its rust-like patina is characteristic of the material, Cor-ten steel. The manufacturers were *Hartlepool Fabrications Ltd*; body and wings came by road at night, were assembled on site, and revealed to the world on 16 February 1998. It stands 65 ft (20 metres) high, with wings, bent slightly forward, 176 ft (54 metres) across. The total cost amounted to £1 million, mostly from the National Lottery fund.

At first, the Angel was loathed and loved in equal parts; it has now become accepted as part of local character and is rarely without visitors strolling around its feet. Gormley has said it has three functions: to remind us that below this site coal miners worked in the dark for 200 years, to grasp hold of the future, expressing our transition from the industrial to the information age; and to be a focus for our hopes and fears. Its gigantic welcoming figure has become a symbol of regeneration.

Further Reading

For both towns there are excellent C20 **histories**: S. Middlebrook, *Newcastle upon Tyne, its Growth and Achievement*, 1950 and 1963, and F.W.D. Manders, *A History of Gateshead*, 1973. For the wider setting, C.M. Fraser and K. Emsley, *Tyneside*, 1973, N. McCord, *North East England, an Economic and Social History*, 1979, and Richard Thompson, *The Northern Counties from A.D. 1000*, 1998, are especially useful. The economic and social background of the 1980s is well described in F. Robinson (ed.), *Post-Industrial Tyneside*, 1988.

Newcastle has one of the earliest English town histories, *Chorographia* by William Grey, 1649 (reprinted 1970 from an edition of 1883), and two C18 historians, Henry Bourne, 1736 (1980 reprint), and John Brand, 1789. The next major books were Eneas Mackenzie, *A Descriptive and Historical Account of the Town and County of Newcastle upon Tyne, including the Borough of Gateshead*, 2 vols, 1827, Thomas Oliver, *A New Picture of Newcastle*, 1831 (1970 reprint), and W. Collard and M. Ross, *Architectural and Picturesque Views in Newcastle upon Tyne*, 1841. For historic buildings then surviving, J.R. Boyle, *Vestiges of Old Newcastle and Gateshead*, 1890, is useful and has good drawings by W.H. Knowles.

Most of the **archaeology** of Newcastle and Gateshead has appeared in *Archaeologia Aeliana*, the journal of the Society of Antiquaries of Newcastle upon Tyne. For the Roman period the best starting point is *The Handbook to the Roman Wall* by J. Collingwood Bruce, 14th edn (by D.J. Breeze), 2006. General archaeological research in Newcastle up to 1976 is summarized in *Archaeology in the North*, ed. D.W. Harding, 1976. The most up-to-date account of what is known of Gateshead's development Is by John Nolan, *Archaeologia Aeliana* 5, XXXVI, 2007.

For **individual buildings** there are good detailed accounts by writers such as W.H. Knowles and H.L. Honeyman, who also contributed to periodicals such as *Archaeologia Aeliana*, *Proceedings of the Society of Antiquaries of Newcastle*, and the *Transactions of the Architectural and Archaeological Society of Durham and Northumberland*. The first of these has much concerning the Castle, the Town Wall and Blackfriars (articles by R.B. Harbottle and her colleagues M. Ellison, R. Fraser and J. Nolan), the Quayside area (C. O'Brien), and Trinity House (G. McCombie). The riverside's (mostly lost) buildings are photographed in the RCHME, *An Architectural Survey of Urban Development Corporation Areas, Tyne and Wear,* vol. 1: *Tyneside,* 1990. The English Heritage guide-book *Tynemouth Priory and Castle,* 2008 (by G. McCombie) gives the history of that important excursion destination.

For **c18 and early c19 buildings of Newcastle,** see the Tyne and Wear Museums exhibition catalogue *The Tyneside Classical Tradition,* 1980, L. Wilkes and G. Dodds, *Tyneside Classical: the Newcastle of Grainger, Dobson and Clayton,* 1964 and I. Ayris, *A City of Palaces,* 1997; also T.E. Faulkner in *Planning Perspectives* 5, 1990. For Dobson see also T.E. Faulker and A. Greg's monograph of 2001.

Of **later periods,** buildings of the University up to 1958 are described in A.R. Roberts's B.Arch. dissertation, Newcastle, 1988, interwar buildings in L. Walker and C. Buckley, *Between the Wars, Architecture and Design on Tyneside 1919–1939,* 1982 (Newcastle Polytechnic Gallery catalogue). The redevelopment of central Newcastle is examined by T.E. Faulkner's article in *Northumbrian Panorama* (ed. Faulkner), 1996, with other valuable material. Also useful are the 1945 City Plan and Wilfred Burns, *Newcastle, a Study in Replanning at Newcastle upon Tyne,* 1967. For Gateshead's secular buildings see Simon Taylor's excellent *Gateshead: Architecture in a Changing English Urban Landscape* (English Heritage, 2004); for the Grainger Town regeneration project see F. Cullen and D. Lovie, *Newcastle's Grainger Town: An Urban Renaissance,* in the same series, 2003. Lovie's *The Buildings of Grainger Town,* 2nd edn, 2001, has walks covering that area in detail.

Of specific **building types,** the Tyneside flat was set in context by S. Muthesius, *The English Terraced House,* 1982; B. Lancaster (ed.), *Working Class Housing on Tyneside 1850–1939,* 1994, also has a chapter. L. Pearson, *The Northumbrian Pub,* 1989, and Frank Manders, *Cinemas of Newcastle,* 1991, are excellent. Much on churches is found in W.S.F. Pickering (ed.), *A Social History of the Diocese of Newcastle,* 1982. Two works on railways are essential: J. Addyman and B. Fawcett, *The High Level Bridge and Newcastle Central Station,* 1999, and Fawcett's *History of North Eastern Railway Architecture* (3 vols., 2001–5).

Further reading can usefully include **maps.** Both towns are the subject of James Corbridge's map of 1723, with little pictures of buildings around the border. A superb source is Oliver's large-scale 1830 map of Newcastle and Gateshead, which with its accompanying Book of Reference identifies the owners of all the properties in the towns. Engraved views of Newcastle, especially taking a southern viewpoint, are plentiful. Alan Morgan, *Victorian Panorama,* 2007 reproduces and explains John Storey's lithographic review of 1862. The two prospects (1723 and 1745) by the Buck brothers are wonderful aids to research as well as to the imagination.

A well-illustrated general survey is T. Faulkner, G. Peacock and P. Jones, *Newcastle & Gateshead, Architecture and Heritage,* 2006, which also has a fuller bibliography than can be included here.

Glossary

Acanthus: *see* [1D].

Acroterion: plinth for a statue or ornament on the apex or ends of a *pediment*.

Aedicule: architectural surround, usually a pediment on two columns or pilasters.

Ambo: raised platform or pulpit in a church.

Antae: simplified *pilasters*, usually applied to the ends of the enclosing walls of a *portico* (called *in antis*).

Antefixae: ornaments projecting at regular intervals above a Greek *cornice*.

Apron: raised panel below a window or wall monument or tablet.

Apse: semicircular or polygonal end, especially in a church.

Arcade: series of arches supported by *piers* or columns (cf. *colonnade*).

Architrave: *see* [1A]. Also moulded surround to a window or door.

Ashlar: large rectangular masonry blocks wrought to even faces.

Atlantes: male figures supporting an *entablature*.

Atrium: a toplit covered court rising through several storeys.

Attic: small top storey within a roof. Also the storey above the main *entablature* of a classical façade.

Ballflower: globular flower of three petals enclosing a small ball; *see* [4].

Baluster: pillar or pedestal of bellied form, often grouped as a *balustrade*.

Baptistery: division of a church designed to house the font.

Barbican: outwork defending the entrance to a castle.

Bargeboards: boards fixed beneath a gable to cover and protect the rafters.

Barrel vault: one with a simple arched profile.

Basement: lowest, subordinate storey.

Bastion: defensive semicircular or polygonal projection.

Bay: vertical division of an elevation or interior space.

Beaux Arts: a French-derived approach to classical design, marked by strong axial planning and the grandiose use of the *orders*.

Blind tracery: *tracery* applied to a solid wall.

Blocked column: interrupted by regular projecting blocks.

Bolection: convex moulding covering the joint between two different planes.

Boss: knob or projection, e.g. at the intersection of ribs in a *rib-vault*.

Brace: *see* [3C].

Bracket: small supporting piece of stone, etc.

Brick nogging: *see* [3C].

Brises-soleil (French): screen of fins or slats to deflect sunlight from windows.

Broach spire: *see* [4].

Broken pediment: *see* [4].

Burgage plot: narrow strip of land running back from a street front.

Campanile (Italian): free-standing bell-tower.

Canted: with an angled edge or sides.

Cantilever: horizontal projection supported at one end only.

Capital: head feature of a column or *pilaster*; for classical types *see* [1].

Cartouche: classical tablet with ornate curving frame.

Casement: side-hinged window.

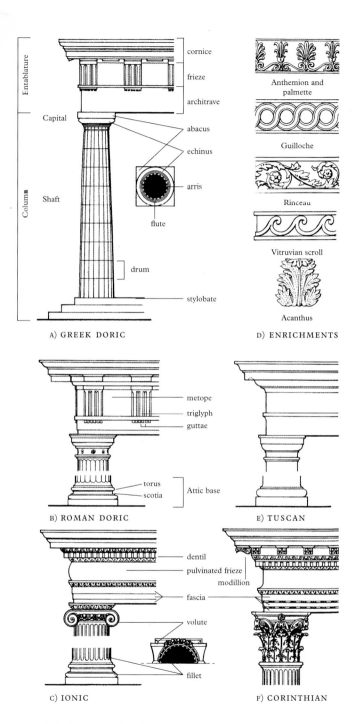

A) GREEK DORIC

- cornice
- frieze
- architrave
- Entablature
- Capital
- abacus
- echinus
- arris
- Column
- Shaft
- flute
- drum
- stylobate

D) ENRICHMENTS

Anthemion and palmette

Guilloche

Rinceau

Vitruvian scroll

Acanthus

B) ROMAN DORIC

- metope
- triglyph
- guttae
- torus
- scotia
- Attic base

E) TUSCAN

C) IONIC

- dentil
- pulvinated frieze
- modillion
- fascia
- volute
- fillet

F) CORINTHIAN

1. Classical orders and enrichments

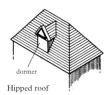
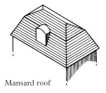
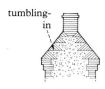

tumbling-in

dormer

Hipped roof

Mansard roof

Tumbled roof

2. Roofs and gables

Chamfer: surface formed by cutting off a square edge.

Chancel: the E part or end of a church, where the altar is placed.

Chapter house: place of assembly for the members of a monastery or cathedral.

Chare (dialect): alley.

Chevron: V-shape used in series on a moulding in *Norman* architecture.

Choir: the part of a great church where services are sung.

Clasping buttress: one which encases the angle.

Clerestory: uppermost storey of an interior, pierced by windows.

Cloister: quadrangle surrounded by covered passages.

Coffered: with decorative sunken panels.

Cogged: (of bricks) a decorative course laid diagonally.

Collar: *see* [3C].

Colonnade: range of columns supporting a flat *lintel* or *entablature* (cf. *arcade*).

Colonnette: small column or shaft.

Composite: classical order with *capitals* combining *Corinthian* features (*acanthus*, *see* [1D]) with *Ionic* (*volutes*, *see* [1C]).

Console: bracket of curved outline.

Corbel, corbel table: projecting block(s) supporting something above.

Corinthian; cornice: *see* [1F; 1A].

Cove: a broad concave moulding.

Crocket: in *Gothic* architecture, leafy hooks or knobs.

Cross-window: with one *mullion* and one *transom*, forming a cross-shape.

Crucks: pairs of inclined timbers set at *bay*-length intervals; *see* [3B].

Cupola: a small dome used as a crowning feature.

Curtain wall: non-load-bearing external wall applied to a framed structure.

Cushion capital: *capital* with rounded edges, like a cushion.

Cusped: with projecting points formed by curves within an arch or *tracery*.

Dado: finishing of the lower part of an internal wall.

Decorated (Dec): English Gothic architecture, late C13 to late C14.

Dentil: *see* [1C].

Doric: *see* [1A, 1B].

Dormer: window projecting from the slope of a roof; *see* [2].

Dragon beam: in a timber-framed building, a beam set diagonally at the corner where two *jetties* meet.

Dripmould: external moulding to protect an opening etc. from water.

Drum: circular or polygonal stage supporting a dome; also part of a column; *see* [1A].

Eared: with side projections at the top.

Early English (E.E.): English Gothic architecture, late C12 to late C13.

Engaged column: one that partly merges into a wall or pier.

Entablature: *see* [1A].

Faience: moulded terracotta that is glazed white or coloured.

Fascia: plain horizontal band; also the upper part of a shopfront.

Flèche: slender spire on the ridge of a roof.

Flemish bond: brickwork with alternating headers (short ends) and stretchers (long sides) showing.

Floor string: horizontal course projecting from of a wall at floor level.

ted: with concave grooves; *see* [1A].

ying buttress: one transmitting thrust diagonally, usually by means of an arch or half-arch.

Frieze: middle member of a classical *entablature*; *see* [1A, 1C]. Also a horizontal band of ornament.

Garderobe: medieval privy.

Giant order: a classical *order* that is two or more storeys high.

Gibbs surround: *see* [4].

Gothic: the style of the later Middle Ages, characterized by the pointed arch and *rib-vault*.

Groin vault: one composed of intersecting *barrel vaults*; hence groined.

Half-timbering: non-structural decorative timberwork.

Hammerbeam: *see* [3A].

Herm: head or bust on a pedestal.

Hipped roof: *see* [2].

Hoodmould: projecting moulding above an arch or *lintel* to throw off water.

In antis: see *anta*.

Intersecting tracery: with interlocking mullions branching out on the same radius but different centres.

Ionic: *see* [1C].

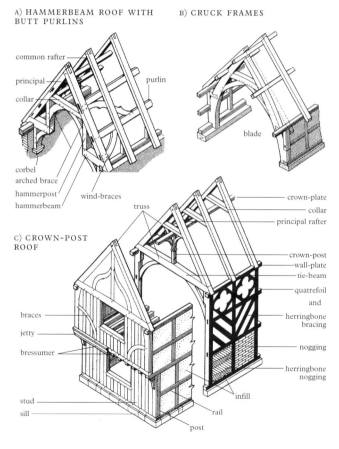

A) HAMMERBEAM ROOF WITH BUTT PURLINS

common rafter
principal
collar
purlin
corbel
arched brace
hammerpost
hammerbeam
wind-braces
truss

B) CRUCK FRAMES

blade

crown-plate
collar
principal rafter

C) CROWN-POST ROOF

crown-post
wall-plate
tie-beam
quatrefoil and
herringbone bracing
nogging
herringbone nogging

braces
jetty
bressumer
stud
sill
rail
post
infill

3. Timber framing

Italianate: a classical style derived from the palaces of Renaissance Italy.

Jacobean: The style of early to mid-C17 England, called after James I's reign (1603–25).

Jamb: one of the vertical sides of an opening.

Jetty: projecting upper storey, usually timber-framed; *see* [3C].

Joists: horizontal timbers laid in parallel to support a floor.

Keeled: brought to a sharp curved point.

Keep: principal tower of a castle.

Keyed: with the central stone or block emphasized.

Kingpost: vertical timber set centrally on a *tie-beam*, supporting the roof ridge.

Lancet: slender, single-light pointed-arched window.

Lantern: a windowed turret crowning a roof, tower or dome.

Light: compartment of a window.

Linenfold: Tudor panelling carved with simulations of folded linen.

Lintel: horizontal beam or stone bridging an opening.

Loggia: open gallery with arches or columns.

Loophole: unglazed slit window.

Louvre: opening in a roof or wall to allow air to escape.

Lucarne: small gabled opening in a roof or spire.

Lunette: semicircular window or panel.

Mannerist: of classical architecture, with motifs used in deliberate disregard of original conventions or contexts.

Mansard roof: *see* [2].

Merlons: the solid uprights of a battlement.

Mezzanine: low storey between two higher ones.

Misericord: shelf on the underside of a hinged choir *stall* seat to support an occupant while standing.

Modillion: *see* [1F].

Mouchette: curved dagger-shaped motif in *tracery*.

Moulding: shaped ornamental strip of continuous section.

Mullion: vertical member between window *lights*.

Nailhead: *see* [4].

Nave: the body of a church w of t' crossing or *chancel*.

Newel: central or corner post of a staircase.

Nook-shaft: shaft set in the angle of a wall or opening.

Norman: the C11–C12 English version of the *Romanesque* style.

Nutmeg: medieval ornament with a chain of tiny triangles placed obliquely.

Oculus: circular opening.

Œil de bœuf (French): small oval ('bulls'-eye') window set horizontally.

Ogee: of an arch, dome, etc., with double-curved pointed profile.

Orders (classical): for types *see* [1].

Oriel: window projecting above ground level.

Ovolo: wide convex moulding.

Palazzo (Italian): compact, ornate, usually classical building like a large Italian town house.

Palladian: following the examples and classical principles of Andrea Palladio (1508–80).

Panel tracery: with even upright divisions made by a horizontal bar.

Parapet: wall for protection of a sudden drop, e.g. on a bridge, or to conceal a roof.

Pargeting: exterior plaster decoration, either moulded in relief or incised.

Patera: round or oval ornament in shallow relief.

Pavilion: ornamental building for occasional use; or a projecting subdivision of a larger building (hence *pavilion roof*).

Pecked: (masonry) with small chipped-out holes.

Pediment: a formalized gable, derived from that of a classical temple; also used over doors, windows, etc. For types *see* [4].

Perpendicular (Perp): English Gothic architecture from the late C14 to early C16.

Piano nobile (Italian): principal floor of a classical building, above a ground floor or basement and with a lesser storey overhead.

Pier: a large masonry or brick support, often for an arch.

Pilaster: flat representation of a classical column in shallow relief.

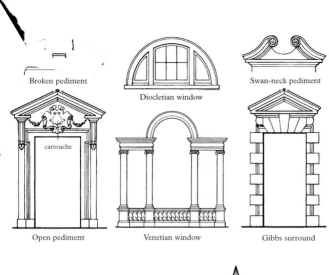

Broken pediment

Diocletian window

Swan-neck pediment

cartouche

Open pediment

Venetian window

Gibbs surround

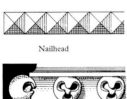

Nailhead

Ballflower

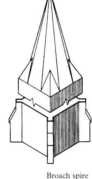

Broach spire

4. Miscellaneous

Pilotis (French): pillars supporting a building above an open ground floor.

Piscina: basin in a church or chapel for washing mass vessels, usually wall-set.

Plinth: projecting courses at the foot of a wall or column.

Podium: continuous raised platform supporting a building; also the lower storeys beneath a multi-storey block of smaller area.

Poppyhead: carved ornament of leaves and flowers on top of a bench end, etc.

Porte cochère (French): porch large enough to admit wheeled vehicles.

Portico: porch with roof and (frequently) *pediment* supported by a row of columns.

Postern: a small gateway at the back of a building or to the side of a larger gate.

Presbytery: a priest's residence; also the part of a major church reserved for the clergy.

Principal: in a roof, a pair of inclined lateral timbers or rafters of a truss; *see* [3A, 3C].

Pulvinated: of bulging profile; *see* [1C].

Purlin: horizontal longitudinal timber in a roof structure; *see* [3A].

Pylon: a large plain vertical stone mass or pier.

Quadripartite vault: a *rib-vault* with four compartments.

Quatrefoil: opening with four lobes or foils.

Queen Anne: the later Victorian revival of the mid-C17 domestic classical manner, usually in red brick or terracotta.

Quoins: dressed or otherwise emphasized stones at the angles of a building; *see* [5].

Rainwater head: container at a *parapet* into which rainwater runs from the gutters.

Ramped: of a stair-rail, etc: with a steep concave curve just short of the *newel*.

Refectory: dining hall of a monastery, college, etc.

Render: a uniform covering for walls for protection from the weather, usually of cement or *stucco*.

Rere-arch: archway across the wide inner opening of a window.

Reredos: painted and/or sculpted screen behind and above an altar.

Respond: attached half-pier or half-column carrying one end of an arch.

Reveal: the surface between the outer face of a wall and the frame of a door or window.

Rib-vault: with a masonry framework of intersecting arches (*ribs*).

Rinceau: *see* [1D].

Rock-faced: masonry cleft to produce a natural, rugged appearance.

Roll moulding: moulding of semicircular or more than semicircular section.

Romanesque: round-arched style of the C11 and C12.

Rood screen: screen to a *chancel*, originally with a Crucifixion (rood) over.

Rubbed brick: soft brick rubbed to a precise surface.

Rustication: exaggerated treatment of masonry to give the effect of strength; for types *see* [5].

Sacristy: room in a church used for sacred vessels and vestments.

Samson post: single upright post supporting a floor.

Sanctuary: in a church, the area around the main altar.

Sash: window that opens by sliding in grooves.

Scalloped: carved with broad flutings or half-cones.

Sedilia: seats for the priests in the *chancel* wall of a church or chapel.

Setts: squared stones used for paving or flooring.

Shaft-ring: a ring around a circular pier or shaft.

Shaped gable: gable with curved sides.

Shouldered: (of a lintel or arch) with arcs in each corner and a flat centre.

Shuttering: temporary framing used for casting concrete.

Sleeper wall: supporting wall under a floor at ground level.

Slype: a covered way or passage leading from the cloisters.

Snecked: (masonry) with courses broken by smaller stones.

Soffit: underside of an arch, *lintel*, etc.

Spandrel: space between an arch and framing rectangle, or between adjacent arches; also a panel below a window.

Spirelet: a small slender spire.

Splayed: wider on one side than the other.

Stalls: fixed seat in a church for the clergy or choir.

Stiff-leaf: carved decoration in the form of thick uncurling foliage; originally late C12–early C13.

Strapwork: decoration like interlaced leather straps.

Stringcourse: horizontal course projecting from a wall surface; *see* [5].

Stucco: plaster shaped into ornamental features, or used externally as a protective coating.

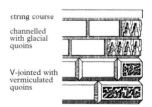

string course
channelled with glacial quoins
V-jointed with vermiculated quoins

5. Rustication

⋅: ornament in the form of
~~~~pery suspended from
~~th ends.
~n-necked pediment: *see* [4].
~ beam: *see* [3C].
Tracery: openwork pattern of
masonry or timber in the upper
part of an opening.
Transept: transverse portion of a
church.
Transom: horizontal member
between window lights.
Trefoil: with three lobes or foils.
Truss: braced framework, spanning
between supports.
Tudor arch: with arcs in each
corner joining straight lines
to the apex.

Tumbled-in brickwork: *see* [2].
Tuscan: *see* [1E].
Tympanum: the area enclosed
by an arch or *pediment*.
Undercroft: room(s), usually
vaulted, beneath the main
space of a building.
Venetian window: *see* [4].
Vermiculated: *see* [4].
Vitruvian scroll: *see* [1D].
Volutes: spiral scrolls, especially
on Ionic columns (*see* [1C]).
Voussoirs: wedge-shaped stones
forming an arch or *lintel*.
Wall-post: structural timber
set upright in or against a wall.
Weatherboarding: wall cladding
of overlapping horizontal boards.

Index
of Artists, Architects and Other Persons Mentioned

The names of architects and artists working in the area are given in *italic*, with entries for partnerships and group practices listed after entries for a single name. Page references in italic include relevant illustrations.

Ekins, L. G. 35, 172–3, 174
Eldon, John Scott, Lord 105
Ellis Williams Architects 43, 88–9
Ellison, Henry 13
Elswick Court Marble Works 182
Emley & Sons 250
Engle (Bernard) & Partners 172
Eno, J. C. 161
Errington, Charles E. 139
Erskine, Ralph 37, 232–6
Evans & Shalev 273
Evetts, L. C. 54, 170, 255

Faber (Oscar) & Partners 137
Fairbairn, R. 140
Fairhurst (W. A.) & Partners 101
Farrell (Terry) & Partners 41, 43, 134, 182–3, 201, 204
Farrier, Gordon 135
Fatkin, J. Newton 242
Faulkner-Brown Hendy Watkinson Stonor 38, 40, 203, 238–9, 256
FaulknerBrowns 43, 203, 209, 211, 239
Feilden Clegg Bradley 264
Fenwick family 145
Fenwick, Alderman 11, 41, 144–5
Fenwick, J. J. 199
Fiennes, Celia 10, 15
Fisher 56
Fitzroy Robinson & Partners 147
Flaxman, John 14, 56, 57
Fletcher Priest 142
Ford (Hubbard) & Partners 118, 230
Foster & Partners 2–3, 43, 91
Fowler, A. M. 20, 108
Fox, Charles 143
Frampton, E. R. 55
Frampton, George 32, 210–11, 250
Fraser (Malcolm) Architects 44, 182
Fulcher, Raf 136, 238–9

Garrett, Daniel 13, 48
Gateshead Borough Architect's Department 224–5, 263
Gateshead Council 222
Gateshead Stained Glass Co. 29, 242
Gibb, Dr 179
Gibberd, Sir Frederick 255
Gibbs, James 13, 46, 48, 129–30
Gibson 170
Gibson, A. B. 117, 122
Gibson, John 20, 163, 224
Gibson, Thomas 143
Gifford & Partners 42, 94–6
Gilbert, Sir Alfred 32, 162
Gilbert, Walter 241
Gillett & Johnson 222–3
Glass, M. K. 29, 242
Glover, Alfred 186

Goldie, Edward 58
Goldie, George 58–61
Goldsworthy, Andy 222
Goodman, T. W. 241
Gormley, Anthony 42, 88, 280–1
Gort, S. R. G. P. Vereker, 7th Viscou. 106–7, 110
Goulden, Richard 264
Gracie, Vernon 234
Graham, Matthew H. 160, 177
Grainger, Richard 16–18, 22, 24, 30, 41, 56, 82, 108, 114, 141–2, 146, 149, 152–66, 178, 180, 182, 184, 188, 212
Grant, Keith 226
Green, Benjamin 17, 20, 30, 47, 153, 162
Green, G. 255
Green, John 20, 30, 46–8, 99, 112, 116–17, 244
Green, John & Benjamin 18, 22, 26, 30, 48, 136, 139, 142, 153, 164–5
Greenhow, C. I. 106
Grey, 2nd Earl 17, 18, 153–4
Grey, W. G. Townsend 182
Grey, William 46, 105
Grey of Fallodon, 1st Viscount 54
Gueritte, T. G. 135
Gustaffsson, Pär 234
GWK Architects 136–7

Hadfield Cawkwell Davidson & Partners 139
Halliday & Agate 171
Hancock, Albany 265
Hancock, John 265
Hardman 59–61
Harris, Augustus 178
Harris, F. E. L. 24, 135
Harris, Renatus 53
Harris, Richard 222
Harrison, Charles A. 87, 102
Harrison, T. E. 26–7, 99–100
Hartlepool Fabrications Ltd 280
Hartwell, C. L. 154
Haskoll 172
Hawks, George 226
Hawks Crawshay 85, 100
Hayton, Lee & Braddock 230
Headlam, T. E. 252
Heatherwick, Thomas 42, 186
Heaton, Butler & Bayne 256
Hebburne, Rauff 124
Hedley, Ralph 29, 53, 170, 195, 250, 250–1, 256
Hendrie, H. 241
Hennebique 24, 135, 179
Henry III, King 62
Henry VIII, King 276
Henry, Sean 161
Hetherington & Wilson 171

ndex
f Localities, Streets and Buildings

Principal references are in **bold** type; page references including relevant illustrations are in *italic*. 'dem.' = 'demolished'

St Peter, Oxford Street (dem.) 29, **192**, 236

St Thomas, Barras Bridge 20, 108n., **196–7**

St Thomas the Martyr (bridge chapel; dem.) 8, 20, 108, 196

St Thomas's Crescent **212**

St Thomas's Square **212**

St Thomas's Street 20, **212**

St Willibrord with All Saints *see* All Saints

Sallyport Crescent 35, **130**

Sallyport (or Wallknoll) Tower 8, **130–1**

Saltwell Park, Gateshead **266–7**

Saltwell Towers, Gateshead 32, 34, **266–7**

Salvation Army, former Men's Hostel 39, **132**

Sand Gate (dem.) 169

Sandgate 121, 131, 132, **134–5**

Sandgate House **135**

Sandgate Square **134**

Sandgate Steps **134**

Sandhill 8–9, 15, 70, **104–11**, 121, **122**, 149, 150

houses 8, 9, 10, 11, **105–7**, 208

Sandyford Road 243, **244**

Saville Place **190**

Saville Row 15, **189**

Science City **215**

Scotswood Road 18

Scottish & Newcastle Brewery (former) **215**

Scottish Provident House 25, 143, **162–3**

sculpture park, Gateshead 42, **222**

Seven Stories **136–7**

Shakespeare Street 17, 142, 153

Shipcote, Gateshead 19, 32, 34, 37, 41, **261–8**

Shipley Art Gallery, Gateshead 34, **263–4**

Shipley Street Baths **235**

Side, The 9, *19*, 46, 69, 87, **117–18**, 150

Sidgate *see* Percy Street

Sinclair Building **178**

South African War memorials:
Gateshead **266**
Newcastle 32, **198**

South Cross Street **256**

South Gosforth 253

South Gosforth Station **254**

South Street 26, 42, **112**

Spiller's Flour Mill **137**

station hotels:
Gateshead (dem.) 22, **221**
Newcastle *see* Central Station Hotel

Stephenson Locomotive Works (former) 26, 42, *112*

Stephenson Monument 32, **113**

Stephenson Quarter 41, *112–19*

Stepney Bank **136**

Stowell Street 16, 169, 172, **174**

Strawberry Place **215**

Summerhill 201

Summerhill Grove **215**

Summerhill Square 16, *214–15*, 216

Summerhill Terrace **215**

Sun Alliance House (former) **139**

Sun Insurance Building 21, *161*

Sunlight Chambers **140**

Swallow Hotel (former) **172**

Swan House (former) *147*

Swinburne Street, Gateshead **222**

Swing Bridge 26, **98**, 104, 108, 122, 220

Swirle Pavilion **136**

Sycamore Close **246**

synagogues (former):
Jesmond 29, **242**
Leazes Park Road **215**

Team Valley Trading Estate 35

Technical College, Gateshead 41

Theatre Royal:
Grey Street 18, 22, 30, 142, 153, 163, *164–5*
Mosley Street (dem.) 22, **162**

Thomson House **139**

Thornton Street **182**

Three Indian Kings House **122**

Time Central **171**

Times Square **182**

Tom Collins House **235**

Tower of the Manors **149**

Towers Avenue **250**

Town Court *see* Guildhall

Town Ditch **175**

town halls:
Gateshead (former) 20, 41, **222–3**, 224, 226
medieval (dem.) 10
St Nicholas' Square (dem.) 20, 72, 76, 139, 198, 235

Town Moor 34, 76, 201, **202**, **211**, 237, 253

Town Quay 22, 121

Town Wall, gates and towers 8–9, 10, 16, 62, **111**, **112**, 121, 122, **130–1**, 132, 136, 141, 154, *168–9*, **170**, **174**, 177, 186, **189**, 215

Trinity Building **195**

Trinity Chare 122, 125, **127**

Trinity Gardens 44, **127–9**

Trinity House 9, 11, 108, 123, *124–* 129, 148

Illustration Acknowledgements

Every effort has been made to contact or trace all copyright holders. The publishers will be glad to make good any errors or omissions brought to our attention in future editions.

We are grateful to the following for permission to reproduce illustrative material:

Martin Brown: 1, 72, 83, 90, 95, 104, 115, 125, 137, 147, 157, 167, 172

Julia Craig-McFeely: 121, 142, 180, 181

Crown Copyright (NMR): 179

English Heritage (Keith Buck): 6, 12, 18, 20, 23, 26, 32, 39, 42, 47, 52, 58, 62, 63, 69, 71, 73, 74, 78, 79, 81, 85, 86, 94, 96, 98, 103, 106, 109, 112, 116, 117, 118, 119, 120, 126, 128, 129, 136, 143, 144, 154, 162, 163, 164, 165, 166, 169, 170, 171, 175, 176, 177

English Heritage (James O. Davies): 2, 3, 4, 9A, 9B, 10, 11, 16, 17, 19, 22, 24, 28, 33, 34, 36, 38, 40, 41, 43, 44, 46, 48, 49, 50, 51, 53, 55, 56, 57, 60, 61, 65, 66, 67, 68, 75, 76, 80, 82, 84, 87, 88, 91, 92, 93, 97, 99, 101, 105, 108, 110, 111, 114, 122, 123, 124, 127, 131, 132, 134, 135, 138, 139, 140, 141, 145, 146, 148, 149, 155, 159, 160, 161, 183

English Heritage (NMR): 7, 15, 21, 27, 31, 150, 151, 152, 173, 174, 178

English Heritage: 25

Alan Fagan: 37

Bill Fawcett: 59

Foster & Partners: 64

Institution of Civil Engineers: 70

National Trust Picture Library/Mark Sunderland: 102

Newcastle Upon Tyne City Architect's Department: 54

Robert Read Graphic Services: 156

Tyne and Wear Archives and Museums: 113, 182

Tyne and Wear County Council: 29

Dr Thomas Yellowley: 30, 89, 107, 133, 158, 168